"An authoritative guide and must-buy for anyone who lives in the area and owns a mountain bike."

– *Mountain Bike* magazine on our companion guide, *Mountain Biking Southern California's Best 100 Trails*

"Mandatory reading for locals and visitors alike, *Mountain Biking Northern California's Best 100 Trails* is the cyclist's most thorough guide yet to the beauty of Northern California."

–Brian Hemsworth,
Editorial Director
Mountain Biking magazine

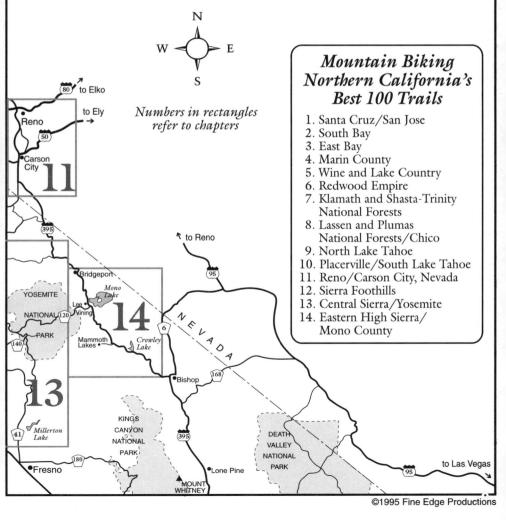

Numbers in rectangles refer to chapters

Mountain Biking Northern California's Best 100 Trails

1. Santa Cruz/San Jose
2. South Bay
3. East Bay
4. Marin County
5. Wine and Lake Country
6. Redwood Empire
7. Klamath and Shasta-Trinity National Forests
8. Lassen and Plumas National Forests/Chico
9. North Lake Tahoe
10. Placerville/South Lake Tahoe
11. Reno/Carson City, Nevada
12. Sierra Foothills
13. Central Sierra/Yosemite
14. Eastern High Sierra/ Mono County

MOUNTAIN BIKING
Northern California's
BEST 100 TRAILS

by

Delaine Fragnoli & Robin Stuart

with chapters by

R.W. Miskimins, Carol Bonser, and
Don Douglass and Réanne Hemingway-Douglass

FINE EDGE
Productions
BISHOP, CALIFORNIA

Important Legal Notice and Disclaimer

Mountain biking is a potentially dangerous sport, and the rider or user of this book accepts a number of unavoidable risks. Trails by nature have numerous natural and man-made hazards; they are generally not signed or patrolled and they change with time and conditions.

While substantial effort has been made to provide accurate information, this guidebook may inadvertently contain errors and omissions. The maps in this book are for locator reference only. They are not to be used for navigation and are intended to complement large-scale topo maps. Your mileages will vary from those given in this book. Contact land managers before attempting routes to check for suitability and trail conditions.

The editors, authors, contributors, publishers and distributors accept no liability for any errors or omissions in this book or for any injuries or losses incurred from using this book.

LIBRARY OF CONGRESS CATALOGING-IN-PUBLICATION DATA

Fragnoli, Delaine, 1962–
  Mountain biking northern California's best 100 trails / by Delaine Fragnoli & Robin Stuart ; with chapters by Ray Miskimins ... [et al.].
    p.   cm.
  Includes bibliographical references and index.
  ISBN 0-938665-31-6 (trade pbk.)
  1. All terrain cycling—California, Northern—Guidebooks.
2. California, Northern—Guidebooks. I. Stuart, Robin. II. Title.
GV1045.5.C22C2545   1995
796.6'4'09794—dc20   95-2838
                                                CIP

Fine Edge Productions, Route 2, Box 303, Bishop, CA 93514

TABLE OF CONTENTS

Acknowledgments and Contributors 9
A Letter from the U.S. Bureau of Land Management 10
A Letter from the U.S. Forest Service 11
IMBA Rules of the Trail 12
Welcome to Mountain Biking Northern California 13
Special Considerations 15

Chapter 1: Santa Cruz/San Jose
By Robin Stuart.. 19

1. Wilder Ranch 21
2. Henry Cowell Redwoods State Park 24
3. Forest of Nisene Marks/Sand Point Overlook 25
4. Grant Ranch Loop 29
5. Grant Ranch/Antler Point.. 30
6. Henry Coe State Park/Middle Ridge Loop 31

Chapter 2: South Bay
By Robin Stuart.. 35

7. Old San Pedro Mountain Road/North Peak 36
8. Harkins Fire Trail to Whittemore Gulch 38
9. Borden Hatch to Grabtown Gulch 41
10. Crystal Springs Reservoir/Sawyer Camp Trail 43
11. Saratoga Gap 44

Chapter 3: East Bay
By Robin Stuart.. 47

12. Lake Chabot Loop 49
13. Redwood Regional Park/West Ridge to East Ridge Loop 50
14. Tilden Park/Wildcat Loop 53
15. Briones Regional Park/Short Loop 55
16. Briones Crest Loop 57
17. Mount Diablo/Wall Point Loop 59
18. Mount Diablo/Mitchell Canyon to Devils Elbow 61

Chapter 4: Marin County
By Robin Stuart.. 63

19. Headlands Loop 64
20. Angel Island Double Loop 65
21. Hoo Koo E Koo to Phoenix Lake 68
22. Pine Mountain to Repack 71
23. Pine Mountain Loop 73
24. Bolinas Ridge 74
25. Samuel P. Taylor State Park/Barnabe Peak Loop 77
26. China Camp State Park/Bay View Loop 79
27. Ridge Fire Trail Loop 80

Chapter 5: Wine and Lake Country
By Robin Stuart.. 83

28. Annadel State Park/Short Loop to Lake Ilsanjo 84
29. Annadel State Park/Long Loop to Ledson Marsh 87
30. Sugarloaf Ridge State Park/Bald Mountain Loop 88
31. Robert Louis Stevenson Memorial State Park/The Peaks 90
32. Boggs Mountain Loop 92
33. Cow Mountain Recreation Area 94

Chapter 6: Redwood Empire
By Delaine Fragnoli 99

34. King Range/Kings Peak 101
35. Humboldt Redwoods State Park/Grasshopper Peak 104
36. Humboldt Redwoods State Park/Peavine Ridge Road 106
37. Redwood National Park/Holter Ridge Loop 108
38. Prairie Creek Redwoods State Park/Gold Bluffs Loop 109
39. Jedediah Smith Redwoods State Park/Howland Hill Road 112
40. Smith River/Old Gasquet Toll Road 113
41. Smith River/Camp Six Lookout 116

Chapter 7:
Klamath and Shasta-Trinity National Forests
By Delaine Fragnoli 119

42. Upper Klamath River 121
43. Gunsight Peak Loop 123
44. Canyon Creek/Buker Ridge Loop 125
45. Forks of the Salmon/Sawyers Bar Loop 127
46. Carter Meadows Loop 130
47. Martin Dairy/Ball Mountain Loop 133
48. Herd Peak Lookout Loop 135
49. Mount Shasta Loop 137
50. Clikapudi Trail 140
51. Boulder Creek 141

Chapter 8:
Lassen and Plumas National Forests/Chico
By Delaine Fragnoli 145

52. Upper Bidwell Park 148
53. Feather Falls 150
54. Mills Peak Lookout 151
55. Crystal Peak 155
56. Dixie Mountain Loop 156
57. Three Lakes 157
58. Spencer Meadow Trail 160
59. Bizz Johnson Trail 161

Chapter 9: North Lake Tahoe
By R.W. Miskimins and Carol Bonser 165

60. Downieville Downhill 166
61. Relief Hill Loop 169
62. Shotgun Lake 170
63. Old Emigrant Trail to Donner Peak 173
64. Sardine Peak Lookout Loop 175
65. El Dorado Canyon Loop 179
66. Ward Creek Loop 182
67. Miller Lake Loop 184
68. Tahoe to Truckee 187
69. The Great Flume Ride 189

Chapter 10: Placerville/South Lake Tahoe
By R.W. Miskimins and Carol Bonser 195

70. Ellicotts Crossing/Hunters Trail 197
71. Pony Express Historical Trail 199
72. Loon Lake Loop 201
73. Angora Lakes 203
74. Mr. Toad's Wild Ride 205
75. Horse Canyon/Carson-Mormon Emigrant Trail 207
76. Burnside Lake 209

Chapter 11: Reno/Carson City, Nevada
By R.W. Miskimins 213

77. Keystone Canyon Loop 215
78. Spanish Springs Canyon 217
79. Virginia Mountains to the Valley 219
80. Lagomarsino Petroglyphs 221
81. Long Valley Loop 223
82. Jumbo Grade Climb 226
83. Carson River Loop 228
84. Kings Canyon Climb 230

Chapter 12: Sierra Foothills
By Robin Stuart 233

85. Salmon Falls Trail 234
86. Olmstead Loop 236
87. Lake Clementine Loop 238
88. Stevens Trail 241
89. Pioneer Trail 242

Chapter 13: Central Sierra/Yosemite
By Delaine Fragnoli 245

90. Spicer Meadow Reservoir to Sand Flat 247
91. Calaveras Big Trees State Park/South Grove Loop 248
92. Yosemite Nationl Park/Valley Floor and Mirror Lake 251
93. Merced River Trail 255
94. Squaw Leap National Recreation Trail 257

Chapter 14: Eastern High Sierra/Mono County
By Don Douglass and Réanne Hemingway-Douglass 261

95. Lower Rock Creek Trail 262
96. Rock Creek Lake/Sand Canyon 265
97. Great Wall of Owens River Gorge 266
98. Minaret Summit to Deadmans Pass 267
99. Inyo Craters Loop 270
100. Sagehen Loop 273
101. Bodie via Cottonwood Canyon 274
102. Bodie to Bridgeport via Geiger Grade/Aurora Canyon 279

Appendixes 281

A. The Care and Feeding of a Mountain Bike, *by R.W. Miskimins* 283
B. Roadside Repair, *by R.W. Miskimins* 286
C. Basic Skills for Mountain Biking, *by R.W. Miskimins* 289
D. Agencies and Visitor Centers 294

About the Authors 297
Recommended Reading 298
Route Index 300
Outdoor Publications from Fine Edge Productions 303

Acknowledgments

The authors wish to thank Ray Miskimins and Carol Bonser for their help in documenting the great riding around Lake Tahoe and northern Nevada. Thanks also go out to Don Douglass for his inspiration and oversight, to Réanne Douglass for all her copyediting and detail work, and to book designer and map maker Sue Irwin for her hard work in producing this book.

We are indebted to the many United States Forest Service, Bureau of Land Management, National Park, State Park and other land management personnel for their advice, support and cooperation. Thanks, too, to the many bike shop employees and bike club members who volunteered a favorite trail. In addition, many cyclists and agency employees took time to round up much-needed photographs at short notice, and we thank them whole-heartedly.

On a personal note, Delaine Fragnoli would like to thank her husband, Jim MacIntyre, for his unflagging support, patience and understanding — and for househusband feats beyond the call of duty.

Robin Stuart sends her thanks to Cathy Jensen and dog Harry for their trail-scouting help.

Delaine Fragnoli and Robin Stuart
Altadena, California
June 1995

Contributors

Design/layout: Sue Irwin, Eastside Desktop Publishing, Mammoth Lakes, California
Cover design: Laura Patterson, Mammoth Lakes, California
Maps: Sue Irwin, Eastside Desktop Publishing, Mammoth Lakes, California
Copyediting: Réanne Hemingway-Douglass, Cindy Kamler
Printing: Gilliland Printing, Inc., Arkansas City, Kansas
Front cover photograph: Cathy Jensen, Pacifica, California
Back cover photograph: Brad Peatross, Mammoth Lakes, California

Photographers:
Carol Bonser: pages 149, 165, 168, 174, 178, 198, 200, 209, 302
Wende Cragg: pages 70, 73, 86, 287
Brian Hemsworth: page 240
Ben Hipple, Lassen Velo: pages 159, 161
Chris Houtanian: page 100
Fran Hull, BLM: pages 126, 134, 142
Cathy Jensen: pages 2, 17, 23, 26, 30, 33, 36, 47, 52, 56, 58, 81, 92, 95, 107, 115, 236, 290
Brian Klock, State of California Parks and Recreation: page 139
Chris Lombardo: pages 261, 268, 270, 276, 293
Ray and Bette Miskimins: pages 146, 188, 192, 203, 213, 218, 227, 256, 278
Robert S.P. Parker: pages 233, 251, 252
Mike Troy: pages 40, 152
Kevin Woten: page 120

United States Department of the Interior

BUREAU OF LAND MANAGMENT
California State Office
2800 Cottage Way, Room E-2845
Sacramento, California 95825-1889
May 25, 1995

Welcome to some of the best mountain biking in the United States...the Public Lands of Northern California. From the subtle to the sublime, vivid and exciting riding opportunities await your exploration. Thrill your senses to a variety of environments that range from the desolation of the Great Basin, to the Gold Country, to the Pacific Ocean.

The Bureau of Land Management administers millions of acres of Public Land in California. A few of these areas are explored in this book. Imagine the remoteness and majesty of what these lands have to offer. Imagine yourself and your family passing through tunnels of time along the Fernley and Lassen Branch Railway which has recently been converted to the Bizz Johnson National Recreation Trail. No matter what your experience level is, you will find a myriad of roads and trails that will challenge and enlighten.

During the past several years I have had the pleasure of working with many in the mountain biking community. I have watched the evolution and growth of the industry and activity. I have discovered that mountain bikers care deeply about the environment and have a tremendous volunteer ethic. Don and Reanne Douglas, pioneers of the mountain bike movement, have contributed greatly to raising public awareness of access and other related needs. Most importantly, they have worked tirelessly to codify the International Mountain Bike Association (IMBA) Rules of the Trail for bikers to aspire to. The IMBA Rules have become a well-known standard of courtesies supported by industry, public agencies and mountain bikers.

Apply these courtesies to others you encounter on the trail. It will increase the acceptance of you and your fellow mountain bikers with all of the customers of the Public Lands. Through these courtesies and your sensitivity to others, I commend your efforts and invite you to some of the best riding in California.

Contact us at any of our many offices throughout the state for information on specific trail restrictions, information on recreation opportunities or on becoming a partner in managing your Public Lands. Your interest and involvement in your Public Lands is invaluable.

Sincerely,

Ed Hastey
State Director

| United States
Department of
Agriculture | Forest
Service | Inyo
National
Forest | 873 N. Main St.
Bishop, CA 93514
(619) 873-2400
(619) 873-2538 TTY |

Reply to: 2320

Date: May 15, 1995

Dear Mountain Bike Enthusiast:

Welcome to some of the best mountain biking country in the United States--the public lands of California. Extraordinary scenic and exciting riding opportunities await your exploration.

The United States Forest Service administers millions of acres of public land. A few of these areas are described in this book, inviting you to experience a variety of environments. You will discover the remoteness and majesty that these lands have to offer. No matter what your experience level, you will find roads and trails that will challenge and enlighten you.

The publishers of Fine Edge Productions continue to educate the public about a wide range of recreational opportunities, as well as stressing the need for responsible riding habits. During all your rides, please practice good mountain bike ethics by following the International Mountain Biking Association Rules of the Trail, particularly by staying on existing and open roads and trails, being considerate of other users, leaving gates as you find them, controlling your speed, and packing out your trash. You are generally responsible for your own personal safety, which includes knowing what hazards might exist and using proper safety procedures and equipment to minimize the inherent risks associated with mountain biking.

Contact the nearest ranger station for specific trail restrictions or information on recreation opportunities. Your interest and involvement in your public lands is invaluable, and we encourage you to share with us your ideas on how we can improve our services and facilities.

Sincerely,

BILL BRAMLETTE
Recreation Staff Officer

FS-6200-28a (5/84)

IMBA RULES OF THE TRAIL©

Thousands of miles of dirt trails have been closed to mountain bicycling because of the irresponsible riding habits of a few riders. Do your part to maintain trail access by observing the following rules of the trail:

1. **Ride on open trails only.** Respect trail and road closures (ask if not sure), avoid possible trespass on private land, obtain permits and authorization as may be required. Federal and State wilderness areas are closed to cycling. Additional trails may be closed because of sensitive environmental concerns or conflicts with other users. Your riding example will determine what is closed to all cyclists!

2. **Leave no trace.** Be sensitive to the dirt beneath you. Even on open trails, you should not ride under conditions where you will leave evidence of your passing, such as on certain soils shortly after a rain. Observe the different types of soils and trail construction; practice low-impact cycling. This also means staying on the trail and not creating any new ones. Be sure to pack out at least as much as you pack in.

3. **Control your bicycle!** Inattention for even a second can cause disaster. Excessive speed maims and threatens people; there is no excuse for it!

4. **Always yield trail.** Make known your approach well in advance. A friendly greeting (or bell) is considerate and works well; startling someone may cause loss of trail access. Show your respect when passing others by slowing or even stopping. Anticipate that other trail users may be around corners or in blind spots.

5. **Never spook animals.** All animals are startled by an unannounced approach, a sudden movement, or a loud noise. This can be dangerous for you, others, and the animals. Give animals extra room and time to adjust to you. In passing, use special care and follow the directions of horseback riders (ask if uncertain). Running cattle and disturbing wild animals is a serious offense. Leave gates as you found them or as marked.

6. **Plan ahead.** Know your equipment, your ability, and the area in which you are riding, and prepare accordingly. Be self-sufficient at all times, keep your machine in good repair, and carry necessary supplies for changes in weather or other conditions. A well-executed trip is a satisfaction to you and not a burden or offense to others. Keep trails open by setting an example of responsible cycling for all mountain bicyclists.

WELCOME TO MOUNTAIN BIKING NORTHERN CALIFORNIA

As the birthplace of mountain biking, Northern California holds a special appeal to mountain bikers. It was here that the sport's pioneers transformed the balloon-tired bike into the mountain bike. In doing so they revolutionized both the bicycle industry and backcountry recreation.

No one who has experienced Northern California's trails should be surprised by this. There is plenty of inspiration to be found in the area's natural lands. From the rolling oak woodlands of San Jose to the fabled headlands of Marin, from the volcanic splendor of Mt. Lassen and Mt. Shasta to the holy quiet of a redwood forest, from the alpine serenity of Lake Tahoe to the granite glory of Yosemite, there is scenery and terrain for all abilities and tastes. It's hard to look at these areas and not want to get on a bike to explore them!

Working with land management personnel, bike shop employees and local trail experts, we have compiled Northern California's top rides, many of which have never before been documented in print. We can say with confidence that this is the most thorough, wide-ranging mountain bike guidebook yet published for the area.

How To Use This Book

With so many great trails to choose from, selecting the best was difficult. (This book could easily have become *Mountain Biking Northern California's Best 200 Trails!*) Obviously *best* means different things to different people. Some rides were included for their outstanding scenic value, others for their historical significance, others simply for their high fun factor. A few were included because they represented the quintessential California in some way.

We have also attempted to include a variety of terrain and levels of difficulty, as well as a certain geographic diversity, although we have erred on the side of accessibility. Thus we have included numerous rides in the heavily populated and highly visited areas of Northern California, namely the San Francisco Bay Area and the greater Lake Tahoe region.

We have tried to organize all this information in an easy-to-use way. Each chapter is dedicated to a particular area, usually a county or national forest. The chapters are organized in a loop starting, appropriately enough, in the birthplace of mountain biking, the San Francisco Bay area, before moving north up the coast to the redwood parks, east to Klamath National Forest and back down along Interstate 5 to Lake Tahoe. We complete the loop by circling back to Sacramento before visiting Yosemite National Park and the Eastern Sierra. Within each chapter we have tried to group rides in the same vicinity.

At the beginning of each ride you will find capsule information to let you decide quickly if a ride is for you or not. Ride distance is included, as is a rating of difficulty. Mileages shown are approximate and may vary among riders and odometers. We rated the rides for strenuousness (from easy to very strenuous) and for technical difficulty (from not technical to extremely technical). The ratings are a subjective assessment of what the average fit rider (acclimatized to elevation) might consider the route.

If you are a racer, you might find some of our difficult rides to be moderate. If you are new to the sport, you may find our mildly technical rides challenging. Know your limits and be honest in evaluating your skill level. We also recommend that you check with local bike shops and land managers for their evaluation of your fitness for a particular ride. We do not know your skill level and consequently cannot be responsible for any losses you may incur using this information. Please see the important legal notice and disclaimer in the front portion of this book.

For elevation we include whatever elevation information seems pertinent to that particular ride, usually net elevation gain and loss. Rides at high elevation will include such information. Ride Type lets you know if the ride is a loop, an out-and-back trip, a multiple-day tour or if it requires a car shuttle. It also tells you the trail surface; for example, "fire road loop with singletrack return." Next, we suggest the best season for riding each route. Last, we recommend the best maps of the area. Unless otherwise indicated, the map names refer to USGS 7.5-minute topographical maps.

If, after reading the capsule information, you are not sure if a ride is for you, the text of each ride description should give you additional information with which to make a decision. The Overview section contains general information on the area and describes the ride's highlights. Getting There directs you to the trailhead, and the Route portion gives you a turn-by-turn guide to the ride.

Please note that the routes described in this book are not patrolled and contain natural hazards. Trail conditions and surfaces are constantly changing. Also be aware that the trail access situation is very volatile in certain regions, particularly in the San Francisco area. Some areas are just now turning on to mountain biking and may have new trails and information by the time you read this. Check with local land managers for the latest trail and access conditions. A complete list of pertinent agencies is included in the Appendix.

Throughout we have tried to be consistent in presentation. We have made an effort, however, to retain some of the character and tone of each individual author. Mountain biking is a very individualistic sport, and we think that should be reflected in any writing about the sport. Remember also that each odometer gives different results and yours may vary from each author's.

We hope you think of this book as a group of friends getting together to tell you about the best riding they've discovered. But enough talk! Get on your bike and start discovering Northern California for yourself. You've got 100 — well, actually 102—trails to explore and the best trail guide available!

SPECIAL CONSIDERATIONS

To enhance your pleasure and safety we ask that you observe the following Special Considerations:

1. **Courtesy.** Extend courtesy to all other trail users and follow the golden rule. Observe the IMBA Rules of the Trail. The trails and roads in Northern California are popular with many user groups: hikers, equestrians, fishermen, ranchers, 4WD enthusiasts, hunters, loggers and miners. Mountain bikers are the newest user group, so set a good example.

2. **Preparation.** Plan your trip carefully; develop and use a check list. Know your equipment, your ability, and the area in which you are riding and prepare accordingly. Be self-sufficient at all times, wear a helmet, keep your machine in good repair, and carry necessary supplies for changes in weather or other conditions. A well-executed trip is a pleasure to you and not a burden or offense to others.

3. **Mountain Conditions.** Be sensitive at all times to the natural environment: the land, beautiful and enjoyable, can also be frightening and unforgiving. The areas covered by this book often provide extremes in elevation, climate and terrain. If you break down, it may take you longer to walk out than it took you to ride in! Check with your local Red Cross, Sierra Club, or mountaineering textbooks for detailed mountain survival information. Know how to deal with dehydration, hypothermia, altitude sickness, sunburn and heatstroke. Always be prepared for:

Intense Sun: Protect your skin against the sun's harmful rays by wearing light-colored, long-sleeved shirts or jerseys. Some of the rides in this book are at relatively high altitude, and the higher you go, the more damaging the sun becomes. Use sunscreen with a sufficient rating. Wear sunglasses that offer adequate protection. Guard against heatstroke by riding in early morning or late afternoon when the sun's rays are less intense.

Low Humidity: East-facing slopes and high elevation usually have low humidity. To avoid headaches or cramps, start each trip with a minimum of two or more full quart water bottles. (*Gallons* of water may not be sufficient for *really* hot weather or hard rides.) Force yourself to drink before you feel thirsty. Carry water from a known source or treat water gathered from springs, streams and lakes. Untreated drinking water may cause Giardiasis or other diseases.

Variations in Temperature and Weather Conditions: Carry extra clothing —a windbreaker, gloves, stocking cap—and use the multi-layer system so you can quickly adapt to different weather conditions. You may find it cool and foggy on the coastal side of a ridge, and hot and dry on the other. Afternoon thundershowers occur frequently in the high country, so keep an eye on changing cloud and wind conditions and prepare accordingly.

Fatigue: Sluggish or cramping muscles and fatigue indicate the need for calories and liquids. Carry high-energy snack foods such as granola bars, dried fruits and nuts to maintain strength and warmth. To conserve energy, add clothing layers as the temperature drops or the wind increases.

Closures: Many mountain and foothill areas are closed to the public during times of high fire danger. Other areas may be temporarily closed during hunting season or because of logging activity. Please check ahead of time with local authorities, and observe such closures. Always be very careful with fire.

4. **Navigation.** The maps in this book are not intended for navigation but as guides to the appropriate forest or USGS topographic maps which we recommend you carry and use. Have a plan ready in advance with your cycling group in case you lose your way (it's easy to do!). En route, record your position on the map(s), noting the times you arrive at known places. Be sure to look back frequently in the direction from which you came, in case you need to retrace your path. Do not be afraid to turn back when conditions change or if the going is tougher than you expected.

In certain cases, it may be difficult to determine which roads and trails are open to public travel. When in doubt, make local inquiries. Follow signs and leave all gates either opened or closed, as you found them, or as signed. Park off the road, even in remote areas, so you do not block possible emergency vehicles.

Before you leave on a ride, tell someone where you're going, when you expect to return, and what to do in case you don't return on time. Ask that person to call the proper officials if you are more than six hours overdue, giving full details about your vehicle and your trip plans.

5. **Horses and Pack Animals.** Some of the trails in Northern California are used by recreational horse riders as well as cyclists and hikers. Some horses are spooked easily, so make them aware of your presence with a friendly greeting or bell *well in advance of the encounter.* A startled horse can cause serious injuries both to an inexperienced rider and to itself.

If you come upon horses moving *toward* you, yield the right-of-way, even when it seems inconvenient. Carry your bike to the downhill side and stand quietly, well off the trail in a spot where the animals can see you clearly. If you come upon horses m*oving ahead of you in the same direction,* stop well behind them. Do not attempt to pass until you have alerted the riders and asked for permission. Then, pass on the downhill side of the trail, talking to the horse and rider as you do. It is your responsibility to ensure that such encounters are safe for everyone. Do not disturb grazing sheep or cattle.

6. **Respect the Environment.** Minimize your impact on the natural environment. Remembe*r, mountain bikes are not allowed in Wilderness Areas and in certain other restricted areas.* You are a visitor, so ask when in doubt. Leave plants and animals alone; historic and cultural sites untouched. Stay on established roads and trails, do not create any new ones, and do not enter private property. Follow posted instructions and use good common sense. If you plan to camp, you may need a permit. Contact the nearest land management agency for information.

Be sensitive to the dirt beneath you. Even on open trails, you should not ride under conditions where you will leave evidence of your passing, such as on certain soils shortly after a rain. Observe the different types of soils and trail construction; practice low-impact cycling. Be sure to pack out at least as much as you pack in.

7. **Control and Safety.** Crashes usually don't cause serious injury, but they occasionally can and do. Stay under control and slow down for the unexpected. Wear protective gear—helmet, gloves and glasses—to protect yourself from scrapes and impacts with rocks, dirt and brush. Guard against excessive speed. Avoid overheated rims and brakes on long or steep downhill rides. Lower your center of gravity by lowering your seat on downhills. Lower your tire pressure on rough or sandy stretches. In late summer and fall, avoid opening weekend of hunting season, and inquire at the appropriate land management agency as to which areas are open to hunting. Carry first aid supplies and bike tools for emergencies. *Avoid solo travel in remote areas.*

8. **Trailside Bike Repair.** Minimum equipment: pump, spare tube, patches, 2 tubes of patch glue, 6" adjustable wrench, Allen wrenches, chain tool and spoke wrench. Tools may be shared with others in your group. Correct tire inflation, wide tires, and avoiding rocks will prevent most flats. Grease, lube, and proper adjustment prevent most mechanical failures. Frequent stream crossings wash out chain lube, so carry extra.

9. **First Aid.** Carry first aid for your body as well as your bike. If you have allergies, be sure to bring your medicine, whether it's for pollen or bee stings. Sunscreen saves your skin, and insect repellent increases your comfort in many seasons. Bring bandages and ointment for cuts and scrapes, and aspirin for aches that won't go away. Additional first-aid items you might carry in your kit are antiseptic swabs, moleskin, a single-edged razor blade, a needle, elastic bandage, Tums or other stomach remedy, and waterproof matches. For expedition trips, consult mountaineering texts on survival for more suggestions.

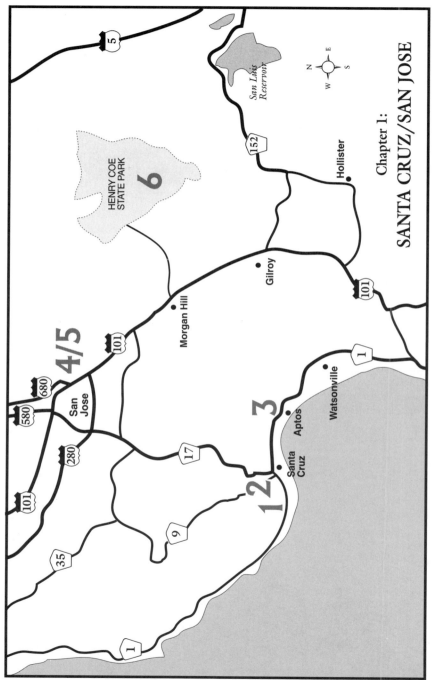

Chapter 1:
SANTA CRUZ/SAN JOSE

CHAPTER 1

Santa Cruz/ San Jose

by Robin Stuart

Thanks to the Santa Cruz Mountains, the lands bordering the Bay Area to the south are the most beautiful in the region. On the western side of the range, you'll find breathtaking ocean views and the university town of Santa Cruz, with its famous beach and boardwalk. The eastern slopes face inland, surrounding San Jose, the heart of the Silicon Valley, and the rolling hills of the East Bay. Although the Santa Cruz and San Jose areas are sides of the same mountain range, they are as different as night and day, with only one thing in common: killer singletrack. On the ocean side, you'll find dense, often moist forests of redwood and eucalyptus. The inland side tends to be drier, favoring oak, laurel, and pine. One thing's for sure: it smells good down here.

Although geographically considered to be part of the South Bay (see Chapter 2), this area deserves special attention. The trails in the parks around Santa Cruz and San Jose are among the best in northern and southern California combined. But don't just take my word for it—go out and ride! On any given day you may see test riders for Rock Shox, Specialized, Bontrager, and Mountain Cycles, along with scores of locals out enjoying these rides.

So what makes this area so great? If you're a beginner, unfortunately, not much. Most of the trails are at least a little technical in nature, generally due to rocks. Once you've mastered those basic handling skills, however, you'll find trails as technical as you can stand, including long and winding fire roads rolling over ridges and topping mountain peaks, and some of the sweetest singletrack winding down, over, and through aromatic forests.

You can thank the local mountain biking community for continued access to the singletrack here, and the best way to show your gratitude is by behaving yourself. Clubs and organizations such as ROMP (Responsible Organized Mountain Pedallers) work long and hard to keep the trails open and available to us. Please don't give land managers and landowners any reasons to consider banning mountain bikes from these trails.

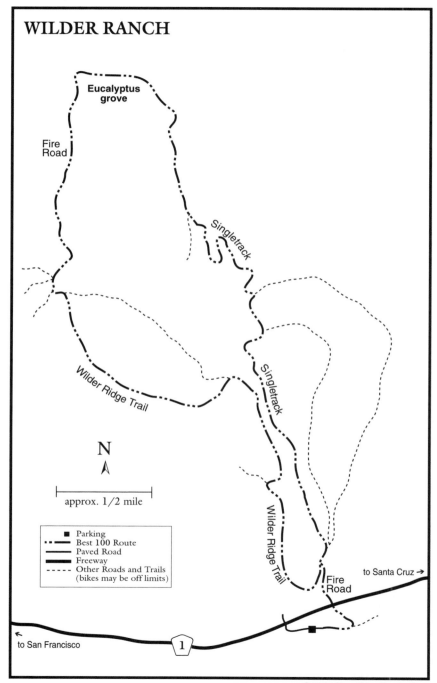

WILDER RANCH

Eucalyptus grove

Fire Road

Singletrack

Wilder Ridge Trail

Singletrack

N

approx. 1/2 mile

Wilder Ridge Trail

■ Parking
Best 100 Route
Paved Road
Freeway
Other Roads and Trails
(bikes may be off limits)

to Santa Cruz →

Fire Road

to San Francisco

1

© 1995 Fine Edge Productions

1 Wilder Ranch

Distance: 9.5 miles
Difficulty: Moderately strenuous, technical sections
Elevation: 800' gain/loss
Ride Type: Loop on fire roads and singletrack
Season: Year-round
Map: Available for free at the ranger kiosk
Comments: Restrooms are available in the parking lot but drinking water is not; keep the map with you as few of the trails are signed.

Overview: Wilder Ranch is a favorite with regional mountain bikers, well worth the hour or so drive from the Bay Area. Located on Santa Cruz's northwest border, the Wilder Ranch State Park and Cultural Preserve is considered to be the local version of a mountain bike park. Nestled within Wilder's 3,900 acres are 28 miles of roller-coaster fire roads, twisting and technical singletrack, water crossings, rockbeds, loose and steep climbs and descents; just about everything the fat-tire heart desires. And thanks to the tireless efforts of the local mountain biking community, it's all legal!

Wilder Ranch also offers a bit of historical enrichment as well. The cultural preserve is a sort of living history center; a collection of restored buildings and artifacts found within the park's boundaries depict its early days as a Native American habitat to its later life as a Spanish ranch during the mission period. In the late nineteenth century, the park was the site of a thriving dairy ranch, which continued through the early twentieth century. To illustrate its past, a small number of livestock are raised on the grounds as part of the exhibit.

Past the cultural preserve and into the parklands, the trails wind through stands of eucalyptus, windswept chaparral overlooking the ocean, and dense forests of oak and redwoods. There are a number of awesome trails and combinations to be ridden here; the following is a favorite short loop which introduces some of Wilder's best features. Few of the trails are signed and nobody seems to know the names anyway, so pay attention to the route directions!

Getting There: From San Francisco, take Highway 1 south towards Santa Cruz, about 60 miles. Wilder Ranch is on Highway 1, just past Davenport and about a mile north of Santa Cruz. The park entrance and parking lot is on the right, well signed with their own turning lane. Parking is $6, a little high but the increased parking fee has kept the park open. Smile as you pay it.

Route: From the south end of the parking lot, follow the path leading through the gate past the restrooms. The path runs into a paved service road; turn right and head down, turning left into the cultural preserve. The preserve is a popular picnic spot so ride slowly or walk through. Veer left at the fork. The path leads through a tunnel (beneath Highway 1) which deposits you onto a fire road at the trailhead.

Head straight on the fire road, and then make the first hairpin left turn onto the Wilder Ridge Trail.

The Wilder Ridge fire road starts climbing immediately, getting very sandy and steep as you round the bend. This marks the beginning of a steep roller-coaster section. At the first fork, turn right for a final steep roll to a level section that heads into the trees. The bad news is the next climb; it's steep, it's rutted, it's rocky, and it's about a 0.25 mile long. The good news is that once it's over, the rest of the climbs are comparatively easy.

At the top, the trail levels and leads to another fork (not shown on ride map). If you go straight, the trail dead ends in about 50 feet at a great overlook, complete with a view of the coast. Veer left to continue. For the next mile, the trail rolls along the chaparral ridge on rocky hardpack, ending with a loose and rocky downhill that leads out to a crossroads, 3.5 miles.

Turn right, heading into a stand of eucalyptus. As the trail starts to head downhill, you'll see a singletrack branch off to the right; you can take it or stay on the fire road since they rejoin on the other side of the knoll. I recommend the singletrack. So, bear right onto the singletrack, which climbs a little bit before pitching into a fast downhill. Turn right at the bottom, back onto the fire road.

The next mile or so is a somewhat steep and rutted climb up to the Eucalyptus Grove. The Grove is the park's northern boundary and a frequently mentioned landmark. Along the way, there are a couple of level spots where you can catch your breath. There's even a brief descent before the last big push up to the ridge and the Eucalyptus Grove.

At the ridge, the trail levels and winds around to the right, through the eucalyptus and along a fire road that flanks the outer perimeter of the oak and redwood forest on the left. Although the trail rolls, it's mostly downhill, which makes it very easy to pick up speed. But stay alert! The turnoff onto an unnamed singletrack is easy to miss.

At about 6.3 miles, you'll see a singletrack split off to the left that dips into a meadow and disappears into the trees. Turn left here. The going gets technical from this point. The smooth and damp singletrack winds its way down through the trees, leading to a tight switchback. Be on the lookout for calf-gashing branches and tire-grabbing tree roots. Past the switchback, the trail continues down to a tight S cut through a fallen redwood and ending in a seasonal water crossing.

On the other side of the creek, the trail climbs steeply up through the forest and back toward the ridge. Along the way, you'll encounter a short, steep climb over tree roots and a rocky, wall-hugging switchback before you come out through a small meadow onto another fire road. Turn right onto the fire road, which starts off fairly level then heads decidedly downhill. Again, it's easy to pick up a lot of speed but the next turn is easily missed.

At about 7.5 miles, there is a singletrack turnoff on the right. You won't see it until you're almost right on top of it because of the thick underbrush. Turn right onto the singletrack.

After a quick, gently descending straightaway, the trail makes a sharp turn down and to the right, around an off-camber tree. Just to make it more interesting, there's a tall rubber waterbar (slippery when wet) protruding just before the apex of the turn. Past this little challenge, the trail swoops and rolls further into the redwoods, around and between more trees. About halfway down, the trail dries out, getting loose and rocky. The rocks seem to get bigger the further down you go until you reach the creek at the bottom. The rocks thin out as you follow the creek and just when you thought you were past them, you come to the amazing all-rock creek crossing. In the winter, this area can get kind of slippery.

Past the rocks, leaving the creek behind you, the trail heads out of the shade of the redwoods and onto level land. The last 0.5 mile is a straight shot through the meadows and stands of oak back out to the main fire road. Turn right on the fire road to get back to the trailhead, and continue straight to go back through the cultural pre- serve to the parking lot.

2 Henry Cowell Redwoods State Park

Distance: 6.5 miles
Difficulty: Moderate, mildly technical
Elevation: 600' gain/loss
Ride Type: Loop on fire roads and pavement
Season: Year-round
Map: Available at the park headquarters for 75 cents
Comments: Water is available at the trailhead.

Overview: Located farther south off Highway 1 in Santa Cruz, this 1,600-acre park epitomizes the Northern California coast with its towering redwoods, cool river canyons and wide open ridges. Its namesake, Henry

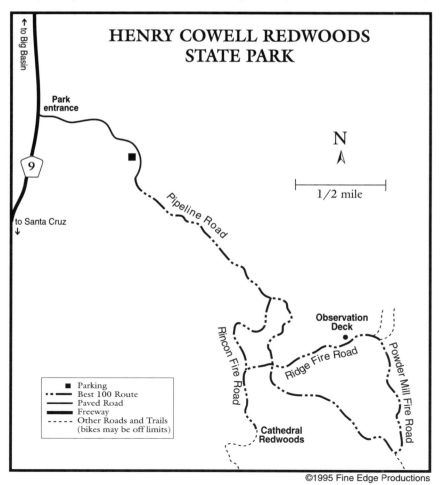

HENRY COWELL REDWOODS
STATE PARK

↑ to Big Basin

Park entrance

9

to Santa Cruz ↓

N
A

|——————|——————|
1/2 mile

Pipeline Road

Observation Deck

Rincon Fire Road

Ridge Fire Road

Powder Mill Fire Road

■ Parking
■··— Best 100 Route
——— Paved Road
■■■■ Freeway
- - - - Other Roads and Trails
(bikes may be off limits)

Cathedral Redwoods

©1995 Fine Edge Productions

Cowell, owned pretty much all of Santa Cruz in the late 1800s. Drawn from Massachusetts by the gold rush, Cowell and his brother operated a drayage service that hauled equipment from the Bay Area to the minefields in the Sierra Nevada foothills. As his success grew, so did his business interests until he became the richest man in Santa Cruz County. Cowell's son made a gift of land to the State of California in 1953. It became a state park in 1954.

The trails are fairly easy, with some sand and rocks, and wind through amazing forests of redwoods, along the San Lorenzo River and up to an overlook with an expansive view of the coastal mountains and valleys.

Getting There: From San Francisco, take 280 south to Highway 1 and follow it to Santa Cruz. Turn left onto Highway 9 and follow it for 5 miles. The park entrance is on the right. Parking is $3.

Route: The trailhead is just past the Nature Center. Follow the paved Pipeline Road past an impressive stand of redwoods and through the trees. After passing under a railroad bridge, the trail begins to climb, getting markedly steeper after crossing Eagle Creek. At the top of the rise, the trail rolls the rest of the way through forests of pine and fir.

At about 2.5 miles, you come to an intersection with the Powder Mill Fire Road. Turn left onto Powder Mill and begin the steady climb up to the Observation Deck. Parts of the fire road get pretty sandy, especially in the later summer months. The worst of the climb is over as you reach the crossroad with the Ridge Fire Road. Stay left and follow Ridge the last quarter mile to the Observation Deck.

After looking around and oohing and ahhing, it's all downhill from here. And kind of steep. The Ridge trail is a loose and bumpy fire road back down to Pipeline. Keep going past Pipeline to the trail's end at the Rincon Fire Road. Turn left onto Rincon—there's something you gotta see.

Rincon gently descends to the Cathedral Redwoods. This is a stand of redwoods like you've only heard about and well worth the side trip. After feeling appropriately humbled by nature, turn around and go back up Rincon. Keep going past the intersection with Ridge, following Rincon as it winds and descends to Pipeline. Turn left on Pipeline and keep your speed in check as you head back down the pavement to the parking lot.

3 Forest of Nisene Marks/ Sand Point Overlook

Distance: 17 miles
Difficulty: Moderately strenuous, mildly technical
Elevation: 1,400' gain/loss
Ride Type: Out and back on fire road
Season: Year round
Map: Available by mail for 75 cents; call (408) 335-4598
Comments: No services are available at the trailhead.

Overview: The Forest of Nisene Marks State Park is a popular attraction for mountain bikers and hikers. Its rugged terrain is nearly untouched from its original state. Shaped by fault lines that bisect the park, the area's narrow canyons and winding ridges make it undesirable to developers. Even the Ohlone tribes that inhabited neighboring regions kept their distance. In 1883, though, it got touched. Rather severely.

The property was sold to a lumber company that had joined forces with the Southern Pacific Railroad. Using a variety of means, everything from trestles to pack animals, they succeeded in clear-cutting the entire forest by 1923. Cut and stacked logs still remain in some of the remote areas of the park — just because they could cut it down didn't mean they could get it out! When the last of the valuable timber was gone, the loggers moved on.

In the 1950s, the Marks family, Salinas Valley farmers, purchased the land. In 1963, the Marks children donated the acreage to the state in their mother's name.

An interesting little side note: the Marks placed a deed restriction on equestrian access. So while mountain bikes are not allowed on single-track, oddly enough, horses aren't even allowed past the first couple of miles of fire road.

Today, a new generation of trees, including redwoods, eucalyptus, madrone and fir, have taken hold. But it will be a long time before the forest is completely restored.

Home seismologists and current events fans take note: the epicenter of the 1989 Loma Prieta quake, which rocked the Bay Area as the players took the field in the third game of the World Series, is located off the main fire road near the park's southeast boundary. I mention the game because it's responsible for saving the lives of countless numbers of Bay Area residents who had left work early to catch the 5:00 p.m. play time; the quake hit at 5:04, causing major damage (some still not repaired) to

freeways and the collapse of a section of the Bay Bridge.

Getting There: From San Francisco, take 280 south to Highway 1, and follow it past Santa Cruz. Turn left at the Aptos turnoff and make the first right onto Soquel Drive. Follow Soquel for about half a mile and turn left onto Aptos Creek Road. Park in the large dirt turnout on the right.

Route: From the parking area, follow Aptos Creek Road for a little under a mile. At that point, it turns to dirt (welcome to the park) and becomes the Aptos Creek Fire Road. You follow this trail all the way up to the Sand Point Overlook. The trail starts out fairly level as it carries you inland, over the steel bridge, where you can look down into a deep and narrow gorge, and past the remains of the loggers' turn-of-the-century housing.

At about 4.5 miles, you reach a point known as the Bottom of the Incline. This marks the end of the gentle ride. To the right is the hiking trail that leads to the Loma Prieta quake epicenter, about half a mile up. Ahead, the going gets a little on the steep side as you enter into a series of switchbacks that climbs about 600 feet in a little under a mile.

At about 6 miles, just past the Top of the Incline, the trail straightens out a bit and continues uphill at an easier grade. As you make your way up, the views start to get nice, especially as you close in on Sand Point. You reach the Sand Point Overlook at 8.5 miles or so. Feel free to ogle at will at the coast and Monterey Bay, the Santa Cruz Mountains and Big Basin.

Turn around here for the fun and frolicking downhill ride back to your car.

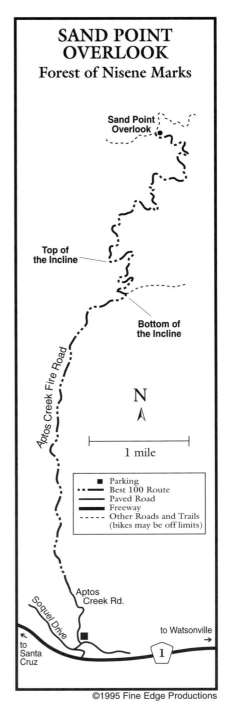

SAND POINT OVERLOOK
Forest of Nisene Marks

Sand Point
Overlook

Top of
the Incline

Bottom of
the Incline

Aptos Creek Fire Road

N

1 mile

■ Parking
∎∙∎∙ Best 100 Route
▬▬ Paved Road
▬▬▬ Freeway
- - - - Other Roads and Trails
(bikes may be off limits)

Aptos
Creek Rd.

Soquel Drive

to
Santa
Cruz

to Watsonville
→

1

©1995 Fine Edge Productions

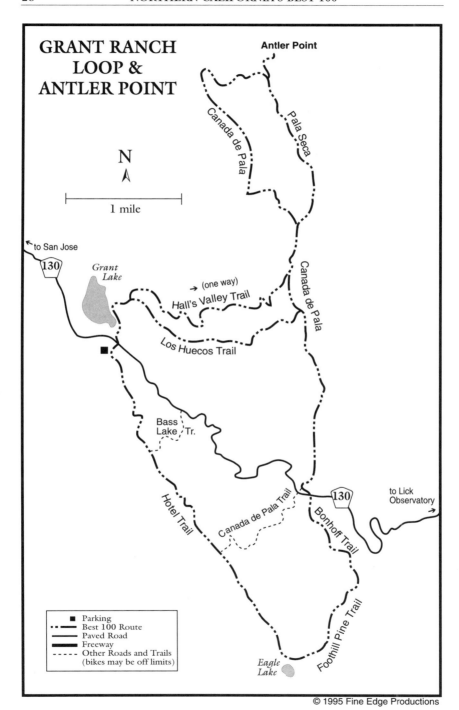

GRANT RANCH LOOP & ANTLER POINT

Antler Point

N

1 mile

to San Jose

130

Grant Lake

Cañada de Pala

Pala Seca

→ (one way)

Hall's Valley Trail

Cañada de Pala

Los Huecos Trail

Bass Lake Tr.

to Lick Observatory

130

Hotel Trail

Cañada de Pala Trail

Bonhoff Trail

Foothill Pine Trail

■ Parking
▪▪▪ Best 100 Route
─── Paved Road
━━━ Freeway
- - - Other Roads and Trails
    (bikes may be off limits)

Eagle Lake

© 1995 Fine Edge Productions

4 Grant Ranch Loop

Distance: 9.6 miles
Difficulty: Strenuous, moderately technical (sand, loose rock, seasonal water crossing)
Elevation: 1,000' gain/loss
Ride Type: Loop on sometimes narrow fire roads
Season: Year-round; heavy rains may temporarily close some trails
Topo Map: Lick Observatory. (Not all trails appear on the USGS map, so pick up a County Parks and Recreation map of Grant Ranch at the Visitor Center)
Comments: Helmets required; water available at the Visitor Center area. Please close all gates behind you.

Overview: Located at the base of Mount Hamilton in San Jose is the Joseph D. Grant County Park, better known as Grant Ranch. The largest recreational area in Santa Clara County, the 9,522-acre park boasts over 20 miles of trails open to mountain bikers.

The park is named for the family which held the land from 1880 until 1972, at which time the property was willed to the Save-the-Redwoods League and the Menninger Foundation. Santa Clara County purchased the land in 1975.

Most of the trails follow the peninsula mold of long and sometimes gnarly climbs, but here you are rewarded with equally long and downright thrilling descents. A local favorite, this playground is a popular site on the Northern California race circuit and, in 1994, was featured as a stop on Evian's Ride for the Wild series.

The loop ride, which follows several trails, illustrates the best that Grant Ranch has to offer: rolling gentle and not-so-gentle climbs and descents by mountain lakes, through meadows and along panoramic ridges, all populated with oak and pine woodlands.

Getting There: From San Francisco,

San Jose is about an hour's drive down either southbound 101 or 280. Both have an Alum Rock turnoff. Head east on Alum Rock for about 2 miles, turning right onto Mt. Hamilton Road/Highway 130. The park entrance is on the right, 8 miles up Mt. Hamilton Road. The park charges a $3 day-use fee.

Route: Starting from the visitor's center, turn right and head down the Hotel Trail. Follow the trail as it makes its way gently up to the Circle Corral, 1.4 miles. Past the corral, the going gets a bit steeper as you climb up to Eagle Lake, which you reach at 3.2 miles. There are several steep climbs along this route; since heat is often a factor in these parts (temperatures can soar above 100 degrees) walking is not only permissible, it may be required.

Stop to admire the view (i.e, catch your breath) before bearing left at the lake and following the Foothill Pine Trail as it drops blissfully down a short hill before climbing up again for another 1.1 miles, bringing your total to 4.3 miles. Hang a left at the next trail intersection, onto the Bonhoff Trail, and enjoy or endure (depending on how you look at it) the next steep ascent. Fortunately, it's over fairly quickly and the trail levels off for a bit along the ridge before dropping down to the cattle-guard at Mt. Hamilton Road (Highway 130).

Go across the road, through the gate on the other side, and continue north for a nasty little ascent up Canada de Pala Trail. Upon reaching the ridge line, after you stop swearing, you can see the Santa Clara Valley laid out below and all around you.

Now you're at the good part. The trail rolls along the ridge until you reach the 7.1-mile point in your journey and come to the intersection with the Los Huecos Trail. Turn left here for the payoff you so well deserve. All that lovely elevation you have gained is lost in 1.8 miles of rollicking downhill.

The trail ends at Grant Lake; turn left to head to the parking lot.

5 Grant Ranch/Antler Point

Distance: 11.2 miles
Difficulty: Strenuous, moderately technical
Elevation: 1,400' gain/loss
Ride Type: Loop on sometimes narrow fire roads
Season: Year-round
Topo Maps: Lick Observatory, Mt. Day. (Not all Grant Ranch trails appear on the USGS map, so pick up a County Parks and Recreation map of the park at the Visitor Center.)
Comments: Helmets required; water available at the visitor center area.

Overview: This is the ride of choice for thrill seekers at both ends of the fat-tire spectrum—mountain goats who like the views from the highest attainable point and the downhill types who enjoy viewing the world through saucer-shaped pupils.

On this ride, you traverse the trails leading to Antler Point, at 2,995 feet, Grant Ranch's highest peak. As you might guess, the views are spectacular. The ride also incorporates many people's favorite downhill, the ever-lovin' Los Huecos Trail.

Getting There: Follow the directions for the previous ride.

Route: Starting from the visitor's center, head left and cross Mt. Hamilton Road to Grant Lake. Follow the trail to Hall's Valley Trail. The Hall's Valley Trail is open to bikes going uphill only; it's a popular route to the Canada de Pala Trail that's not as long as the Hotel to Bonhoff Trails and not as steep as the Los Huecos Trail. Bear left on Hall's Valley Trail and begin the climb toward the ridge. At about 1.3 miles, the grade steepens a bit for the next 0.25 mile, suddenly gaining 200 feet. Take heart, however; the next 200-foot gain comes with twice the distance.

The trail meanders around and up until the 2.7-mile point, when it ascends sharply to the junction with Canada de Pala. Turn left here and follow the trail as it ascends slightly to the next intersection of Canada de Pala and the Pala Seca Trail.

Bear right and head up the Pala Seca Trail. After a steep but brief climb, it rolls along the high ridge. When you've gone 4.9 miles, you come to a very steep trail going up on your right. Feel free to walk it, but you just have to go the 0.2 mile to see the world from almost 3,000 feet. This is Antler Point.

After spending a few moments, or a long time, feeling that top-of-the-world feeling, go back down to the Pala Seca Trail and turn right. The trail drops steeply down to a line shack, used for herding the cattle that sometimes graze here. Bear left at the shack and continue descending to the stream.

You are now back on the Canada de Pala Trail, which follows the stream until the junction with the Washburn Trail, which is off limits to bikes. Bear left and stay on the Canada de Pala Trail. This all starts looking familiar as you approach first the intersection with Pala Seca, then Hall's Valley. Stay on Canada de Pala; you've got a date with a downhill.

When you reach the trail marker for Los Huecos at 8.7 miles, turn right and get ready for the fun. Once again, at the bottom, turn left and follow along the lake to get back to the parking lot.

6 Henry Coe State Park/ Middle Ridge Loop

Distance: 9.5 miles
Difficulty: Strenuous, moderately technical
Elevation: 1,900' gain/loss
Ride Type: Loop on fire roads and singletrack
Season: Spring through fall
Topo Maps: Mount Sizer, Mississippi Creek. (The Pine Ridge Association produces a map, available at the park, with suggested mountain bike routes and trail mileages.)
Comments: Water is available at park headquarters. All park singletrack is closed for 48 hours after a half-inch or more of rain. There's a 15-mph speed limit on roads.

Overview: At over 79,000 acres, Henry Coe is California's largest state park. Some 22,000 of those acres are designated wilderness and, thus, are closed to bikes. Look on the bright side—that still leaves 57,000 acres to explore! The land is an amalgamation of ranch lands acquired by the state, beginning with Henry Coe's Pine

Ridge Ranch. In 1953, Pine Ridge Ranch was donated to the county by Henry Coe's daughter, in her father's name. The county park was bought by the state in 1958, which then added to it as the state acquired the neighboring ranch properties.

What exists now is a wonderland of challenging, well-marked trails and pristine wilderness with over 70 lakes and ponds. The trails take you through forests of oak and pine, mountain meadows lush with seasonal wildflowers, creek crossings, and cool canyons. The park's rolling hills dotted with oaks are as classic a California landscape as the Sierras or the redwoods. This is quintessential Northern California.

Most of the riding in this park is strenuous with very steep climbs and descents. (Beginning mountain bikers may want to try the relatively easy 5.4-mile trip out to Manzanita Point instead of this ride.) The Middle Ridge Loop is a short loop and, by far, the most popular loop trail in the park.

It's got everything—classic singletrack, tight switchbacks, challenging climbs and descents, rocks, sand, water crossings, you name it.

Whenever you ride at Henry Coe, keep your eyes peeled for riders on high-tech bikes. The park is a favorite testing ground for employees of nearby Specialized Bicycle Components.

Getting There: From San Francisco, take 101 south to Morgan Hill and take the East Dunne Avenue exit. Head east on East Dunne, following the signs to the park entrance, about 13 miles. The park charges a $5 per vehicle day-use fee.

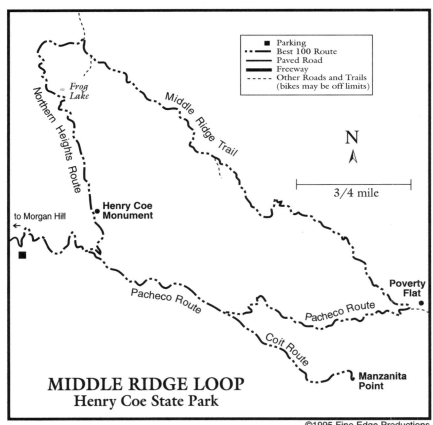

MIDDLE RIDGE LOOP
Henry Coe State Park

©1995 Fine Edge Productions

Route: Starting from the park headquarters, make a left turn onto the Northern Heights Route, 0.7 mile from the gate. At the top of Pine Ridge, you pass a monument to Henry Coe. Give him your regards and descend to and cross Little Fork Coyote Creek on your way to Frog Lake. Just past the lake and up a small climb, at 3.0 miles, turn right onto the Middle Ridge Trail. This singletrack delight rolls along the ridge with a few short, steep climbs.

Just over 4.0 miles, you pass a junction with Fish Trail. Stay on the Middle Ridge Trail. At 4.7 miles, after passing through a meadow, the trail pitches steeply downhill along a forested ridge. Keep your speed under control and be prepared for the steep, tight switchbacks that begin about halfway down.

The wild ride ends at Poverty Flat, the ride's low point of 1,200 feet. At about the 6.2-mile mark, cross Coyote Creek and take a few deep breaths; you're about to pay for all that fun. Bear right onto the Pacheco Route and granny it up a steep, 1,400-foot, dang-blasted hill.

When you pass the trail junction with Coit Route, at 8.0 miles, the worst is over. Mercifully the last 1.5 miles are an easy spin back to Pacheco Route gate and the parking lot.

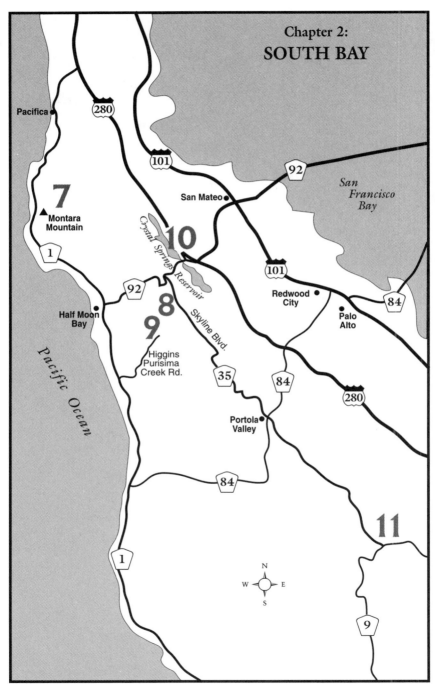

Chapter 2:
SOUTH BAY

Pacifica

280

101

92

San Mateo

San Francisco Bay

7

▲Montara Mountain

1

Crystal Springs Reservoir

10

92

8

101

Redwood City

84

9

Half Moon Bay

Palo Alto

Skyline Blvd.

Higgins Purisima Creek Rd.

35

84

280

Portola Valley

Pacific Ocean

84

11

1

N
W — E
S

9

©1995 Fine Edge Productions

CHAPTER 2

South Bay

by Robin Stuart

Mountain bikers who enjoy the San Francisco's South Bay area have a lost Spaniard with poor navigation skills to thank. In 1769, Gaspar de Portola "discovered" the San Francisco Bay from a spot near what is now the San Pedro State Beach on the Bay Area peninsula. De Portola had actually been hunting for Monterey, about 100 or so miles south, but he must have been distracted on his trek north from San Diego. His mistake was to our advantage. With only a little imagination, it's still possible to see what Gaspar saw in his unplanned discovery. Much of the area down the peninsula remains undeveloped as protected land, open space, national parks and game preserves.

Within 30 minutes drive south of San Francisco, literally hundreds of miles of trails await your tire treads. Driving down Highway 1, past and through the laid-back coastal communities between Pacifica and Half Moon Bay, you have the Pacific Ocean on your right and the western-most end of the Santa Cruz Mountains on your left. The terrain varies from windswept and weather-carved sandstone and granite to redwood rainforests.

Thanks to the marine layer, the weather is fairly pleasant year-round, with temperatures ranging from the forties to the sixties in the winter, and the sixties through eighties in the summer months. In the winter and early spring, wearing removable layers of clothing is strongly recommended as the temperature can vary as much as 10 degrees on a 1,000-foot climb. Particularly in redwood forests, the farther you get away from the valley floor, the warmer it gets.

Those preferring warmer climes and drier conditions need only turn left at Half Moon Bay and head a few minutes east. On the inland side of the coastal range lies the South Bay region. Home of Silicon Valley, political conservatives and great weather, the South Bay also boasts a smorgasbord of trails ranging from long, easy spins to lung-busting climbs. The parks, open spaces and game preserves are all heavily forested with redwood, eucalyptus and several species of pine.

On weekends, the trails in this region are sometimes crowded, but so far everyone is well-behaved, if not downright polite. There's plenty of great riding and hiking for all.

7 Old San Pedro Mountain Road/ North Peak

Distance: 12.4 miles
Difficulty: Strenuous, mildly technical
Elevation: 1,800' gain/loss
Ride Type: Out-and-back on access roads
Season: Year-round
Topo Map: Montara Mountain

Overview: Awesome views and a wild downhill make this one of the most popular rides in the area. The top of North Peak (1,898') offers a 360 degree panorama of the entire Bay Area. On clear days, you can see as far north as Point Reyes and Napa County, as far south as Santa Cruz, and as far east as the Sierras hiding behind Mount Diablo. To the west, the Farallon Islands are the only land mass interrupting the Pacific Ocean.

Old San Pedro Mountain Road runs north along the western side of Montara Mountain, from Montara to Pacifica. As the name suggests, it was once an automobile route between San Francisco and Half Moon Bay. Known as Coastside Boulevard, it opened in 1915 and was abandoned in 1937, in favor of the "new" state highway, Highway 1, although some folks still used it until after World War II. The trail that exists now is made up of sandstone and deteriorating asphalt. Every winter, a little more of the asphalt gives way to dirt.

The top of Old San Pedro Mountain Road becomes the North Peak Access Road, a jeep trail used by park rangers and various agencies to reach the communications towers at the top. The trail turns into an all-sandstone adventure in traction at this point, rolling steeply to the Peak. The descent is what made this trail famous—a high-speed roller coaster

on a surface that sometimes feels like marbles.

The Old San Pedro Mountain Road portion of the trail is the busiest, used year round by mountain bikers, hikers and equestrians. The closer you get to North Peak, the more traffic thins out.

Getting There: From San Francisco, drive 22 miles south on Highway 1. The trailhead is on the left side of the highway just past Devil's Slide, easily identified by a metal gate and trail marker. Although the area in front of the gate will accommodate only four cars, the Montara State Beach parking lot is almost directly across the highway (and a lot easier of access both in and out).

Route: Follow the trail of broken asphalt, rocks and sand to the first fork at the ranger's house. Hang a left here and keep following the gradually disintegrating trail of broken pavement. Don't worry, about halfway up, it gives way completely to dirt.

Along the way, you'll come across several singletrack offshoots, none of which are signed and all but one of which are legal for bikes (the exception has a circle-slash-bike marker). Almost all of these dead-end within a mile but they make a nice diversion. On this particular ride, however, you'll need to save your strength.

About 1.0 mile up, you come to a fun little S-shaped whoop-de-do.

In the winter, it becomes a whoop-de-wet, filling with rainwater runoff. Continue snaking your way up the mountain.

As you gain elevation, you can see behind you the towns of Montara and Moss Beach. A little higher up, you can see Half Moon Bay and Pillar Point Harbor, marked by the radar tower which is used to track satellites. You'll also notice a couple of overturned rusting automobiles dotting the mountain side, remnants of what once was.

At 2.5 miles, you come to another fork. To the left, Old San Pedro Mountain Road continues on, descending into Pacifica. On this ride, keep going straight and shift into

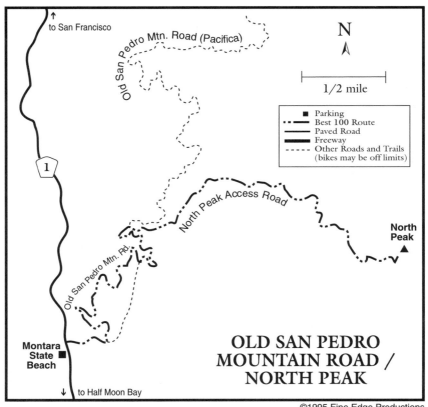

↑ to San Francisco

Old San Pedro Mtn. Road (Pacifica)

N

1/2 mile

■ Parking
▪▪▪ Best 100 Route
── Paved Road
▬ Freeway
---- Other Roads and Trails
(bikes may be off limits)

1

North Peak Access Road

North Peak ▲

Old San Pedro Mtn. Rd.

Montara State ■ Beach

↓ to Half Moon Bay

OLD SAN PEDRO MOUNTAIN ROAD / NORTH PEAK

your granny gear. You're about to climb a loose, steep section known lovingly as "The Wall." The Wall ascends 500 feet in 0.5 mile. The thought that keeps your legs moving is knowing that you get to ride down this sucker.

Past the Wall, the trail gets a lot more interesting. The foliage flanking the trail becomes more dense with coastal scrub and manzanita, and there are just enough short descents to keep your spirits up as you continue to gain altitude. And then, of course, there are the views. As you wind your way up to the ridge line, you'll see alternately the north coast (San Francisco, Mt. Tam and Point Reyes) on the left and the south coast (Half Moon Bay, Pescadero and Santa Cruz) to the right.

You know you're just about there when you reach the first communication tower, which is basically a bunch of antennas and generators. Keep heading straight past the first tower and head up to the next one. When you see the sharp left turn, take it. It will be obvious. This is followed by a deeply rutted right turn. Within a few feet, you'll find yourself in a small clearing, sharing level ground with the fenced-in communication set up. There's a short, narrow trail of loose granite rocks rising up to the left. Follow it to the dead end, about 10 feet. Look around. Amazing, huh?

After ample gawking time, comes the best part; you get to go back down. There is no speed limit but in the warm spring and summer months, keep your speed in check because you will likely encounter other bicyclists and hikers. In the wet winter months, when traction is at its best, use caution but don't expect to see too many other fools like you traipsing around up here.

8 Harkins Fire Trail to Whittemore Gulch

Distance: 6.8 miles
Difficulty: Moderate, somewhat technical
Elevation: 1,400' gain/loss; begin/end 400'; high point 1,800'
Ride Type: Loop on fire road and singletrack
Season: Harkins, year-round; Whittemore Gulch, spring through fall
Topo Map: Woodside. (The Midpeninsula Open Space District produces a brochure with trail map available by calling 415-691-1200.)
Comments: Helmets required. Speed limit of 15 mph suggested but currently not enforced. Whittemore Gulch Trail is closed to bikes and equestrians during the rainy season.

Overview: Nestled on the western slopes of the Santa Cruz Mountains just east of Half Moon Bay is the Purisima Creek Redwoods Open Space Preserve. The 2,519-acre park offers a variety of bike trails, including one of the region's most awesome singletracks, the Whittemore Gulch Trail. This is what mountain biking is all about: tight switchbacks, precarious dropoffs, negotiating through rocks and winding around trees, all in a spectacular redwood forest.

The Harkins Fire Trail is no slouch, either. Its name is deceiving; this "fire trail" has two stretches of singletrack, a wide fire road section and the rest is roughly the width of

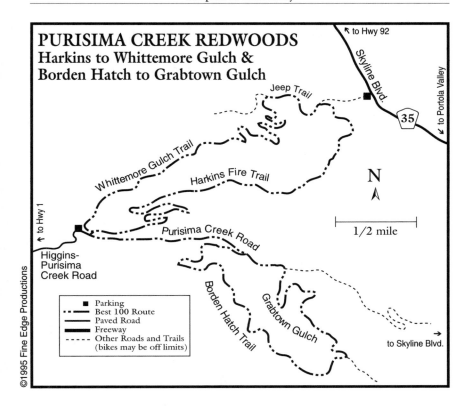

PURISIMA CREEK REDWOODS
Harkins to Whittemore Gulch &
Borden Hatch to Grabtown Gulch

Legend:
■ Parking
•─•─ Best 100 Route
─── Paved Road
▬▬▬ Freeway
- - - Other Roads and Trails
(bikes may be off limits)

©1995 Fine Edge Productions

doubletrack. Harkins presents you with fast sweeping turns, steep technical sections through loose rocks and tree roots, seasonal bouts with mud, and a climb that tests your levels of fitness and determination.

Whittemore Gulch is a popular hiking trail and, as always, bicyclists are at the bottom of the right-of-way pecking order. Although there are signs of the presence of horses, the most likely place that you will encounter equestrians is on the Harkins Fire Trail.

Both trails afford ample views of the Pacific and the lower coastal hills. Most of your riding time, however, is spent among the redwoods and Douglas fir. It's a great place to enjoy being alive.

Getting There: From San Francisco, take Highway 280 south to Highway 92, about 27 miles. From 92, take the Highway 35/Skyline Boulevard turn-off, which comes up quickly. The preserve's main entrance and parking lot is on Highway 35/Skyline Boulevard, 4.5 miles south of 92.

To get to the preserve's lower entrance, take 92 down to Highway 1. Turn left onto Highway 1 and left again onto Higgins-Purisima Creek Road, about 1 mile south of Half Moon Bay. Keep going straight at the fork. The parking lot is about 2 miles past the fork, on the right.

Route: The traffic on the trail system at Purisima seems to move counter-clockwise or by shuttle. This is due to the elevation changes; if you want to do a loop, you'll have to climb one trail to get to the other. Because I prefer going out with a bang instead of a whimper, I suggest starting from the lower parking lot and climbing up Harkins Fire Trail. This also makes a convenient segue to the next ride.

So, from the lower gate, pedal 50 yards or so along Purisima Creek Road, the main trail along Purisima Creek, and turn left onto the wooden bridge. On the other side of the bridge, turn right onto Harkins (all of the trails at Purisima are well marked). The climb begins in the cool shade of towering redwoods, accompanied by Purisima Creek.

As you climb out of the redwoods, the trail turns from mud to dry powder while the temperature goes up a few degrees. The landscape changes from lush rainforest to the wide open feeling of the Sierras. If you can take your eyes off of the pine, scrub and wildflowers flanking the trail, you have views of the neighboring Santa Cruz Mountains while the ocean is behind you.

The trail narrows and widens, and alternates between gentle rolling slopes and steep, out-of-the-saddle grunters. The last 0.5 mile is an easy wall-hugging singletrack that offers a beautiful view of the coast.

The trail ends at a jeep trail. To the right is the upper parking lot. Turn left and keep your eyes peeled for the Whittemore Gulch trailhead, about 0.5 mile down. The trailhead is on the left, and if you go by too fast, you'll miss it. It's set back off the jeep trail a couple of feet, in a thickly

wooded area, and is identified by a wooden fence with a trail marker.

Now for some serious fun. The trail starts with a gentle downslope through the trees and leads to a test of your switchback skills. The first 1.5 miles are made tricky due to half a dozen very tight switchbacks that wind down the face of the mountain. After the last switchback, the trail goes from an open meadow to an E-ticket roller coaster through the redwoods. The scenery, if you take time to notice, is impossibly beautiful with huge redwoods and ferns everywhere.

Too quickly, you find yourself back at the bridge by the lower parking lot. Turn right and cross it to get back to the parking lot.

9 Borden Hatch to Grabtown Gulch

Distance: 6 miles
Difficulty: Strenuous, somewhat technical
Elevation: 1,200' gain/loss; begin/end 400'; high point 1,600'
Ride Type: Loop on jeep trails
Season: Year-round
Topo Map: Woodside. (The Midpeninsula Open Space District produces a brochure with trail map available by calling 415-691-1200.)
Comments: Helmets required. Speed limit of 15 mph suggested but not enforced.

Overview: Although it's short, this is the second most popular ride in Purisima Creek Redwoods Open Space Preserve. The Borden Hatch Trail is a 3.5-mile climb along a canyon wall, through a forest of redwoods and eucalyptus. If you go to the end of the trail, you will find yourself at a country road that takes you to another park, Skeggs Point. Borden Hatch also leads to Grabtown Gulch, a hair-raising 1.25-mile descent back down the canyon to Purisima Creek. As if the grade didn't make it lively enough, there are water bars every 50-100 feet, for those who prefer to fly.

This loop is most populated by bicyclists; Borden Hatch, albeit one of the prettiest trails in the park, is considered an out-and-back by loop-happy hikers for whom the steep Grabtown Gulch holds little appeal. Once in a while you may encounter hearty souls making their way up Grabtown Gulch, but not often.

Because this loop is short, most riders incorporate it into other rides. Therefore, it gets less populated later in the day. Depending on the time of year, the terrain is almost-but-not-quite dry to very muddy.

Getting There: This loop can only be directly accessed from the lower parking lot. Of course, you can ride across the park from the upper lot to get to the trailhead. Follow the driving directions for the previous ride.

Route: From the gate at the lower parking lot, follow Purisima Creek Road for 1.0 mile to the Borden Hatch trailhead, which is on the right. You begin to climb immediately, but the severity of the grade eases past the first turn. After that point, it alternates from "this isn't so bad," to kind of hard to downright steep. There are also several coasting sections and a couple of downhills just to keep things interesting. You get to use pretty much all of your gears on this trail.

The only time you do not have towering trees as a ceiling is when you come to a trail junction in a small meadow, 3.5 miles up. Turn left onto Grabtown Gulch and quickly descend back into the trees. The turns on this trail are mostly blind and the waterbars seem to get taller the farther down you go. It also gets slippery in spots. Again, it is a beautiful trail, guarded by redwoods, eucalyptus and ferns.

The last two waterbars are the steepest and may require a bit of lifting to get your front wheel onto them. The trail ends back on Purisima Creek Road, about 0.25 mile from the Borden Hatch trailhead. Turn left onto Purisima Creek Road to get back to the parking lot.

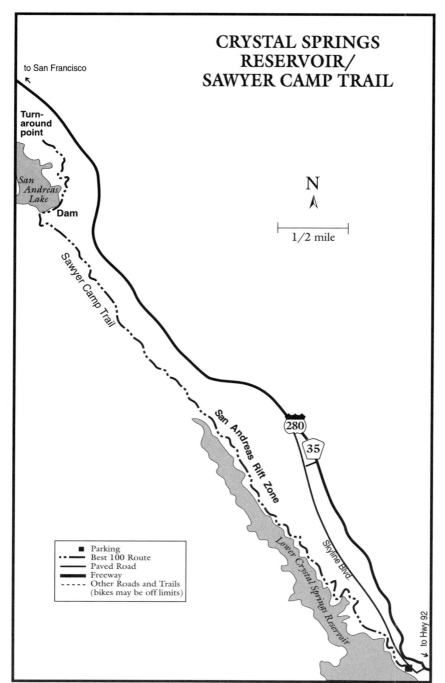

CRYSTAL SPRINGS RESERVOIR/ SAWYER CAMP TRAIL

to San Francisco

Turn-
around
point

San
Andreas
Lake

Dam

Sawyer Camp Trail

N
A

├─── 1/2 mile ───┤

San Andreas Rift Zone

280

35

Lower Crystal Springs Reservoir

Skyline Blvd.

to Hwy 92

■ Parking
·-·-· Best 100 Route
─── Paved Road
━━━ Freeway
- - - Other Roads and Trails
(bikes may be off limits)

10 Crystal Springs Reservoir/ Sawyer Camp Trail

Distance: 12 miles
Difficulty: Easy, not technical
Elevation: 300' gain/loss
Ride Type: Out-and-back on pavement
Season: Year-round
Topo Maps: Montara Mountain, San Mateo
Comments: Mosquito repellent is a must. Enforced speed limits.

Overview: Although not a "real" mountain bike trail, under the strictest definition, the Sawyer Camp Trail warrants attention because it's such a great family trail; an easy, rolling out-and-back with plenty of benches and bathrooms. In fact, families are the dominant user group, so keep an eye out for wandering toddlers and small children wobbling on their first bikes.

This trail is also a popular winter destination for local mountain bikers when rains close the nearby trails or as an easy spin on warm summer evenings. At any given time, you're as likely to see the latest in full-suspension high-zoot technology as you are a kid on a Big Wheel.

The path winds along the lower branch of the Crystal Springs Reservoir and the southern end of San Andreas Lake. Beneath the lake is the site where our old friend Gaspar de Portola camped after making his exhausting discovery. The surrounding land is now a fish and game reserve; woodland creatures may shadow you on the hillside above the trail as you make your way through stands of live oak, Monterey pine, eucalyptus and laurel.

Speaking of laurel, you'll be passing by the oldest and largest one. Over 600 years old, the Jepson Laurel is named for California botanist Willis Linn Jepson. Signs in both directions point out the tree.

The Sawyer Camp Trail parallels the infamous San Andreas Fault, which was responsible for the "Great Earthquake" of 1906 that devastated San Francisco. Most of the trail runs approximately a mile parallel to the fault although once you cross the dam, you'll be just a few feet away.

Getting There: From San Francisco, drive 27 miles south on Highway 280 to the Bunker Hill exit and veer right. Turn right onto Skyline Boulevard. The reservoir entrance is about 0.5 mile away, on the left. There's a small parking lot just south of the gate, or you can park on the road.

Route: The minute you pass through the reservoir's main gate, you're on the trail. There are no turns or tricky parts, making this one of the all-time easiest trails to follow. Scattered alongside the paved path are several taste-tempting morsels of singletrack. Unfortunately, as a multitude of signs and your fellow trail users will gleefully point out, these are strictly off-limits to bikes. Violators are not only subject to fines, but to serious doses of poison oak and insect bites as well.

You'll be sharing the trail with walkers and in-line skaters until about the 3.0-mile mark, at which point the crowds thin out. The famed Jepson Laurel towers off to your left at 3.5 miles. Its moss-shrouded cousins keep you company for the next 1.0 mile or so, until you start a mild climb.

At the top of the rise, just past the 5.0-mile mark, you ride along the San Andreas Dam, at the southeast end of San Andreas Lake. The dam was built in 1869 and its claim to fame is its strength; it survived the 1906 earthquake unscathed, although pipes leading in and out of it sheared right off. The dam also serves as a scenic overlook. As you cross it, the Crystal Springs Valley is laid out to the right. From this point of view, there's no sign of civilization, or even the bike path you just came up, only rolling green hills and lots of trees.

On the other side of the dam, an easy 0.5-mile climb takes you to the end of the path at the park's north gate. Turn around here and head back, keeping in mind that foot traffic starts getting heavy again at about the halfway mark.

11 Saratoga Gap

Distance: 9.5 miles
Difficulty: Moderate, somewhat technical
Elevation: 1,200' gain/loss
Ride Type: Loop on fire roads and singletrack
Season: Year-round; heavy rain closes portions of the trail
Topo Maps: Mindego Hill, Cupertino. (Existing topos do not show the Saratoga Gap Trail or the Canyon Trail/Charcoal Road junction that leads over Table Mountain.)

Overview: This is one of the most popular loops in the Bay Area. A series of trails leads through grasslands and forest, replete with pine, oak and the ever-present ferns. The terrain rolls, steeply at times, along the ridges and down the canyon to Stevens Creek and back up, making for a truly scenic adventure.

The trails join together three open-space areas: Saratoga Gap, Montebello and Long Ridge. While each open-space preserve offers its own share of mountain biking opportunities, this particular loop provides a sort of sampler plate.

Getting There: The trailhead is located at the junction of Highways 9 and 35. From San Francisco, take 280 south to the Highway 92 turnoff. Head west on 92 to Highway 35 (Skyline Boulevard), which pops up right away. Turn left onto Skyline and follow it to the parking lot at the junction with Highway 9, about 25 miles.

Route: From the gate, follow the first stretch of singletrack, the Saratoga Gap Trail, to the intersection with the Charcoal Road. Tantalizing as it looks, the Charcoal Road is only bike-legal going uphill (you'll be climbing it at the end of the ride). Turn left instead onto the Long Ridge Trail and follow it back out to Skyline. Cross the highway and pick up the trail again on the other side, in the Long Ridge Open Space.

As the name suggests, the trail rolls along a ridge. Ignore any spurs that drop toward the west (your left). Also ignore ones that go east until you reach a four-way intersection, at about 2.5 miles. Here you want to bear right onto a semi-steep singletrack descent. Bear left and stay on

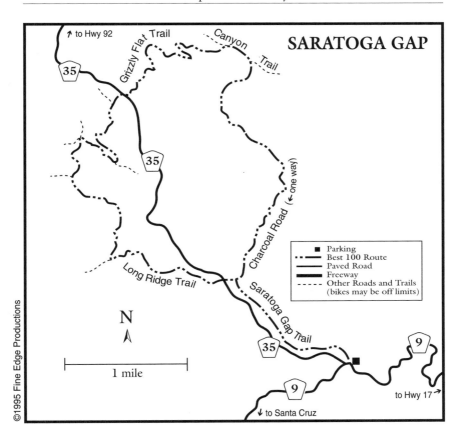

SARATOGA GAP

↑ to Hwy 92

Grizzly Flat Trail

Canyon Trail

35

35

Charcoal Road (←one way)

Long Ridge Trail

Saratoga Gap Trail

35

9

9

to Hwy 17 ↗

↓ to Santa Cruz

■ Parking
··· — Best 100 Route
—— Paved Road
▬▬ Freeway
---- Other Roads and Trails
(bikes may be off limits)

N
Λ

|— 1 mile —|

©1995 Fine Edge Productions

the singletrack when it makes a dog-leg turn above Peters Creek. At the bottom, follow the trail through the meadow and across the seasonally-technical stream and climb back up to your old friend, Skyline Boulevard.

Cross the highway again, enter the Montebello Open Space and head onto the Grizzly Flat Trail. This trail has a lot to do with the loop's popularity. The sometimes steep yet always enjoyable trail leads you down to and over Stevens Creek. A series of switchbacks brings you to the junction with the Canyon Trail.

Turn right onto the Canyon Trail and enjoy the last bit of downhill you'll taste on this ride. At 6.0 miles, turn right onto Charcoal Road. This nasty yet picturesque climb gets easier as you reach Table Mountain, around 7.0 miles into the ride, at which point you bear right to continue climbing on Charcoal Road. Remember the uphill-only trail that you saw at the beginning of the ride? This is it.

The trail ends back at the intersection with Saratoga Gap Trail. Turn left to get back to the parking lot.

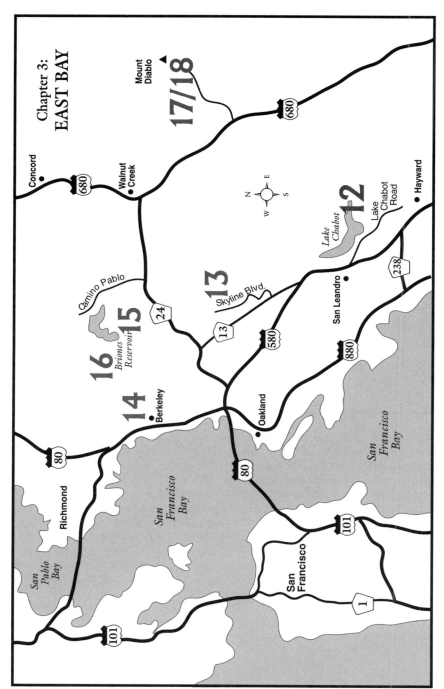

Chapter 3:
EAST BAY

Mount Diablo

17/18

680

Concord

680

Walnut Creek

N W E S

Lake Chabot

12

Lake Chabot Road

Hayward

Camino Pablo

13

Skyline Blvd.

Briones Reservoir

15

16

24

13

San Leandro

238

14

Berkeley

580

880

80

Oakland

San Francisco Bay

80

Richmond

San Francisco Bay

101

San Pablo Bay

San Francisco

101

1

East Bay

by Robin Stuart

If you live in the Bay Area, the chances are that you or someone you love lives in the East Bay. Just across the Bay Bridge from San Francisco proper, this sprawling suburbopolis is comprised of dozens of mini-suburbs with names like Hayward, San Leandro and Castro Valley; upscale bedroom communities like Danville, Pleasant Hill and Blackhawk; and the cities-within-the-suburbs of Oakland, Richmond and Berkeley. Doesn't exactly sound like a mountain biker's paradise, does it?

Don't be fooled. Lurking within and beyond each of the aforementioned locales are several of the most popular trails in Northern California. The allure of the East Bay parks is their knack for containing some of the most spectacular ridge rides this side of the Sierras. On any given trail, the views may range from the Bay to Yosemite. The trails themselves are visions in eucalyptus and live oak, with smatterings of pine and redwood.

Another likely reason for the East Bay's popularity is the accessibility of its trails; while some of the climbs and descents may be, shall we say, invigorating, few of them are technically difficult. Tree roots and loose rocks pop up here and there, but the most common technical challenge is sand-like pulverized soil. The later it gets in the season, the looser the trails become, owing to the region's arid summer and fall months.

One of the drawbacks of the East Bay is its lack of legal singletrack. However, as the number of mountain bikers continues to grow, hopefully, so too will our clout. In the meantime, there are plenty of fire roads, jeep trails and doubletrack with spectacular views to keep us busy and breathless.

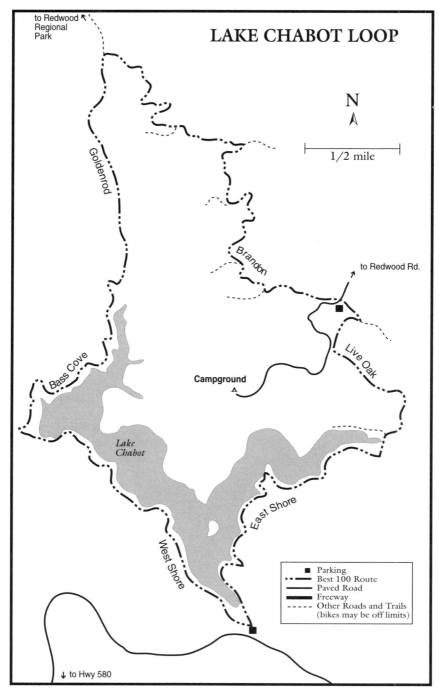

LAKE CHABOT LOOP

to Redwood
Regional
Park

N
∧

1/2 mile

Goldenrod

Brandon

to Redwood Rd.

Bass Cove

Live Oak

Campground
∧

Lake
Chabot

East Shore

West Shore

■ Parking
·—·— Best 100 Route
—— Paved Road
▬▬ Freeway
- - - Other Roads and Trails
(bikes may be off limits)

↓ to Hwy 580

© 1995 Fine Edge Productions

12 Lake Chabot Loop

Distance: 11.2 miles
Difficulty: Moderately strenuous, mildly technical
Elevation: 600' gain/loss
Ride Type: Loop on fire roads
Season: Year-round
Map: Olmsted & Bros. Rambler's Guide to the Trails of the East Bay Hills (Central)
Comments: Water is available at each entrance and along the paved portions of the path. Bells are required.

Overview: This loop is an area favorite with riders of all abilities. Beginners will find a couple of the climbs challenging, but they are paid for in spades by the overall roller-coaster ride around the lake and through forests of madrone, pine and live oak in the park's southern end, and eucalyptus, bay and pine in the north.

The ride follows a circuit around the 4,900-acre Anthony Chabot Regional Park, better known as Lake Chabot. The park sits on the boundaries of Castro Valley, San Leandro and Oakland and has entrances in each city. The lake itself is actually a reservoir built in 1875 by a placer mining engineer, Anthony Chabot. It's now used as an emergency water supply for the East Bay.

Getting There: From the Bay Bridge, head east on 580 towards Hayward. Take the Fairmont Drive exit, turning left at the second light onto Fairmont. Follow Fairmont over the hill into Castro Valley where the road becomes Lake Chabot Road. Just past the first left is the left turn into the park. Expect to pay a $1 day-use fee during the summer and on weekends.

Route: Starting from the main parking lot, follow the paved footpath into the barbecue area at the marina. Make the first right turn over a small bridge

and turn left onto the East Shore path. This is a popular walking path with a bike speed limit of 15 mph. Keep right and beware around blind turns of fishermen holding their poles straight out in front of them.

At about 1.5 miles, you'll reach a gate that signifies the end of the pavement as well as the foot traffic. Just past the gate, turn left and walk down the narrow steps to the bridge. On the other side of the bridge, gear down and get ready for the worst climb of the day.

Bear right and bear with the Live Oak Trail. It's graded regularly which ensures loose conditions. To the right is the southwestern boundary of the Willow Park Golf Course. As you creep your way up, you can feel superior to the golfers until you round a bend which hides the plaid bunch from view. To the left, you have a great view of Honker Bay and the southern half of Lake Chabot.

The worst of the climbing is over as you reach the 2.5-mile point. The trail levels for a short while, ending at a road that leads to a campground. Turn right on the trail that parallels the road, and follow it as it winds up to the ridge.

At the top, at about 3.0 miles, make a hairpin turn to the left, onto the Brandon Trail. The trail quickly leads to a gate and another parking lot. Go out the gate, cross the parking lot and the road, and pick up Brandon through the gate on the other side. The next 1.0 mile or so is a washboard, the result of being a popular thoroughfare for equestrians. Keep an eye out for them.

At approximately 3.5 miles, you come to an intersection; bear right to stay on the Brandon Trail. A second intersection quickly follows; again, stay right. About this time, you'll probably also notice the sound of gunfire. On the other side of the ridge is a shooting range. Although it is disconcerting, you're not in any danger.

The trail dives down, then swoops back up again, which is a recurring pattern for the rest of the ride. At the top of the first brief climb, you'll reach the next intersection; bear right and keep on Brandon. Within 0.5 mile, at the next intersection, turn left. Believe it or not, you'll still be on Brandon.

Not all trails are signed, so late spring through fall the trail intersections are marked with white arrows painted on the ground; the arrows point in the direction of the Brandon Trail to minimize the confusion.

After a few more swoops, the trail leads down a rocky hill. At the bottom of the hill, at about 6.0 miles, you'll come to a stone bridge. If you turn right, you can follow the East Bay Skyline Trail to the Redwood Regional Park. On this ride, though, turn left and out of the oak and begin the climb through the eucalyptus up the Goldenrod Trail. The climb levels at 6.6 miles and rolls along the northwestern ridge before diving back down towards the lake. This ridge skirts the back side of a eucalyptus forest; it smells good but you won't see much.

At approximately 8.0 miles, the trail dead ends at a paved path used by golf carts (this time, it's the Lake Chabot Golf Course). Turn left for a quick paved descent, then left again at the bottom and back to the dirt to catch the Bass Cove Trail. This trail is a fun stretch of twisting downhill leading back to the water's edge.

You come to a fork at 9.1 miles; bear left followed by a quick right to the trail's end at the paved West Shore Trail and the dam. Turn left and follow the rolling path back to the marina and the parking lot.

13 Redwood Regional Park/ West Ridge to East Ridge Loop

Distance: 9.0 miles
Difficulty: Moderately strenuous, some technical sections
Elevation: 900' gain/loss
Ride Type: Loop on fire roads
Season: Year-round
Map: Olmsted & Bros. Rambler's Guide to the Trails of the East Bay Hills (Central Section)
Comments: Water is available at park entrances; bells are required.

Overview: Slightly north of Lake Chabot (and connected by the East Bay Skyline Trail) is the regal Red-wood Regional Park. As the name implies, one of the park's highlights is its inviting forest of redwoods; the

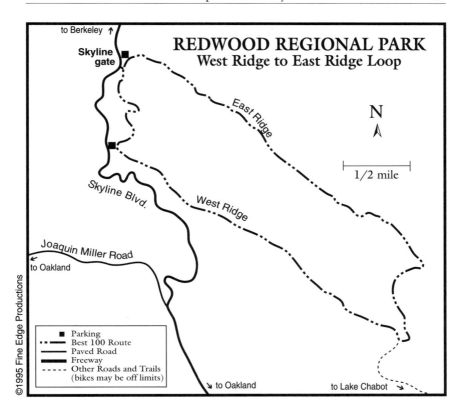

REDWOOD REGIONAL PARK
West Ridge to East Ridge Loop

Parking
Best 100 Route
Paved Road
Freeway
Other Roads and Trails
(bikes may be off limits)

©1995 Fine Edge Productions

West/East Loop begins and ends under their cool canopy. Believe me, in the heat of summer, it's very much appreciated.

Although shorter, this trail is a little more exciting than the Lake Chabot Loop, which is why riders with the time and energy like to combine the two (such a loop would be 22.5 miles). Here in Redwood Regional, the loop begins on a redwood-forested ridge, drops down into the canyon and climbs back up. Sounds simple enough, right?

What makes this ride so popular is that it starts with a few tree roots and drops down along great slabs of rock which lead to a loose and dusty screaming downhill. You have a chance to catch your breath on the level traipse across the canyon floor to a grunting uphill followed by a roller-coaster ride back to the car.

Although some people have different names for it, nearly every Bay Area rider you talk to mentions this ride as one of their favorites.

Getting There: From the Bay Bridge, take 580 to 24 (Walnut Creek). From 24, take Highway 13 (Warren Freeway) south to the Joaquin Miller Road exit. Head east on Joaquin Miller to Skyline Boulevard. Turn left on Skyline and follow it for approximately 3 miles to the parking lot at the Redwood Regional Skyline Gate which is on the right.

Route: From the gate, turn right into the redwoods and onto the West

Ridge Trail. Along the way, you'll have to ignore several beckoning singletracks that lead down to a creek trail; all of the singletrack here is illegal. Just over 1.0 mile from the gate, the West Ridge Trail seemingly ends at a second parking lot. Shoot straight across and you'll see where it continues on the other end.

Right away, you get to test your technical prowess with a section of gnarled, twisty, tall tree roots on the trail. They look kind of like a large primeval nest. At that same point, the left bank of the trail drops off, so you can't really go around them.

Once you've crossed the roots, the trail winds up and through the forest, leading out of the redwoods and to the next adventure, the rock slabs. The rock is almost shaped like giant, off-kilter stairs and the traction is better than you think it would be. Head on down and keep in mind that the last "step" is kind of tall; beginners should lay off the front brake while more advanced riders should raise their front wheel to smooth out the landing.

From this point, the trail levels and gets dusty for the next 1.0 mile or so. Then the trail veers off to the right and starts to slope downhill. The grade is gentle at first, leading to a wide turn after which it pitches into a loose and steep straightaway. At the bottom, the trail levels as you wind out of the forest and into a grass clearing. Follow the path through and around the picnic area.

The dirt briefly becomes a paved path as you bear left onto the connector to East Ridge, at 6.0 miles. (Heading straight on West Ridge leads you out of the park to Lake Chabot, a little over 2.0 miles away.) At the sign for East Ridge, the dirt begins again and so does a short, nasty climb.

At the top, there's a brief level spot before the trail pitches uphill again, this time for about 1.0 mile. There are periodic level spots in the climb that make it bearable. There are also great views of the surrounding parklands in between the trees.

Right around 7.0 miles, you reach the redwoods and the end of relentless climbing. From here, the trail rolls along the canyon wall back to the parking lot.

14 Tilden Park/Wildcat Loop

Distance: 13.3 miles
Difficulty: Moderate, mildly technical
Elevation: 600' gain/loss
Ride Type: Loop on fire roads
Season: Spring through fall
Map: Olmsted & Bros. Rambler's Guide to the Trails of the East Bay Hills
(North Section)
Comments: Water is available at the trailhead. The claylike soil turns into a quagmire in
the rain; in the event of spring rains, let it dry out for several days before attempting to
ride here.

Overview: Often mentioned in the same breath as Redwood Regional Park is Tilden, one of the East Bay's oldest parks. Nestled in the Berkeley hills, this particular loop stretches north beyond the boundaries of Tilden and into the adjacent Wildcat Canyon Regional Park. The ride is akin to the Lake Chabot Loop; rolling fire roads through forests of live

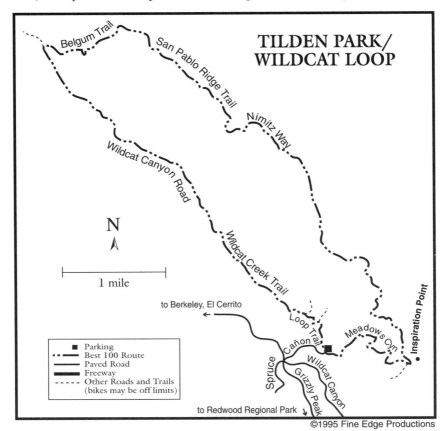

TILDEN PARK/
WILDCAT LOOP

©1995 Fine Edge Productions

oak and eucalyptus, a portion of paved bike path and a climb thrown in for good measure.

There are two features that make this ride a crowd-pleaser; first, it's relatively easy and second, you can catch a glimpse of the Hayward Fault. The loop takes you past an unused road and parking lot, abandoned as a result of the damage wrought by the road's placement literally right on top of the active fault. What Californians don't secretly fancy themselves junior seismologists?

Getting There: From the Bay Bridge, take 80 north (Berkeley/Richmond) to the University Avenue exit. From University, turn left onto Martin Luther King Drive. Follow MLK for

about a mile and turn right onto Marin Avenue. About a half mile up Marin, turn left onto Spruce. Follow Spruce to the intersection at the Spruce Gate with Grizzly Peak, Wildcat Canyon and Cañon Drive. Make a left onto Cañon Drive. Take the first right onto Central Park Drive and left on Lone Oak Road to the Lone Oak parking lot and trailhead.

Route: From the parking lot, head up through the picnic area to the Loop Trail. This quickly leads to Jewell Lake, a popular stop for walkers and bikes. At the lake, bear right onto the Wildcat Creek Trail. This part of the loop is fairly level, leading out of Tilden Park and into Wildcat Canyon. Once inside the Wildcat bound-

BRIONES REGIONAL PARK
Short Loop & Briones Crest Loop

N

1/2 mile

Briones Crest Trail
Briones Crest Trail
Old Briones Road
Crescent Ridge Trail
Homestead Valley Trail
to Tilden Park, Orinda
Bear Creek Road

■ Parking
▪-▪-▪ Best 100 Route
—— Paved Road
▬▬ Freeway
- - - - Other Roads and Trails
        (bikes may be off limits)

©1995 Fine Edge Productions

ary, the trail rolls very gently to the cracked abandoned road. Welcome to earthquake country.

Past the damaged road, the trail rolls pleasantly to the intersection with the Belgum Trail at about 5.0 miles. Hang a right onto Belgum and start climbing. This trail takes you out of the canyon and up to the views. Within 1.0 mile, you emerge from the trees to the ridge line and the San Pablo Ridge Trail. Bear right and follow San Pablo along the ridge.

There are a couple of nasty little climbs along the way that reward you with views of the Bay to one side and Mount Diablo to the other. With a final descent, the trail joins the paved Nimitz Way at 7.5 miles. This path continues rolling along the ridge to Inspiration Point where you turn right, and back onto dirt, on the Curran Trail.

At the next intersection, which comes up quickly, turn right again, onto the Meadows Canyon Trail. Meadows Canyon takes you on a loose washboarded 1.5-mile downhill that ends back at the parking lot.

15 Briones Regional Park/ Short Loop

Distance: 5.7 miles
Difficulty: Moderately strenuous, mildly technical
Elevation: 800' gain/loss
Ride Type: Loop on sometimes narrow fire roads and doubletrack
Season: Spring through fall
Topo Map: Briones Valley. (The East Bay Regional Park District makes a free brochure and trail map available at the park or by calling 510-562-PARK.)
Comments: Water is available at the staging area. Cattle regularly graze here; please close all gates behind you.

Overview: Briones Regional Park is truly the East Bay's best-kept secret. Tucked away in a remote corner of Contra Costa County, Briones is a virtual wonderland of winding trails, breathtaking views, miles of rolling woodlands and wild downhills. And the best part is, not many people know it's there.

At Briones, a smorgasbord of trails awaits you, leading up from the forests in the Bear Creek Canyon and the Alhambra Valley to grassland ridges and peaks. Although the singletrack is illegal for bikes, there's nearly 40 miles of legal fire roads and doubletrack, ranging from short and easy valley forays to day-long adventures filled with thigh-burning climbs and hair-raising downhills.

This particular ride is reserved for the downhill aficionados: a relatively easy climb followed by a twisting, screaming descent that can feel, at times, like a freefall along a loose and dusty fire road with the occasional rock outcropping.

Getting There: From the Bay Bridge, take 580 east to Highway 24 (Walnut Creek). Past the Caldecott Tunnel, take the Orinda exit and turn left, onto Camino Pablo. From Camino Pablo, turn right onto Bear Creek Road. The Briones Park Bear Creek Staging Area is on the right, about 4.5 miles up the road. There's a $1 day-use fee during the summer and on weekends.

Route: Starting at the gate at the

upper parking lot, head up the paved road. The pavement ends around the first turn at a fork where you bear left onto the Old Briones Road Trail. It looks like you're about to climb up into a yucky ol' dry grass wasteland until you round the first turn. Personally, it reminds me of the Yosemite Valley, sans the big rocks. Whatever impression you get, you'll find yourself winding around a tree-studded meadow, complete with a creek. The climb starts out very subtly, giving your journey an all-around pleasant beginning.

Just past the corral, turn left at the intersection with the Valley Trail to stay on Old Briones. The climb gets a little tougher, interspersed with a couple of short descents, as you roll your way up to the ridge. As the valley starts to fall away, you can see the San Pablo Reservoir behind you.

At the next trail junction at 1.7 miles, turn right onto the Briones Crest Trail towards Briones Peak. The trail is fairly level at this point and for the next 1.0 mile or so. Between the trees, you can catch glimpses of the surrounding hillsides and Mount Diablo.

At the fork with Table Top and Spengler Trails, make a hard right to stay on the Briones Crest Trail. At this point, the roller coaster begins in earnest. The trail heads in an overall downhill direction in a series of sweeping descents followed by sometimes steep climbs.

The trail ends at a cattle gate. Turn right past the gate; this continues to be the Briones Crest Trail. Within 0.5 mile, you'll see another gate on the right. Turn in here to experience a killer downhill—the often steep, but totally cool Crescent Ridge Trail.

The first hundred feet or so is level, but once the downhill starts it's like a carnival ride. Most of the turns are completely blind so keep your speed in control at all times; you may be greeted by a herd of cows grazing their way across the trail or a couple of startled equestrians.

At about 4.0 miles, at the top of a short climb, the trail levels briefly before pitching down through a very steep granite outcropping. Just wanted to warn you.

The grade eases to almost level at about 4.5 miles, at the junction with the Yerba Buena Trail. From here, you can see your valley destination but you can't see the trail that awaits around the turn. Keep going straight down Crescent Ridge and be prepared for a steep and bumpy ride. The rest of the downhill is a steep, loose and severely hoof-rutted straightaway down to the meadow.

The trail ends at the Homestead Valley Trail; turn right and follow Homestead Valley across the meadow and through the gate for a last descent to a seasonal water crossing. After a short climb, the trail ends at the junction with the trailhead of the Old Briones Trail. Bear left back onto the paved road to head back to the parking lot.

16 Briones Crest Loop

Distance: 8 miles
Difficulty: Moderately strenuous, mildly technical
Elevation: 800' gain/loss
Ride Type: Loop on sometimes narrow fire roads and doubletrack
Season: Spring through fall
Topo Map: Briones Valley. (The East Bay Regional Park District produces a free map of the park available at the park or by calling 510-562-PARK.)
Comments: Water is available at the staging area; please close cattle gates behind you.

Overview: This loop is the most popular ride at Briones Regional Park and a great way to acquaint yourself with the type of trails that the park has to offer. The loop follows the Briones Crest Trail as it rolls around the central portion of the park, through dense forests of live oak and fruit trees, the John Muir Nature Area, past mountain lagoons and back down to the Homestead Valley meadow and Bear Creek. This trail is less taxing than the previous loop; although there are a couple of brief steep climbs and descents, it's suitable for most riders.

Getting There: See the directions for the previous ride.

Route: Beginning at the lower parking lot, go through the gate for the Briones Crest and Deer Creek Trails, making the first right onto the Briones Crest Trail. The trail meanders gently up through the trees to the ridge line. At 1.6 miles, you'll come to an intersection with the Santos Trail; bear left to stay on Briones Crest.

Just past the 2.0-mile mark, you'll enter the John Muir Nature Area. From this point, the next 2.5 miles roll along the ridge, in and out of the trees and through sweeping turns. Again, be on the lookout for roving herds of grazing cows.

At 3.2 miles, the trail takes you between the two Sindicich Lagoons. The trail may get a little more populated here, by horses and bikes, as this is a convergence point between the northern and southern park entrances.

Past the lagoons, bear right briefly onto Old Briones Road, then make the first left back onto Briones Crest. This section takes you past the park's highest point, Briones Peak (1,483'). On a clear day, you have expansive views from Mount Diablo and the Diablo Valley to the Bay.

At the next trail junction, make a hard right to stay on Briones Crest. The trail hugs the canyon wall as you begin to lose elevation. The trail rolls a little steeper back into the trees, followed by a steepish climb and ending at a cattle gate. Turn right past the gate to stay on Briones Crest. The trail widens for 0.5 mile, giving you glimpses of civilization beyond the trees to your left before turning back towards the park and heading down.

The trail ends at a fork at 6.2 miles. Turn right towards the meadow and onto the Homestead Valley Trail. Just past the next cattle gate, the trail rolls briefly but steeply down to Bear Creek then back up again to the junction with Old Briones Road. Turn left and follow the trail as it leads out of the park and into the upper parking lot. Cut across the lot to the lower lot and your car.

17 Mount Diablo/Wall Point Loop

Distance: 9.5 miles
Difficulty: Strenuous, mildly technical, seasonal water crossings
Elevation: 1,300' gain/loss
Ride Type: Loop on fire roads and singletrack
Season: Late winter through fall
Topo Maps: Diablo, Clayton. (The Mount Diablo Interpretive Association publishes an excellent Trail Map of Mount Diablo State Park and Adjacent Parklands, $5 and worth it at park headquarters.)
Comments: It gets very hot here; carry extra water (available at the trailhead).

Overview: The feather in the East Bay's cap, the icing on its cake, the heart and soul of the East Bay mountain biking world is Mount Diablo. With a summit elevation of 3,849 feet, Mount Diablo is the tallest mountain in the Bay Area and is visible from all corners.

Speaking of views, this mountain has some jaw-droppers. On a clear day, you can get a clean look at Yosemite's Half Dome. At closer range is the Diablo Valley, Sonoma Valley, the Santa Cruz Mountains, Mount Tamalpais and the Marin Headlands.

If it's trails you want, Mount Diablo has them, too. Lots of them. All of the mountain's fire roads are legal, with the added bonus of three singletrack segments. The trails range from almost-easy to forget-it-and-push, which twist and turn and wind and roll all over the mountain.

While each of the available trails seems to be somebody's favorite, the following rides are known and loved by many. This particular loop is a popular race site, with a couple of challenging climbs and long, sweeping descents. The loop leads through forests of live oak, across a couple of creeks, up to a chaparral-covered ridge before turning back towards the trees and through the Diablo Ranch.

Getting There: From the Bay Bridge, take eastbound 580 to 24 (Walnut Creek). Follow 24 to the 680 split, taking 680 south (Dublin/Sacramento). Next take the Diablo Road exit and turn right at the light. At the intersection of Diablo and El Cerro Roads, turn right again, staying on Diablo Road. Turn left onto Green Valley Road and follow to end at dirt parking lot and the Macedo Ranch trailhead.

Route: The ride begins with a granny-gear climb up the Wall Point Road trail. You'll come immediately to a fork where you bear right to stay on Wall Point. Around the next bend, the grade eases, and begins to roll through forests of live oak. The first descent leads through a seasonal water crossing followed by a semi-steep climb.

At the bottom of the next descent, turn left and go through another seasonal creek onto Stage Road for a brief level section. At the pond, turn right onto Burma Road. At the top of the first short but steep climb, turn right to stay on Burma.

The trail levels at this point and crosses the paved North Gate Road. Bear right at the fork on the other side of the road and climb up and past two-humped Camel Rock. Bear left

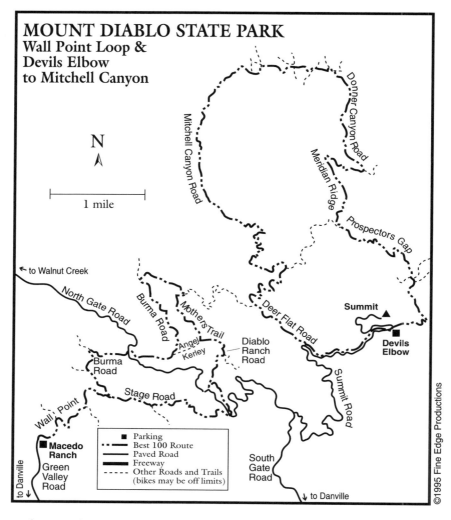

MOUNT DIABLO STATE PARK
Wall Point Loop &
Devils Elbow
to Mitchell Canyon

N
A

|—————————————|
      1 mile

←— to Walnut Creek

North Gate Road

Burma Road

Mother's Trail

Angel Kerley

Burma Road

Stage Road

Wall Point

Macedo Ranch

Green Valley Road

to Danville ↓

Parking
Best 100 Route
Paved Road
Freeway
Other Roads and Trails
(bikes may be off limits)

Mitchell Canyon Road

Donner Canyon Road

Meridian Ridge

Prospectors Gap

Deer Flat Road

Summit ▲

Devils Elbow

Diablo Ranch Road

Summit Road

South Gate Road

↓ to Danville

©1995 Fine Edge Productions

at the next intersection to stay on Burma. Again, the climb eases for a brief respite.

At a fork at the bottom of a short descent, turn right (still on Burma Road) and do a little more climbing. At about 4.7 miles, you reach one of the park's three legal singletracks, Mother's Trail. Hang a right and enjoy it as it leads down, then around, ending in a short rise at Angel Kerley Road. Turn left onto

Angel Kerley and then make the first right onto Diablo Ranch Road.

Diablo Ranch starts with a steep downhill that levels past the switchback then rolls back across the road and through the actual Diablo Ranch. At the ranch, head west back onto Stage Road for a fast fire road descent to the junction with Wall Point. Bear left to connect with Wall Point, endure the last climb, and then it's all downhill back to the trailhead.

18 Mount Diablo/Mitchell Canyon to Devils Elbow

Distance: 12.3 miles
Difficulty: Strenuous, moderately technical
Elevation: 2,800' gain/loss
Ride Type: Loop on singletrack and fire roads
Season: Spring through fall
Topo Map: Clayton. (The Mount Diablo Interpretive Association publishes an excellent Trail Map of the park and adjacent parklands—$5 (and worth it) at park headquarters.)
Comments: Carry extra water; water is available at the half-way point.

Overview: This ride begins just a few hundred feet from Mount Diablo's summit, affording some amazing views. It begins with a thrilling downhill, the terrain changing from high scrub to forest to a rocky canyon before climbing back up along a creek. Some parts of this ride may be a bit too hair-raising for some folks, but experienced riders will relish it.

Getting There: From the Bay Bridge, take eastbound 580 to 24 (Walnut Creek). Follow 24 to the 680 split, and take 680 south (Dublin/Sacramento). Take the Diablo Road exit, turning left at the light. Follow Diablo Road to Mt. Diablo Scenic Boulevard and turn left. This becomes South Gate Road as you pass through the park gates. Follow the road to the ranger station, about 4 miles. Bear right onto Summit Road. Park at the Devils Elbow turnout/trailhead, about 2 miles up.

Route: From the Devils Elbow trailhead, the ride starts off with a bang, beginning with a loose and rocky singletrack downhill. Some might call it devilish! Hope you like steep descents; in the first 1.0 mile, you'll lose just under 1,000 feet.

Follow the singletrack to the somewhat confusing trail junction with three fire roads and an illegal singletrack. The singletrack is on your left and the other two fire roads on your right. Head straight onto the Prospectors Gap fire road for another gravity lesson. The trail starts off steeply then smoothes out past the switchback and the crossing of Donner Creek.

After a brief spell of level trail, turn right onto Meridian Ridge Road and lose some more elevation. Past a hairpin turn at Meridian Point, there's a short climb up to the next trail junction. Turn left here onto the Donner Canyon Road for the last rolling descent along Donner Creek.

At 4.5 miles, turn left onto an unnamed fire road, heading toward the Clayton entrance of the park. At the ranger station, turn left on Mitchell Canyon Road, which begins as a relatively easy climb along Mitchell Creek. At 6.5 miles, it steepens sharply, and you begin the arduous task of regaining all that lost elevation. Periodic level spots generally appear when you start thinking your heart will jump out of your throat.

At about 9 miles, the trail levels as it approaches Deer Flat Picnic Area. At the fork, turn right onto Deer Flat Creek Trail, a rolling fire road that levels off as it contours around the mountain to Juniper Campground. There you follow the paved footpath to Summit Road, where you go left to return to Devils Elbow parking area.

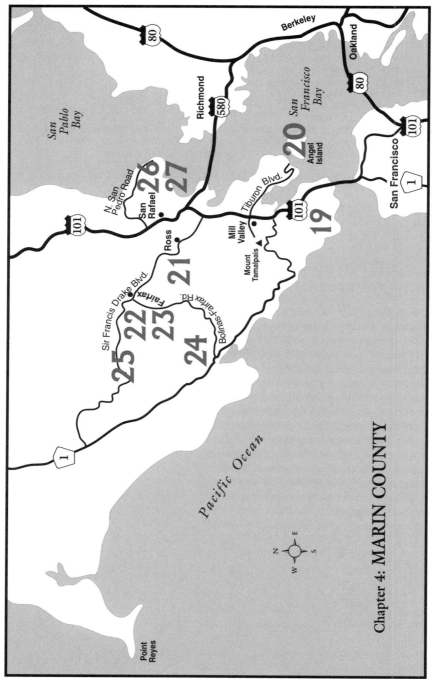

Chapter 4: MARIN COUNTY

CHAPTER 4

Marin County

by Robin Stuart

Marin is probably Northern California's most famous mountain biking county, the cradle of knobby civilization. In the early Seventies, a group of friends got together to play around on their balloon tire Schwinn cruisers, taking to the trails of Mount Tamalpais (affectionately known as Mt. Tam). Guys with names like Breeze, Fisher, Kelly, Ritchey and Cunningham. Tinkers all, they reinvented the bicycle, piece by piece, their dreams and ideas culminating in the lightweight works of art we now ride.

The trails in this chapter take you through mountain biking history. They also take you through some of the state's most beautiful open space and park lands, lush with redwoods, pine and madrone. Riding here, you understand why John Muir fell in love with the place, and why the region continues to draw artists, dreamers and mountain bikers in droves.

It must be noted, however, that trouble has been brewing here for some time now. From the get-go, hikers and equestrians have been waging a battle against mountain bike access. So far, they have successfully closed off dozens of trails to us and persuaded the powers-that-be to establish a universal speed limit on the remaining trails.

If you live here, you owe it to yourself and your fellow mountain bikers to contact the Bicycle Trails Council of Marin at (415) 456-7512. If nothing else, at least add your name to the growing number of riders lobbying to challenge trail closures, present and future. Visitors, once they have seen the great riding available and the sorry state of trail closures, may want to get involved, too.

As for the other problem, if you are caught exceeding the rather low speed limit of 15 mph, you may be slapped with a fine of $200! This rule is most stringently enforced on Mt. Tam, by way of radar guns and road blocks. The interesting part about both of these methods is that they are completely contestable; if you fight the ticket, you will probably win.

How? By instituting a "street" rule, i.e. a speed limit, the rangers have to follow the law as it applies to automobiles. Radar guns are inadmissible as evidence in California courts, and road blocks constitute entrapment—any evidence gathered by entrapment is also inadmissible. So, unless the ranger tags you by following you in a vehicle, or can prove your speed by some other legal means, the ticket is no good.

Riders who have fought tickets have also discovered that rangers, like police, aren't really good about keeping their court dates. No ranger, no witness, no crime. Just thought you might want to know.

19 Headlands Loop

Distance: 6.7 miles
Difficulty: Moderate, not technical
Elevation: 1,000' gain/loss
Ride Type: Loop on fire roads
Season: Year-round
Map: Olmsted & Bros. Rambler's Guide to the Trails of Mt. Tamalpais and the Marin Headlands
Comments: The trails get very muddy after rains; give them time to dry out.

Overview: The Marin Headlands are legendary—open grassland hills overlooking the San Francisco Bay in the shadow of Mount Tamalpais. This ride is a hit with beginners and the proficient alike, thanks (in no small part) to its breathtaking views.

Wildlife watchers will also enjoy Hawk Hill, located centrally within the loop. It's one of the best places in the country to spot soaring hawks, eagles and other birds of prey. Apparently, they don't like to fly over large bodies of water so they congregate here while they get their nerve up to cross the bay.

Getting There: From San Francisco, take Highway 101 north across the Golden Gate Bridge, to the Highway 1/Stinson Beach turnoff. Bear left onto Highway 1, and then take the Tennessee Valley Road exit. The parking lot is at the end of Tennessee Valley Road.

Route: Begin the ride by heading up the gently sloping Old Marincello Trail. The trail winds around as it

levels, hooking up with the Bobcat Trail. Continue ahead on Bobcat. At about 2.5 miles, you come to a fork as you turn towards the ocean. Bear right to stay on Bobcat and don't forget to look around; the views are pretty great.

This next part is everyone's favorite; the road gently descends for about 2.0 miles from the ridge to the Gerbode Valley. At the bottom, you follow a creek for about 0.5 mile before crossing it.

On the other side of the creek, the trail seemingly ends at an intersection with the Miwok Trail. This portion of the Miwok was illegal until recently, when it was widened to accommodate bikes. Turn right onto Miwok for a gentle climb.

As you approach the ridge line, you come to an intersection with Chaparral and Wolf Ridge Trails; turn right and stay on Miwok until you see a fire road on your left. This is Old Springs Road. Turn left and follow Old Springs as it rolls back up, past the stables and to the parking lot.

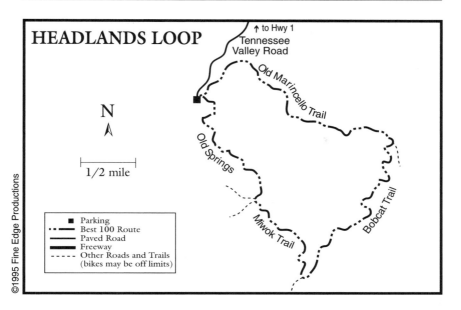

HEADLANDS LOOP

↑ to Hwy 1
Tennessee
Valley Road

Old Marincello Trail

Old Springs

N
A

├─────────┤
1/2 mile

Miwok Trail

Bobcat Trail

■ Parking
•• — Best 100 Route
—— Paved Road
▬▬ Freeway
- - - - Other Roads and Trails
(bikes may be off limits)

©1995 Fine Edge Productions

20 Angel Island Double Loop

Distance: 10.3 miles
Difficulty: Moderate, not technical
Elevation: 500' gain/loss
Ride Type: Loop on fire roads and doubletrack
Season: Year-round
Map: Available for $1 at the Ayala Cove dock.
Comments: Dress in layers; the temperature varies, sometimes wildly, as you make your way around the island. Restrooms and water are available along the way. A snack bar at Ayala Cove offers sandwiches, drinks (including beer and wine), and a variety of trail-mix-type snacks. Mountain bike rentals are also available (rigid Marins, what else!) for $12 per hour or $25 per day.

Overview: When was the last time you got to ride your bike around an island? Angel Island State Park is the largest of the San Francisco Bay islands, comprised of 750 acres of grassland, forests and beaches. Its size and location contributed to its long and sometimes checkered history.

The island's earliest known use was as a favorite hunting and fishing spot for the Miwok Indians, the original Marin natives. In 1775, the Spanish explorer Juan Manuel de Ayala

dropped anchor in what is now Ayala Cove while he and his men developed the first-ever maps of the region. It was Ayala who named the island, "Isla de Los Angeles," adhering to the tradition of Catholic explorers who named their "discoveries" for the nearest religious celebration.

In the early 1800s, the island was the site of Russian sea otter hunting expeditions. In 1814, the British sailing ship, HMS Raccoon was beached at Ayala Cove for repairs,

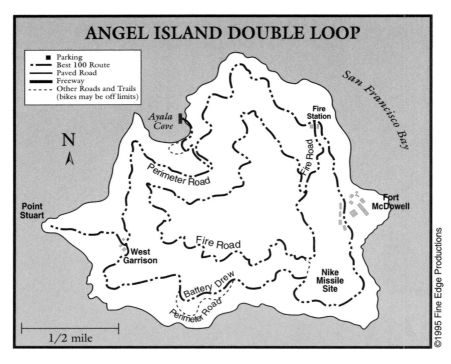

becoming the namesake for the deep-water channel between Tiburon and Angel Island, Raccoon Strait.

After a land grant dispute, the federal government declared owner-ship of the island in 1859, at which time the military took up its long residency. At differing times, the island served as a Civil War defense post, a training and staging area for campaigns against West Coast Indian tribes, a quarantine station to isolate troops exposed to contagious diseases during overseas actions, and a World War I prison for "enemy aliens" arrested on ships harbored on the West Coast.

Angel Island's most infamous incarnation was as the Immigration Station which opened in 1910. Although popularly referred to as the Ellis Island of the West, the detention center was actually used to dissuade and exclude new arrivals, most of whom were Chinese immigrants. (A museum at China Cove depicts this less-than-angelic bit of Angel Island history.) The Immigration Station was abandoned in 1940, shortly before the Chinese Exclusion Acts were repealed by the federal government.

Efforts to make the island a state park began in the late 1940s, led by local conservationist Caroline Livermore. Success was hard-won, and it came piecemeal. During this time a Nike missile-launching facility operated on the south side of the island. In 1963, the missile site was de-activated, and the entire island became state park land.

For those interested in delving into Angel Island's history in more detail, there is a large Visitor's Center located behind the picnic grounds at Ayala Cove and the above-mentioned museum at China Cove. The ride takes you past and through the remains of the abandoned military outposts.

On the lighter side, you also wander through forests of oak, eucalyptus, pine and fir and along a high ledge of Mount Livermore, named in honor of Caroline Livermore's efforts.

Getting There: This is a ride where getting there really is part of the fun. (Unless you really like boats, I wouldn't say it's "half the fun," more like a third.) Angel Island is only accessible by boat, via private crafts or a ferry from San Francisco, Vallejo or Tiburon. Located one mile southwest of the Tiburon harbor, the shortest boat ride is the Tiburon ferry, which takes about 15 minutes from dock to dock.

From the Golden Gate Bridge, follow 101 north to the Tiburon Blvd./E. Blithedale exit. Bear right onto Tiburon Boulevard, following it through Belvedere and into Tiburon. At about 4.5 miles, you reach a turnaround at the marina; park in the lot off the north side of the turnaround ($5). From the parking lot, turn right onto Tiburon Boulevard and bear left onto Main Street. The ferry leaves from 21 Main Street; a sign will direct you through the corridor out to the wooden dock.

The ferry is $5 roundtrip, plus $1 for your bike. The money is collected as you board. Keep your ticket, because you need to show it to return.

Route: From the Ayala Cove dock, head up the paved path to the right, past the snack bar, and turn left toward the Visitor's Center. You see a sign for the bike path pointing left,

directly across the road from the center. The pavement turns to dirt and gravel immediately.

Just past the second switchback, you come to a paved crossroad; head across, bearing right and up, onto Perimeter Road. The trail winds around and rolls through eucalyptus, bay and madrone. Throughout the ride, you are accompanied by great views of the Bay Area on your right.

The pavement intersperses with dirt and gravel all along Perimeter Road. On the first dirt stretch, at about 1.7 miles, you see the West Garrison on the right. Turn off here, following the trail between the buildings and toward a legal singletrack which leads steeply up to Point Stuart. From a clearing at the top of the trail, you get a great view of the San Francisco skyline and have a good little descent back to the main road. It's definitely worth the side trip.

Come back down the singletrack the way you went up and continue on Perimeter Road to a fork with the Battery Drew trail. Veer left up Battery Drew. This steepish climb takes you through a forest of oak and eucalyptus, past a small outcropping of serpentine rocks. At the top of the climb, there's a clearing which looks down on the lower Perimeter Road and out to the bay.

The reason I've led you up this way is for the long, fast descent back to Perimeter Road. It's a straight shot down along a slightly loose surface. At the bottom, veer left and continue on Perimeter.

At 3.1 miles, you reach the second crossroad. Turn right, back onto pavement, to continue on Perimeter Road. At 3.4 miles, you pedal past the Nike missile site. This mileage mark also signifies a long paved descent back to dirt. Technically, you are supposed to walk your bike down the pavement.

Back on the dirt, there's a little washboard followed by smooth dirt and gravel leading to the next historical point of interest: the East Garrison and Fort McDowell. Follow the road as it curves around and between the abandoned military buildings.

Just past the fort area, back on pavement again, you see the park fire station. At 4.5 miles, make the sharp left turn up into the driveway on the right side of the fire house. Within 50 feet, it goes back to gravel, becoming the Fire Road. With the exception of this one tricky turn, the rest of the Fire Road is well signed.

The Fire Road gets a little steep as you pedal up; it's not that hard but, compared to the rest of the ride, it's a little startling. At a big fork at 4.8 miles, bear right for a last little burst of steepness. Welcome to the amazing loop-within-a-loop.

At the top of the short climb, the road narrows and winds around the mountain along a doubletrack ledge. The next few miles of the ride are an unexpected delight, given the tame quality of the Perimeter Road outer loop. The doubletrack is dry and rocky, clinging to the edge of the mountain amid pine trees and manzanita. The trail is mostly level, leading subtly to its highest point, 100 feet below the mountain's summit. The views are, as one might expect, spectacular.

At about 7.5 miles, the scenery changes from reddish clay high country to a grassy pine forest. The trail surface goes from slightly loose and rocky to smooth hardpack as it begins to descend.

At 7.8 miles, you are back at the second paved crossroad. Stay left, crossing the pavement, and then shoot straight onto the dirt again, following the signs for the Fire Road. The doubletrack trail continues to wind around through the pine, leading to a fun downhill. The scenery should start looking familiar as you find yourself back at the fork behind the fire station, this time coming down the other side. Head straight out through the buildings to Perimeter Road.

Turn left and follow Perimeter as it rolls its way back to the very first crossroad. Make a very sharp right turn back onto the dirt switchback trail. At the Visitor's Center, turn right to get back to the dock.

21 Hoo Koo E Koo to Phoenix Lake

Distance: 12 miles
Difficulty: Strenuous, some technical sections
Elevation: 1,300' gain/loss
Ride Type: One-way shuttle on fire roads with short loop option
Season: Year-round
Map: Olmsted & Bros. Rambler's Guide to the Trails of Mt. Tamalpais and the Marin Headlands
Comments: Water is available at the Lake Lagunitas picnic area.

Overview: This ride is a local favorite, a way to get away from the throngs on Mt. Tam. The trails are crowd-ed pleasers, containing everything—famous names, steep climbs, steep descents, rocky technical sections, lakes, trees, wildflowers—everything but legal singletrack.

The Hoo Koo E Koo trail is one of the most famous on the mountain, probably because people like saying "Hoo Koo E Koo." The trail was named for the Native Americans that inhabited the area at the base of Mt. Tam. Knobby pioneer Gary Fisher, in turn, has named one of his bike models the Hoo Koo E Koo.

This ride also contains a section of the Eldridge Grade, another well-known and beloved trail, made famous by our fat-tire forefathers.

Getting There: This ride begins at the Old Railroad Grade trailhead and

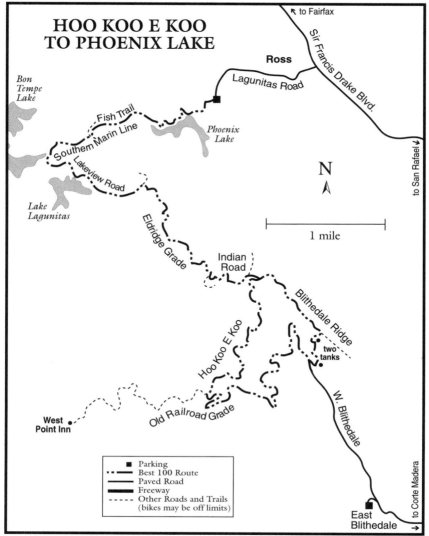

©1995 Fine Edge Productions

ends at Green Park in the town of Ross. To get a return vehicle to the parking lot at Green Park, take 101 north to the San Anselmo/Sir Francis Drake exit, bear left and take Sir Francis Drake west. Follow Sir Francis Drake to Ross and turn left onto Lagunitas Road. The park is at the end of Lagunitas Road.

To get to the Old Railroad Grade trailhead from the Golden Gate Bridge, follow 101 north to the East Blithedale/Tiburon Boulevard exit. Bear left onto East Blithedale and follow it to the heart of Mill Valley, the Mill Valley common. The area resembles a town square with shops and restaurants and several small parking lots around the square. Park here as there is no parking to speak of at the gates of Mt. Tam.

Route: From the Mill Valley common, pedal up West Blithedale Avenue, a narrow and slightly winding paved road, to its end at the park gate. Go over the little bridge and start up the Old Railroad Grade. The trail meanders along in a series of switch-

backs at about the same grade for its entire length. You wander through stands of oak, bay and madrone and along exposed and rocky ridges. Almost 4.0 miles up Old Railroad, past the paved section along the top of Summit Avenue and past the three switchbacks, turn right onto Hoo Koo E Koo.

Hoo Koo E Koo winds and rolls its way down along a rocky and sometimes hairy fire road. If it has rained recently, expect the trail to be even rockier and a little rutty. Hoo Koo E Koo, the legal part of it, anyway, ends at Blithedale Ridge.

If you can't arrange a shuttle or want a slightly shorter loop option, you can turn right here for another mile or so of rocky and rolling downhill. Again, the more it rains, the rockier the terrain as water washes the dirt away. This has been dubbed "The Roller Coaster" by locals who have been known to finish this loop and head back up to do it again. Rigid fork owners beware: the length and harshness of the descent may leave your arms longing for a hot tub.

On this ride, at about 8.4 miles total, you see an unnamed fire road come up on your right; turn onto it. Locals refer to this trail as "Two Tanks"; you see why as you make your way down the trail, past two water tanks. The trail winds between the water tanks and loosely switchbacks its way down to the Old Railroad Grade. At the Old Railroad Grade, turn right to have another go at the Roller Coaster. Turn left to get back out on West Blithedale. This option makes for a 10-mile loop. Of course, the hard core can do the loop *and* go back up to Blithedale and continue to Phoenix Lake for a very strenuous 22-mile ride.

Those of you continuing on the main route should turn left at the Hoo Koo E Koo/Blithedale Ridge junction and mentally prepare yourself for a very steep climb. Thankfully, it's also very short. At the top of the climb, the trail dead ends at Indian Road. Hang a left here. The Blithedale Ridge climb puts things in perspective, making everything else seem pretty easy, including this climb up to the next trail intersection.

Indian Road ends at Eldridge Grade Trail, where you bear right. Eldridge is fairly level at this point, rolling for the next mile or so and briefly climbing before heading back down.

At about 8.3 miles, the trail forks; veer left onto Lakeview Road. This smooth and level fire road takes you past Lake Lagunitas and through a picnic area. When you see the small paved road, turn right and follow it briefly. Make the first right onto the paved footpath, Southern Marin Line. This slopes kind of steeply downhill.

Pretty quickly, you see a fire road turnoff on your left. Veer left here, onto the Fish Trail, not to be confused with Fish Gulch, an illegal singletrack which branches off of the Fish Trail. This is a fun but very steep and rocky descent that leads down to Phoenix Lake. At Shaver Grade Trail, cross the trail to a final short descent and follow the north lake shore route out to the parking lot.

22 Pine Mountain to Repack

Distance: 4.2 miles
Difficulty: Strenuous, very technical
Elevation: 1,200' gain/loss
Ride Type: One-way shuttle on sometimes narrow fire roads
Season: Year-round
Map: Olmsted & Bros. Rambler's Guide to the Trails of Mt. Tamalpais and the Marin Headlands

Overview: It may be short but it's memorable. Slightly northwest of Mt. Tam, the Pine Mountain Ridge area is for advanced riders looking to explore Marin's more sinister side. The going is steep, loose and rocky—and a whole lot of fun.

This particular ride is probably the most famous in mountain biking lore. The Repack Trail got its name in 1976, when it was the site of the first-ever downhill bike race. Of course, it wasn't a big race—just the Marin mountain biking pioneers and their friends. They were racing on Schwinn cruisers with coaster brakes. Seems the rear hubs got so hot from the constant coaster braking, the grease melted right out of them. They needed to be repacked, and so the trail got its name.

Nowadays, sane people don't hit high speeds on Repack. It's a treacherous, rocky, and very rutted screamer of a downhill not for the fainthearted.

Getting There: The ride starts at the Pine Mountain Road trailhead on the Bolinas-Fairfax Road. To get to the trailhead, take 101 north to the San Anselmo/Sir Francis Drake exit. Bear left and take Sir Francis Drake west, following it to Bolinas-Fairfax Road. Turn left and follow Bolinas-Fairfax Road to the trailhead, about 3 miles up. The trail is on the right and parking on the left.

Park the return vehicle along the end of Cascade Drive, at the entrance to the Elliot Nature Preserve. To get there, follow the directions to Bolinas-Fairfax Road, and turn right onto Laurel Drive. Veer left to Cascade Drive, following Cascade to the end.

Route: From the Pine Mountain Road trailhead, climb up the fire road. The trail is loose and rocky, but not too terribly steep. Follow the trail for 1.7 miles to the Repack Trail. Turn right and get ready for one of the wildest descents ever.

Do not attempt to take this trail at high speeds. The terrain can be unsettling, at best: very loose, very rocky and very rutted. Repack drops for 2.5 steep and twisting miles. At the fork near the bottom, bear right and continue on down to the gate at the end of Cascade Drive.

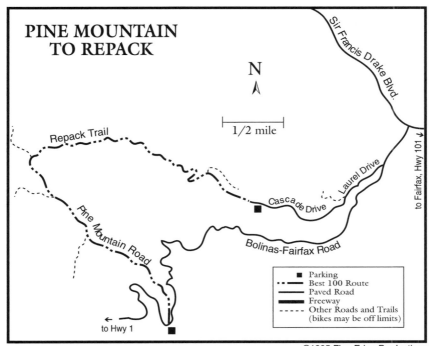

PINE MOUNTAIN
TO REPACK

N

1/2 mile

Repack Trail

Sir Francis Drake Blvd.

to Fairfax, Hwy 101

Laurel Drive

Cascade Drive

Pine Mountain Road

Bolinas-Fairfax Road

← to Hwy 1

■ Parking
·—·—· Best 100 Route
——— Paved Road
▬▬▬ Freeway
- - - - Other Roads and Trails
        (bikes may be off limits)

23 Pine Mountain Loop

Distance: 13 miles
Difficulty: Strenuous, very technical
Elevation: 1,300' gain/loss
Ride Type: Loop on sometimes narrow fire roads
Season: Year-round
Topo Map: Bolinas

Overview: This ride is almost as famous as Repack; nobody raced here, but it's one of the original mountain bike loops in the area. Those early folks seem to have had a penchant for rocks and loose surfaces. You experience plenty of both on this ride, along with steep climbs and steep descents, making for an interesting afternoon all around.

The loop traverses two ridges and a canyon, where you (literally) run across three creeks. And don't let the name mislead you; like most of the surrounding hills, the ridges are wide open grassland, affording spectacular views.

Getting There: From the Golden Gate Bridge, follow 101 north to the San Anselmo/Sir Francis Drake exit. Bear left and take Sir Francis Drake west, following it to Bolinas-Fairfax Road. Turn left and follow Bolinas-Fairfax Road to the trailhead, about 3 miles. The trail is on the right and parking is on the left.

Route: From the trailhead, start up the Pine Mountain Road. The climb isn't too bad, except for one brief steep section. Just past the top of that climb, turn left at the second fork to stay on Pine Mountain Road.

Now the climbing gets nasty. The first mile is the worst—very loose, very rocky and very steep. The good news is that once you've made it, you're at the highest point in the ride, the Pine Mountain summit. Enjoy the panoramic view while you let your heart rate fall back to an acceptable level.

Now the fun begins. The next section is a long roller-coaster ride which ends with a sharp descent to a trail fork and Kent Lake. Turn right at the fork and wind your way through the canyon and across the creeks, subtly climbing. The switchback at the third creek is your signal to start gearing down; the gradual climb gets decidedly steep as you make your way back up to the ridge.

Up on the ridge, you come to a crossroad near the summit of Green

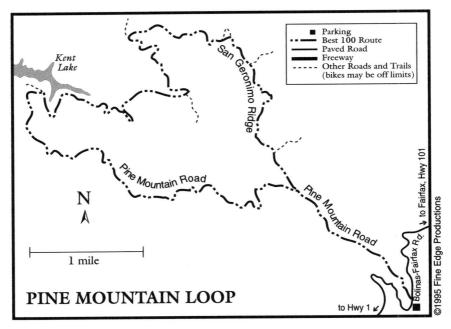

PINE MOUNTAIN LOOP

Hill at about 8.5 miles. Turn right and continue climbing, at a less taxing grade now, toward San Geronimo Ridge. Within a mile, you reach another fork. This is a private property boundary. Make a hard right onto San Geronimo Ridge Road and head up for the last bit of climbing.

At about 10.5 miles, the trail once again becomes a roller coaster. San Geronimo Ridge Road ends at Pine Mountain Road. Bear left for the descent leading back to the trailhead.

24 Bolinas Ridge

Distance: 22.5 miles
Difficulty: Very strenuous, mildly technical
Elevation: 1,100' gain/loss
Ride Type: Out-and-back on fire roads and doubletrack
Season: Spring through fall
Topo Maps: Bolinas, San Geronimo
Comments: It can get very hot and dry during the summer months, carry extra water (none is available); fire danger sometimes closes the trail; rideable in the winter if you don't mind a lot of mud; please close cattle gates behind you.

Overview: This ride has just about everything a person needs to be happy: cool redwoods, wide open grasslands, great views, neat rocks, long climbs doing double duty as long, sweeping downhills, and a little bit of technical stuff (some tree roots, some rocks). There's enough to hold your interest but not so much that you're demoralized if you ain't exactly Hans Rey.

The trail is on land that's part cattle ranch, part parkland and the line of demarcation couldn't be more obvious if it had a sign; past the last cattle gate, the madrones close in and the redwoods suddenly spring up around you. From the grassy slopes of the cowfeteria, you get great views of Tomales Bay; from the highest points in the forest, you look down through the trees to the Pacific Ocean.

This ride can be done as a one-way shuttle that's suitable for beginners. But then you miss half the fun.

Getting There: From the Golden Gate Bridge, take 101 north to the San Anselmo/Sir Francis Drake exit. Bear left and take Sir Francis Drake west, following it to the trailhead, about 20 miles. When you see the sign that says "Olema 1 Mile," the trailhead and parking area are just around the next bend. Park on the wide dirt shoulders on either side of the road.

Route: From the trail gate, the ride starts off with a short singletrack climb up to the fire road. At the outset, the road is steep, rocky and loose, but the worst of it is over quickly. At the top of the first rise, the trail almost levels briefly before climbing again, this time at a more reasonable grade. This short climb is followed by a brief downhill; it's not much, but you take what downhills you can get.

As the trail heads up again, you reach the first of many cattle gates. Upon passing through it, gear down early. After about 100 feet, the trail rises sharply up to the right, through a gnarled, rain-rutted switchback. As an added bonus, in the late summer, the rut becomes sandy, too.

Past the rut, the trail heads straight up, marking the first of four very nasty climbs. At the top, you can see Tomales Bay off to the right and tree-dotted parkland rolling below you.

After a too-brief level section comes the second icky climb. Again, it's severely rutted and seasonally loose. This climb is also the longest of the bad ones, about 0.25-mile long. At least you get it over with right away. The good news is, the next bad one is about a mile away.

At the top, the road again levels before rolling in an overall uphill direction. The little downhills are fast and fun, but all too soon, at about 3.5 miles, you reach the third bad climb. It starts off at a bearable grade before suddenly getting steeper and looser toward the top. The trail surface on this climb is made up of sandy soil and tiny, marble-sized rocks.

Again, the trail plateaus briefly at the top of the hill before rolling toward the last nasty climb. This one is fairly steep but also kind of technical. The trail is rutted and includes rock outcroppings that start halfway up and continue up to the top.

After this climb the trail levels again. You see a large rock outcropping on the left, in front of a cattle gate, marking the 5.0-mile point. This is a popular break spot. If you do stop here, choose your rest spot carefully— the rock has patches of poison oak growing on and around it.

From here the trail starts to roll with a vengeance. Long descents followed by long climbs lead you out of the open grassland and into the redwoods. Once in the trees and for the next 5 miles, the terrain becomes smooth hardpack with intermittent roots snaking across the trail. You can really pick up speed in here but be

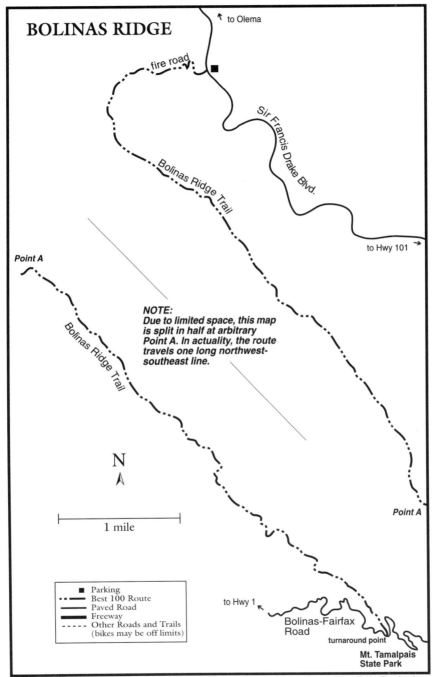

BOLINAS RIDGE

to Olema

fire road

Sir Francis Drake Blvd.

Bolinas Ridge Trail

to Hwy 101

Point A

NOTE:
Due to limited space, this map is split in half at arbitrary Point A. In actuality, the route travels one long northwest-southeast line.

Bolinas Ridge Trail

N

⊢————————⊣
     1 mile

Point A

■ Parking
▪·▪· Best 100 Route
——— Paved Road
▬▬▬ Freeway
- - - Other Roads and Trails
        (bikes may be off limits)

to Hwy 1

Bolinas-Fairfax Road

turnaround point

Mt. Tamalpais State Park

©1995 Fine Edge Productions

careful; if you're going to see hikers, you see them at this end. Also keep an eye out for bicyclists going in the other direction.

At about 10.0 miles, you start to climb out of the redwoods and toward the top of the ridge line. Out in the open for a bit, a final descent leads past a great view of Bolinas to the right and the Pine Mountain Ridge to the left. The last 0.5 mile is a climb back into the redwoods to the park's west entrance on Bolinas-Fairfax Road.

If you're doing the ride as a one-way shuttle, this is the starting point. For those of us going all the way, this is the turnaround. Head back the way you came for a rollicking good time. Going in this direction, the ride is mostly downhill. Although there are a couple of climbs, there's nothing nasty. As I said earlier, while you are in the forest, keep your speed in check and watch for hikers and bikes.

The redwood roller coaster is over way too soon, leading to the free-for-all back through the grazing area. Remember those four steep climbs? Guess what you get to do. Back at the big rock, the last 5 miles are basically a series of long, fast and furious descents back to the trailhead.

25 Samuel P. Taylor State Park/ Barnabe Peak Loop

Distance: 6.9 miles
Difficulty: Moderately strenuous, mildly technical
Elevation: 1,250' gain/loss
Ride Type: Loop on sometimes narrow fire roads
Season: Year-round
Map: Available at ranger kiosk for 50 cents.
Comments: Water and restrooms are available in the campground areas. Let the trails dry out for a few days following rain.

Overview: This is a great date ride. If you happen to be involved with your riding partner and you're looking for a romantic ride, this is it. While you may encounter a few technical challenges, mostly of the mud and tree root variety, the bulk of the ride traverses smooth trails in a drop-dead gorgeous forest of redwood and madrone.

The Samuel P. Taylor State Park encompasses 2,882 acres of redwood canyons and rocky grassland ridges. The property once belonged to Samuel Taylor, a late nineteenth-century entrepreneur who purchased the land with the help of a modest gold strike. He built a paper mill on the property, but rather than use the trees on his land, Taylor instituted a process which utilized scrap paper and rags gathered from other sources. Among his customers were the San Francisco newspapers.

At another site in the canyon, Taylor operated a less successful venture, a blasting powder mill. A huge explosion ended his dream of becoming a major player in the black powder business.

In 1874, a railroad was built through the canyon. Our enterprising friend Mr. Taylor built a hotel next to rail line and opened Camp

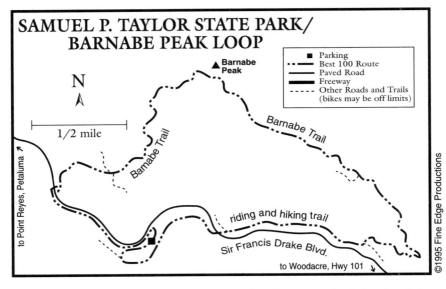

Taylor, one of the first recreational camping areas in the United States.

Getting There: From the Golden Gate Bridge, follow 101 north to the San Anselmo/Sir Francis Drake exit. Bear left and take Sir Francis Drake west. Follow it to the park entrance, about 16 miles. The entrance and parking lot are on the left. Day use parking is $5.

Route: From the ranger's kiosk, head down into the campground area on the paved path, following the signs for the Lower Campground. The path ends at the paved Bike and Horse Trail. Turn left and follow it to the gate at the end. The dirt Hiking and Riding Trail starts once you're through the gate.

The trail follows the Papermill Creek through a forest of towering redwoods, with lots of ferns and moss-covered rocks. Very shortly, you cross the creek and the road on a wooden bridge which takes you to the Irving Group Picnic Area. The well-signed

trail picks up on the left side of the clearing. You can't miss it.

The trail continues to follow the creek, although now slightly above it. At about 2.0 miles, make the first left onto the Barnabe Trail. Barnabe starts with a steep but short climb, then winds somewhat steeply away from the canyon and up through the redwood and madrone. The grade eases considerably after this.

As the climb continues toward Barnabe Peak (1,466'), you emerge from the forest on to the ridge line, with great views of the Inverness Ridge and Point Reyes. As you approach the peak, the trail rolls a little bit before heading back down into the forest.

The remainder of the Barnabe Trail is a 2.5-mile winding, redwood-filled frolic back down to Sir Francis Drake Boulevard. Turn left onto Sir Francis Drake. The park entrance and parking lot are about 0.25 mile up. Fortunately, the road provides an ample shoulder and the drivers out here are pretty used to sharing the road with bikes.

26 China Camp State Park/ Bay View Loop

Distance: 4.7 miles
Difficulty: Moderate, slightly technical
Elevation: 800' gain/loss
Ride Type: Loop on singletrack with a little fire road
Season: Year-round
Map: Available for free at the ranger kiosk
Comments: Water and restrooms are available in the parking lot and in campground areas. Because the park sits on the shore of San Pablo Bay, wet weather turns the trails to goo.

Overview: China Camp is one of the last places in the county where the singletrack is legal (except for one short trail on the bay side that leads to a bird sanctuary). And it's a good thing, too, because more than half of the trails here are singletrack.

China Camp State Park got its name in the late 1800s when it was a Chinese shrimping village. The villagers were fishermen from the Kwangtung Province in China, mostly immigrants seeking to escape racial discrimination in San Francisco. The people supported themselves by exporting shrimp to Hawaii, China and Japan. In 1906, the village provided refuge for thousands of Chinese whose homes were destroyed in the earthquake and fire in San Francisco.

The land remained privately owned until the state purchased it in 1977. Besides the parkland, China Camp is also a wetland sanctuary.

While the park is fairly small, only 1,476 acres, the trails are a blast to ride. The singletrack and fire roads wind through forests of manzanita, bay, live oak and madrone, and through grassy clearings. Most people spend the day and ride both this loop and the following loop, with a scenic lunch break in between.

Getting There: From the Golden Gate Bridge, follow 101 north to the N. San Pedro Road exit. Take N. San Pedro Road east and follow it to the campground entrance and parking lot. The entrance is on the right, 3 miles up. Day use parking on weekends and holidays is $3.

Route: From the parking lot, follow the fire road on the right side of the restrooms around the back of Back Ranch Meadows to a 3-way fork. Go straight onto the Bay View Trail, which quickly becomes a singletrack. The Bay View Trail rolls, winds and climbs up above the campground through the trees and along a narrow ledge before heading up to a clearing just below a ridge.

At the clearing, turn left onto the Back Ranch Meadows Fire Trail and make a quick right back onto the Bay View singletrack. This part of Bay View is mostly level with intermittent rolling as it hugs the mountain's curves.

At the next fire road intersection, at about 2.8 miles, turn left onto the Ridge Fire Trail. This part of the Ridge Trail can get pretty rutted although it is graded periodically. It starts off as a gradual downhill that leads to a junction with the Miwok Fire Trail. Go straight onto Miwok (Ridge veers off to the right) for a steep and loose downhill. (If it's muddy, it may be slippery.)

At the bottom of the descent, make a hard left turn onto the Shoreline Trail. This starts as a level and smooth fire road that leads to a day use picnic area. Follow the trail around the back side of the picnic area, where the trail becomes a singletrack again. It leads to the back wall of a canyon before heading out toward a wetland meadow and around a small hill. The trail ends back at the campground parking lot.

27 Ridge Fire Trail Loop

Distance: 5.6 miles
Difficulty: Moderate, slightly technical
Elevation: 900' gain/loss
Ride Type: Loop on fire roads and singletrack
Season: Year-round
Map: Available free at ranger kiosk
Comments: Water and restrooms available in the parking lot and at campground areas. Trails may be gooey after rains.

Overview: This loop takes you from the San Pablo Bay to a ridge overlooking the San Francisco Bay. This time, there are some fire roads mixed in with the singletrack.

Getting There: Follow directions for the previous ride.

Route: From the parking lot, follow the fire road on the left side of the restrooms to its end at Back Ranch Meadows Fire Trail. Head up the Back Ranch trail, which gets a little on the steep side when you're in the switchback sections. The trail crosses the Bay View Trail before ending at the Ridge Fire Trail.

Turn left onto Ridge, which rolls along the top of the ridge behind the trees. From here, you get a

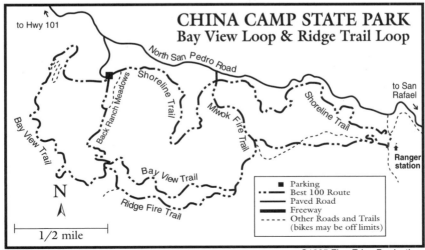

CHINA CAMP STATE PARK
Bay View Loop & Ridge Trail Loop

to Hwy 101

North San Pedro Road

Shoreline Trail

Back Ranch Meadows

Bay View Trail

Miwok Fire Trail

Shoreline Trail

to San Rafael

Ranger station

Bay View Trail

Ridge Fire Trail

N
∧

1/2 mile

■ Parking
∙∙∙∙ Best 100 Route
─── Paved Road
▬▬▬ Freeway
- - - - Other Roads and Trails
(bikes may be off limits)

©1995 Fine Edge Productions

nice view of the San Francisco skyline and the Golden Gate Bridge.

At about 1.5 miles, you come to another intersection with the Bay View singletrack on the left and an unnamed fire road to the right. Continue straight through, towards the Miwok Fire Trail. Within 0.5 mile, continue straight past the Ridge Fire Trail turnoff, briefly following the Miwok trail.

As the trail starts to pitch downhill, you see a singletrack trailhead on the right. Turn right onto the singletrack to enjoy the handiwork of your compatriots; this unnamed 0.75-mile stretch of roller coaster was built by mountain bikers.

At about 2.8 miles, you once again intersect with the Ridge Fire Trail. Go across to pick up the singletrack on the other side. The trail starts to head down, with three fun switchbacks before a descent into the ranger service area.

Turn left down the road to catch the Shoreline Trail, which comes up quickly on your left. Turn left onto Shoreline and follow it as it snakes its way along the grassy slopes overlooking the bay.

At just under 4.5 miles, Shore-

line drops down onto the Miwok Fire Trail. Turn left and immediately bear right to stay on Shoreline. Follow the fire road to the day use area. Follow the trail to the back side of the picnic area where the trail becomes singletrack again. The trail winds along the canyon before heading back out to the meadow, ending back at the parking lot on the other side of the hill.

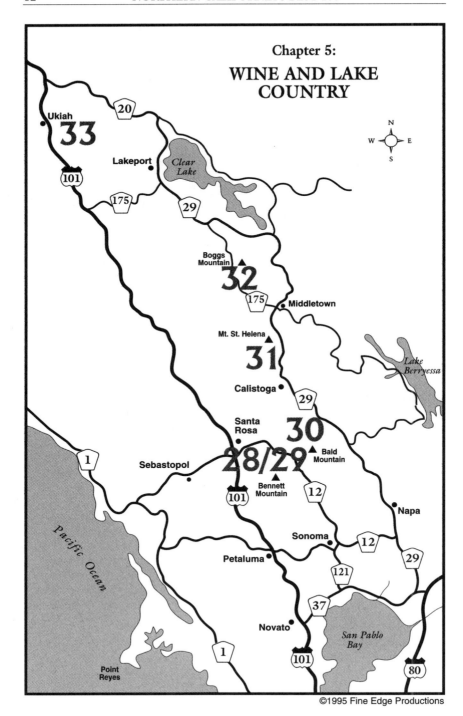

Chapter 5:
WINE AND LAKE COUNTRY

©1995 Fine Edge Productions

Wine and Lake Country

by Robin Stuart

Just above the Marin County line lies a land of vineyards and farms, pine forests and redwoods, state parks and (happy sigh) legal singletrack. When folks in the Bay Area say they are "going to the country," it's a safe bet they are headed up here. Although the recent real estate boom has pushed the northern border of the "Bay Area region" well into Sonoma County, once you get past Santa Rosa, you notice that people move a little slower and they're quicker to smile and say hello. It may only be an hour away from San Francisco, but it seems like light years.

Aside from the trails and the tranquillity, this area has another well-known feature. Located in the heart of the county is the world-famous California Wine Country. Most of the wineries have tasting rooms and some offer tours of their facilities. A bike is a great way to get around since many of the wineries are located along winding country roads and auto traffic can get pretty congested, especially on weekends. A word of advice for those who want their wine-tasting trip to be a pleasant experience: don't drink the whole glass. Take a sip, swish it around your mouth, then pour the rest out. No one will think you're rude or silly; au contraire, you'll look like a pro. Plus, you get the flavor without the headache.

To the west of the Wine Country, the more coastal region gets increasingly rugged and wooded. To the east, more open oak- and pine-covered ranges rise up to dominate the landscape before giving way to the expanse of the Central Valley. From some of the higher points in the following rides, you'll even be able to see Mount Shasta and Mount Lassen to the north and northeast on very clear days.

Thanks to smatterings of maple and black oak here and there, the North Bay counties featured in this chapter bear the classic colors of fall. Nothing as vivid as New England, of course, but hey, it beats California's usual brown. Winters are typically very wet in these parts, but the reward is warm sunshine and spectacular displays of wildflowers in the spring. The summer temperatures get surprisingly high, so coastal dwellers are advised to plan for early morning playtimes and to bring twice as much water as you think you need. As for those of us who think the term "hotter than hell" is a selling point, bring lots of water and bask—or is it bake?—in it.

28 Annadel State Park/ Short Loop to Lake Ilsanjo

Distance: 10 miles
Difficulty: Strenuous, technical (very technical in spots)
Elevation: 1,100' gain/loss
Ride Type: Loop on sometimes narrow fire roads
Season: Year-round
Map: Available for 75 cents from a vending machine in front of the park office.
Comments: The only water available is in front of the ranger station; it gets very hot in the summer so bring as much water as you can carry. Restrooms are strategically placed at locations throughout the park. Speed limit of 15 mph.

Overview: You haven't truly "done" the Wine Country until you have rolled your tire tread upon the trails of Annadel State Park. This is definitely not a place for beginners. The terrain at Annadel is most often described as "really rocky," but that doesn't quite tell the whole story. The trails vary between loose and bumpy to "you call that a trail?" The rocks here come in all shape and sizes and in all stages of exposure; from lurking just below the surface, to felt but not seen, to quarry conditions. If you want to practice your technical skills, this is certainly the place.

Not surprisingly, the history of Annadel State Park is linked closely to its geology. Long ago it was considered an important source of obsidian to the Native Americans who inhabited the region. The hard and shiny obsidian was used to make tools and weapons that were hot-ticket items for trade among the Northern California tribes (think titanium and you get an idea of its appeal). With

the Spanish settlement in 1770 came a stint of agricultural use until the land was included in a Mexican grant. The first quarrying operations began in 1880.

At the turn of the century, the land was held by two families, the Wymores and the Hutchinsons. They continued the quarrying business, churning out cobblestone which was used in the original Bay Area building efforts as well as the rebuilding of San Francisco after the 1906 earthquake. The park is named for Annie Hutchinson, the granddaughter of one of the owners. The area was known as "Annie's Dell" and the name stuck.

With the advent of the automobile came the demise of the cobblestone business. The land changed hands in the 1930s, reverting back to agricultural use and obsidian mining, which continued through the 1960s. The state then purchased the property in 1971.

At 5,000 acres, Annadel contains 35 miles of legal fire roads with

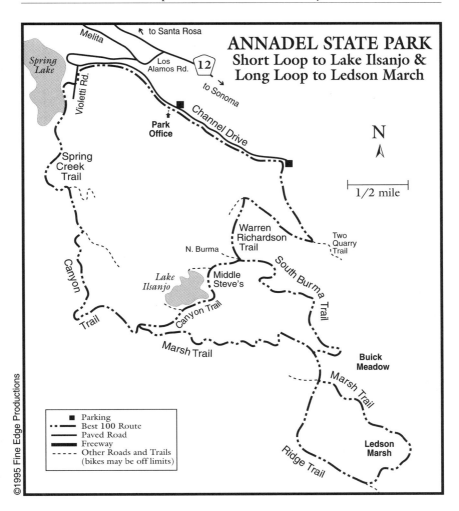

ANNADEL STATE PARK
Short Loop to Lake Ilsanjo & Long Loop to Ledson March

some legal singletrack. The trails are all well-signed (trails not marked or named have been developed illegally) and fairly easy to follow. The following rides are the most popular loops around the park, bypassing a couple of the ridiculously technical singletrack sections. Obviously, these only scratch the surface of the many riding possibilities here.

Getting There: From San Francisco, take 101 north to the Sebastopol/ Sonoma Highway 12 turnoff. Bear right, taking Sonoma East. Follow the signs through downtown Santa Rosa to stay on Highway 12. Turn right on Los Alamos Road, bearing left at the fork with Melita. Just before crossing the second bridge, turn left onto Channel Drive. Follow the signs to the Annadel State Park entrance. You can park along Channel Drive by the park office or continue to the parking lot at the end of the road. There is a $2 parking fee.

Route: Starting from the park office, go west on Channel Drive, as if you were leaving the park. Within a mile, you'll come to Violetti Road; a left turn followed by a quick right takes you into the Spring Lake Park entrance. Follow the path to the left, along the shoreline of Spring Lake, which ends at the Oak Knolls Picnic Area and the Annadel gate. Inside the gate, follow the Spring Creek Trail, a fire road that winds along Spring Creek. Just past the 3-mile point, you cross a bridge. Turn right on the other side of the bridge to stay on Spring Creek. Within 0.5 mile, you see another bridge on your right. Turn here and cross the bridge onto Canyon Trail fire road.

Canyon Trail climbs steadily and, at times, steeply along a wall overlooking forests of Douglas fir and oak, Spring Creek and Lake Ilsanjo. Unless it has rained recently, this trail is a little bumpy and a little loose but not terribly rocky. At about 5.1 miles, you reach a fork with the Marsh Trail. Bear left to stay on Canyon Trail.

This stretch of Canyon leads, at long last, downhill to Lake Ilsanjo. After a short rise just past the junction with Marsh, the trail veers fairly gently down to the lake. The lake shore area is a popular rest stop, particularly in the summer (swimming is allowed and, on some days, is a must). Follow Canyon along the south side of the lake to an intersection with Middle Steve's Trail. To the right is the now illegal singletrack portion of Middle Steve's. Turn left onto Middle

Steve's fire road to continue around the lake.

Middle Steve's ends at the Warren Richardson Trail (named for a local cattle rancher and founder of the Sonoma County Trail Blazers). Turn right onto Richardson, following it as it plunges steeply and roughly away from the lake. Within 0.5 mile, you come to a fork with South Burma. Make a hard left to continue the steep and rocky descent along Warren Richardson. Another fork pops up right away, this time with North Burma. Bear right, staying on Richardson as you descend into the redwoods and fir.

The trail seemingly ends in a redwood grove. Make a hard right and continue the raucous downhill on Warren Richardson. If your arms are tired from the rocky pounding, consider this: this trail is the smoothest of the downhills to Channel Drive. At 8.0 miles, the trail intersects the Two Quarry Trail. Make a hairpin left turn to stay on Warren Richardson. The rest of the descent is relatively smooth and gentle to the parking lot at the end of Channel Drive. Go through the parking lot and head down Channel, back to the park office and the starting point.

29 Annadel State Park/Long Loop to Ledson Marsh

Distance: 16.3 miles
Difficulty: Strenuous, technical (very technical in spots)
Elevation: 1,300' gain/loss
Ride Type: Loop on sometimes narrow fire roads
Season: Year-round
Map: Available for 75 cents from a vending machine in front of the park office.
Comments: The only water available is in front of the ranger station; it gets very hot in the summer so bring as much water as you can carry. Restrooms are available along the way. Speed limit of 15 mph.

Overview: This loop incorporates much of the previous ride's short loop, bypassing Lake Ilsanjo in favor of the high ridge a few hundred feet below the summit of Bennett Mountain, the park's highest peak. The route leads around Ledson Marsh on the park's east side, through meadows and forests and along terrain that is comparatively smooth and darned near level.

Getting There: See directions for the previous ride.

Route: The beginning of this ride is identical to the short loop. From the park office, follow Channel Drive out of the park to Violetti Road. Turn left on Violetti, making the first right into the Spring Lake Park. Follow the path at the lake's shore as it leads left, taking you to the Annadel gate. Inside the gate, follow the Spring Creek fire road which runs parallel to Spring Creek. Cross the first bridge, make a sharp right turn, and continue to follow the creek to the second bridge. Turn right, cross the bridge, and climb up the Canyon Trail.

Upon reaching the fork with the Marsh Trail, bear right this time, onto the Marsh Trail and continue climbing. The trail starts off on the steep side, easing at the top of the first

short rise to a manageable grade. The terrain is, of course, peppered with rocks as you move in and out of stands of oak and redwoods, with a seasonal water crossing about halfway up the ridge.

At about 5.7 miles, you reach a fork with the now illegal Upper Steve's singletrack. Turn left to continue following the Marsh Trail. Just around the bend from the intersection, the trail levels as you move between the mountain peaks through Buick Meadow. At the next fork, at 6.5 miles, bear right onto the Ridge Trail. The first half of Ridge is a relatively easy climb to the park's southern boundary. At the top of the climb, you see the trail marker for the top of Upper Steve's. Stay left and follow Ridge as it rolls along, you guessed it, Annadel's high ridge.

Just under the 8.0 miles, you come to another fork. This time, it's with the top of the Marsh Trail. Turn left onto Marsh and let the fun begin. The trail starts by descending gently to Ledson Marsh. Although there aren't as many rocks around this area, the trail does get pretty rutted. As you make your way down, you see several trails going off to the right. Stay left, following Marsh as it winds around Ledson Marsh, back to Buick Meadow.

Just past the junction with the Ridge Trail, you retrace your steps for a brief stretch, until you reach the trail marker for the South Burma Trail. You see it at about 11.1 miles. Turn right onto South Burma, which winds through Buick Meadow to a scenic overlook with views of the coast. Just past the overlook, you come to another trail intersection; turn left to stay on South Burma. Now the trail returns to Annadel typical terrain, descending steeply at times, and definitely bumpier.

At approximately 13.1 miles, South Burma ends at the Warren Richardson trail. Hang a right and follow Warren Richardson into the redwoods and over the rocks, back down to the parking lot at Channel Drive. Go through the parking lot and down Channel Drive to return to the park office.

30 Sugarloaf Ridge State Park/ Bald Mountain Loop

Distance: 6.5 miles
Difficulty: Strenuous, mildly technical
Elevation: 1,500' gain/loss
Ride Type: Loop on fire roads and pavement
Season: Year-round
Map: Available for 75 cents at the Visitor Center or the ranger kiosk.
Comments: Water is available at the Visitor Center and campgrounds. There's a $5 parking fee (a permit is required to park anywhere on the mountain). Speed limit is 15 mph.

Overview: Sugarloaf Ridge State Park is so close to Annadel State Park that it's often overlooked. Or else people are scared off by the initial climb. That's too bad because Sugarloaf is another of the little gems of Sonoma County. Not only is it generally less crowded than its more famous neighbor, but it's also well-suited to those not up for Annadel's technical challenges.

Sugarloaf got its name from the shape of the mountains within its 2,700 acres. In the late 1800s, sugar was packaged in cone-shaped "loaves" and grocers would break off pieces of the loaf for individual sale. The mountains in and around the park look decidedly conical, resembling those early sugarloaves.

The land was the long-time home of the Wappo Indians. They fought Spanish settlement only to relinquish their land later to American settlers after back-to-back disease epidemics greatly reduced their numbers in the 1830s. Attempts were made to farm the rocky terrain until the state bought the property in 1920. Plans to dam Sonoma Creek were abandoned thanks to the outcry of local property owners. The land was used as a camping and picnic area, and as a Boy Scout camp, until 1942, when it was leased for cattle grazing. Sugarloaf Ridge became a state park in 1964.

Although the first couple of miles of this loop are paved, don't let it deter you. The descent from the summit of Bald Mountain is a roller coaster on loose and rocky fire roads

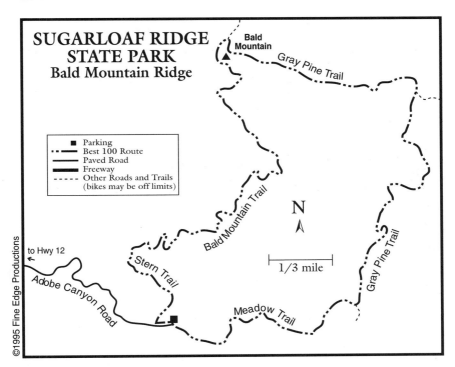

SUGARLOAF RIDGE
STATE PARK
Bald Mountain Ridge

Bald Mountain

Gray Pine Trail

Parking
Best 100 Route
Paved Road
Freeway
Other Roads and Trails
(bikes may be off limits)

to Hwy 12

Adobe Canyon Road

Stern Trail

Bald Mountain Trail

Meadow Trail

Gray Pine Trail

N

1/3 mile

©1995 Fine Edge Productions

through forests of maple, pine, live oak, madrone and redwood. Runoff from winter rains (and occasional snow) creates a seasonal network of creeks (i.e. water crossings) that feed into Sonoma Creek, which runs along the southern portion of the park.

Getting There: From San Francisco, take 101 north to the Sebastopol/Sonoma Highway 12 turnoff. Bear right, taking Sonoma East. Follow the signs through downtown Santa Rosa to stay on Highway 12. Turn left on Adobe Canyon Road, which ends at the park entrance.

Route: From the parking lot, backtrack about 50 yards to the paved Stern Trail, almost directly across the road from the ranger kiosk. Turn right onto Stern, following it to the paved Bald Mountain Trail. The Bald

Mountain Trail takes you all the way up to the mountain's summit at 2,729 feet, which you reach at 2.8 miles. The trail has a few fairly steep sections but when you get to the top, you'll (hopefully) think it was worth it. The views from Bald Mountain are spectacular, reaching from San Francisco all the way to the Sierras, overlooking the Wine Country valleys and nearby Mount St. Helena.

The good news is, it's all downhill from here. Okay, mostly. From the summit of Bald Mountain, head down onto the dirt (at last) Gray Pine Trail. Gray Pine descends rapidly (900 feet in just over a mile), with a couple of short uphill sections, to a fork with the Brushy Peaks Trail. Stay right to continue the rolling descent on Gray Pine. This section of Gray Pine has a tendency to get a bit rutted from both runoff and horse hooves. In the dry summer months, it can be loose.

At about 4.7 miles, the trail flanks a seasonal branch of Sonoma Creek as it runs down into the valley, shortly before crossing the main creek. In winter months, this crossing can be a little tricky, particularly in heavy rain years. Normally, though, it's no big deal.

Gray Pine ends at the Meadow Trail at about 5.3 miles. Turn right onto Meadow for an easy spin along the creek to the campgrounds. Just inside the campground gate, turn left onto the paved service road and follow it back to the parking lot.

31 Robert Louis Stevenson Memorial State Park/The Peaks

Distance: 13 miles
Difficulty: Moderately strenuous, not technical
Elevation: 2,000' gain/loss
Ride Type: Out and back on fire roads
Season: Year-round
Topo Maps: Detert Reservoir, Mount St. Helena
Comments: No water is available; bring plenty, especially in the summer when it can get very hot.

Overview: Robert Louis Stevenson Memorial State Park is really more like an open space. There's no park headquarters, no rangers and no services. It is a beautiful spot located about halfway up Mount St. Helena, overlooking the Napa Valley. The park is named for poet/novelist Stevenson, who briefly made his home here following his marriage to Fanny Osbourne. The remains of their honeymoon cabin can be found a short hike off the main road (no bikes allowed on hiking trail).

Although the park encompasses over 1,000 acres, the Peaks route is the only developed multi-use trail. But it's a fun one—semi-steep climbs followed by fast descents with some awesome views along the way. The trail winds its way up and between Mt. St. Helena's North and South Peaks, both of which offer far-reaching views from San Francisco to Mount Shasta.

Getting There: From San Francisco, head for Napa Valley by going north on Highway 101 to the Black Point Forest/Highway 37 turnoff. Stay left, following 37 to Highway 121. Turn left onto 121, bearing east (right) at the fork with 116. About 2 miles later, bear right as Highway 12 joins 121. In about 8 miles, at the intersection with Highway 29, turn left onto 29, which passes through the heart of the Wine Country.

Robert Louis Stevenson is about 35 miles up Highway 29, between Calistoga and Middletown. When you see the trail gate on the left, park along the road (there are wide shoulders on both sides).

Route: This trail is pretty straightforward and easy to follow. From the gate, head up the fire road and into the forest. Bear left at the first fork, at about 0.7 mile. At 1.5 miles, you see the sign and the hiking trail heading down to the Stevenson cabin. Past this point, the trail rolls a little, but steadily climbs up and out of the pine toward exposed rocky grassland dotted with madrone.

The going gets a little steeper as you wind around three wide switchbacks and out into a clearing. From this point, the terrain is a little bit looser with easily avoided ruts (as long as it hasn't rained recently). Alongside the trail, rock outcroppings and madrone decorate the hillside.

At about 3.5 miles, the trail levels out as it leads to the South Peak turnoff, about 0.5 mile ahead. Turn left at the turnoff for a bit of a steep climb up to the South Peak summit (4,003'). The views up here are pretty nice, stretching as far south as San Francisco and, on clear days, beyond. To the east, you can see the Sierras and to the north, you can make out Mount Shasta (you'll be getting a better view in a few miles).

Head back down to the main fire road, turning left to continue on to North Peak. Along this stretch, the climbing is relieved by a short rolling section. Accompanying you are views of the ocean to your left and Lake Berryessa to the right. At about 6 miles, you'll come to another fork; follow the sign and veer left for the final steep ascent to North Peak.

Slightly taller than South Peak, the North Peak (4,343') offers fabulous views. From here, you can add a better view of Mount Shasta and, slightly east of it, Mount Lassen to your list of sights. After an appropriate amount of gawking time, go back the way you came, enjoying the well-deserved downhill ride to the car.

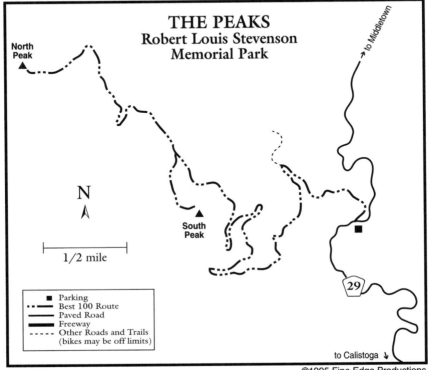

THE PEAKS
Robert Louis Stevenson
Memorial Park

North Peak

to Middletown

N

1/2 mile

South Peak

29

Parking
Best 100 Route
Paved Road
Freeway
Other Roads and Trails
(bikes may be off limits)

to Calistoga

©1995 Fine Edge Productions

32 Boggs Mountain Loop

Distance: 12.4 miles
Difficulty: Moderately strenuous, mildly technical
Elevation: 900' gain/loss
Ride Type: Loop on singletrack and fire roads
Season: Year-round
Map: Available free from the forestry office
Comments: Drinking water is not available. Deer hunting is permitted here in August and September. Either wear a lot of safety orange and make a lot of noise or save this ride for a less hazardous time.

Overview: The Boggs Mountain Demonstration State Forest is a special place for mountain bikers. All of the trails, including approximately 15 miles of buff singletrack, are 100 percent legal. In fact, the singletrack was built with mountain bikes in mind. The men and women of the California Department of Forestry and Fire Protection ride these trails to stay in tip-top shape. To celebrate their efforts (both in building the trails and protecting the forest surrounding them), this loop takes place almost entirely on singletrack.

Boggs Mountain is named after Henry C. Boggs, the timber baron who originally owned the land in 1879. His son operated two sawmills on the northeast side of the mountain between 1880 and 1885. The land's ownership subsequently changed hands several times. It was used primarily for timber and cattle grazing until 1949 when the state bought the property. At the time, all economically viable timber had been cut and hauled out of the area. The state used the 3,500 acres to experiment with forestry and demonstrate the productive and economic possibilities of a

forest; hence the name, Demonstration State Forest. Lest you think the area is barren, the once clear-cut land is now replete with ponderosa and sugar pine, Douglas fir and black oak.

Fortunately for us, one of the management objectives is to promote the forest's full recreational value, maintaining the delicate balance of its other uses as a wildlife habitat and watershed, while it continues to supply trees for wood-based products. Camping and hunting are both permitted, and the trail system is "limited" to non-motorized vehicles, specifically including mountain bikes in its trail uses. The local community knows a good thing when it sees one; charitable organizations from nearby Cobb get together with the Boggs Mountain Forest officials to host an

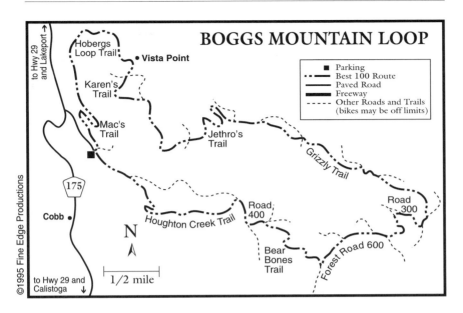

annual mountain bike race here to raise money for the Cobb Community Center. Now, if other land managers would just pay attention....

Getting There: Boggs Mountain lies in the hilly country between Napa Valley and Clear Lake. From San Francisco, take Highway 101 north to the Black Point Forest/Highway 37 turnoff. Stay left, following 37 Highway 121. Turn left onto 121, bearing east (right) at the fork with 116. About 2 miles later, bear right as Highway 12 joins 121 (there are signs listing the highway as both).

In about 8 miles, at the intersection with Highway 29, turn left onto 29, which passes through the heart of the Wine Country. Follow 29 for about 45 miles to Middletown. At the light in Middletown, turn left onto 175. Boggs Mountain is off 175, just past the town of Cobb. Follow the signs for the State Fire Station (there is a sign for Boggs Mountain once you're on the Forest

Road), which will lead you to the parking area at the heliport and forestry office.

Route: The trail begins just past the heliport and forestry office on Forest Road 210. Turn left immediately, onto the singletrack Mac's Trail. After a couple of steep switchback climbs, Mac's levels for a bit before making a quick descent to a fork in the trail. Stay left, following the Hobergs Loop Trail which climbs steeply up through the pine trees. At the ridge line, the trail levels and briefly dips down to a vista point overlooking the Napa Valley.

Past the vista point, the trail begins to climb again, more gently this time. About halfway up the rise, you come to an intersection with a fire road. Cross the road and pick up the trail on the other side. This section of singletrack is Karen's Trail. Karen's continues climbing up an easy grade, ending with a short descent back at the fire road. Turn right onto the fire road, heading up and over a small hill. Within 100 feet or so, the fire road peters out and becomes a singletrack as it descends back into the trees.

Just past the four-mile point, you come to another fire road. Shoot straight across it onto Jethro's Trail, a fun switchbacking downhill that ends at Forest Road 300 and Mill Creek. Turn right onto the fire road, which continues to head downhill. Almost immediately, you see a singletrack turnoff on the right. You can stay on the fire road or take the singletrack; they're roughly the same distance and rejoin again in about a 0.25 mile. I recommend the singletrack.

So, veer off to the right, heading up a short rise that levels to an easy pedal and leads back to the fire road. At the intersection, go straight across the fire road onto the next singletrack, the Grizzly Trail. Grizzly descends, steeply at times, through a forest of black oak. At about 6.7 miles, you reach the next short fire road section, Forest Road 100. Turn right onto the fire road, splash through a seasonal water crossing, and bear right at the next fork, back onto singletrack.

This stretch of trail rolls and climbs back up to the pine trees, ending at another junction with Forest Road 100. Turn right, and quickly make another right onto Forest Road 300. After a short, steep climb the trail levels as it approaches the next fork. Veer left onto Forest Road 600, staying left through the next mini-fork. The fire road meanders its way up, past a couple of tempting singletrack turnoffs. You'll be passing in and out of the trees as the trail rolls a bit before the last big push up to the crossroads.

At about 9.1 miles, you find yourself at the intersection of Forest Roads 600, 610 and the Bear Bones singletrack. Make a sharp, hairpin right turn onto the Bear Bones Trail. The trail begins with a rolling section, then becomes a fast and twisting downhill. It's over too soon, ending at Forest Road 400. Hang a left here, followed by a right turn onto the paved main road. Don't worry, you'll be off the pavement in a jiffy.

At 10.5 miles, turn left onto the first singletrack you see, Houghton Creek Trail. Aptly named, the trail follows Houghton Creek for about a mile before crossing it. After some tight switchbacks, the trail straightens and levels, leading back to the main road and the parking area.

33 Cow Mountain Recreation Area

Distance: 37 miles
Difficulty: Strenuous, mildly technical
Elevation: 4,400' gain/loss
Ride Type: Out and back on fire roads
Season: Spring through fall
Map: Available free from the Bureau of Land Management, (707) 468-4000
Comments: Water is available at the Mayacamas trailhead and at points along the Glen Eden Trail. It can get very hot here in the summer months.

Overview: The Cow Mountain Recreation Area is a 50,000-acre site due west of Clear Lake. While technically not a part of the North Bay/Sonoma area, it's close to Sonoma County's north boundary and a playground this size just had to be brought to your attention! There are over 150 miles (!) of trails included in this land, ranging from short and scenic to rough and tumble.

Named after the longhorn cattle that once roamed wild over this range, the recreation area is, for governing purposes, delineated as North and South Cow Mountain. The majority of the trails and approximately two-thirds of the property are found in the South Cow Mountain area, open to all, including 4WD vehicles and motorcycles. The trails here are steep, rough and rugged, providing endless hours of fun and amusement.

The northern third, North Cow Mountain, has a handful of trails that are restricted to non-motorized vehicles and provide slightly gentler

(and quieter) forms of entertainment. The trails here traverse ridges and meadows and follow seasonal creeks and streams. Fishing and camping are popular in this area, as well as hunting (every place has its drawbacks).

Because of the area's size, wildlife is abundant here. Beyond the usual Northern California-type animals such as coyote, deer, fox and rabbits, some of the grander and more exotic species hang out here, too, namely black bears and mountain lions. More than likely, you won't see the big guys but, for the sake of your own safety and that of the animals, wear a whistle around your neck. I've found whistles to be extremely effective when encountering wildlife bigger than a German shepherd. Not only will a couple of short, shrill blasts alert anyone within earshot that you're there and possibly in trouble, it frightens away most animals. (Did you know that bears can jump? Pretty high, too, considering their girth.)

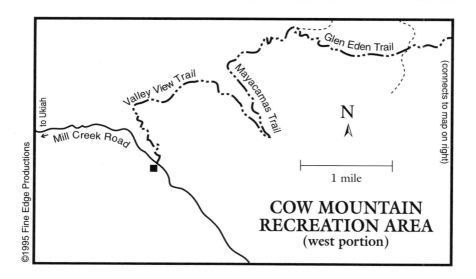

Valley View Trail

Mayacamas Trail

Glen Eden Trail

(connects to map on right)

to Ukiah

← Mill Creek Road

N

1 mile

**COW MOUNTAIN
RECREATION AREA**
(west portion)

©1995 Fine Edge Productions

While there are obviously an abundance of trails and combinations in the area, the following route, one of the most popular, is set forth here as an introduction to Cow Mountain. It runs across the North Cow Mountain Recreation Area, from the west boundary to the east boundary. It can be done as an 18.5-mile one-way shuttle or the more popular 37-mile out-and-back.

Getting There: From San Francisco, go north on 101 to Ukiah and take the Talmadge (Ukiah) exit. Take Talmadge Road east to East Side Road, then make the first left onto Mill Creek Road. The trailhead gate is on the left, about 4 miles up Mill Creek Road. Park in dirt turnouts on either side of the road.

For one-way shuttlers, the second vehicle should continue on Mill Creek Road and follow it through the South Cow Mountain area to Scott Creek Road. Bear left onto Scott Creek and follow it to Riggs Road, just past the U-Wanna Campground (I didn't name it, folks). Turn left on Riggs, which quickly ends at Scotts Valley Road. Turn left onto Scotts Valley and park at Kelly's Kamp, about 8 miles up.

Route: From the trail gate, follow the Valley View Trail as it climbs up along a grassland ridge. The trail starts as a series of switchbacks that takes some of the sting out of the climb. At the end of the first 1.5 miles, the grade eases considerably while the trail straightens out. From this point, the rest of Valley View rolls to its end at a junction with dirt Mendo Rock Road and the Mayacamas Trail (at the Willow Creek Recreation Site).

Turn left onto Mayacamas, which crosses Willow Creek and then follows its bank. A long downhill section leads to the north fork of Mill Creek. The trail turns to follow Mill Creek through a forest of pine and oak. Mayacamas rolls along the bank of the creek, through a seasonal water crossing, and up to a fork with the Glen Eden Trail, at about 7.5 miles.

The fun is temporarily over as

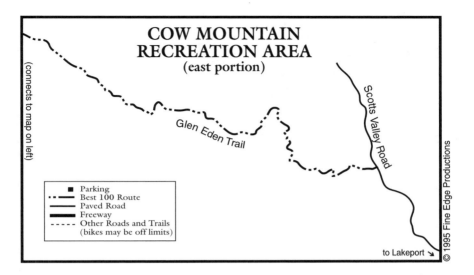

you turn right onto Glen Eden. Glen Eden climbs steeply up a short rise, about 0.5 mile. As you move away from the creeks, the scenery gets a little less green, opening up to grassland dotted with oak.

At the top of the first rise, the fun is back. The trail becomes a roller coaster that continues for the next 10.5 miles. Glen Eden rolls and turns, up ridges and down again, with great views of Clear Lake in front of you and the Mayacamas Range behind you. At about 12 miles, you cross the seasonal Scotts Creek in the Goat Rock Recreation Site. There are a few more trees here until you make your way up to the next ridge, where the grass and chaparral once again take over.

At approximately 15.7 miles, just past a water refill point, you enter private property. The remainder of the trail is a rolling downhill to the BLM gate (and another water refill point) on Scotts Valley Road. This is the end of the line for one-way shuttlers. Those riding the whole distance turn around here and go back the way you came.

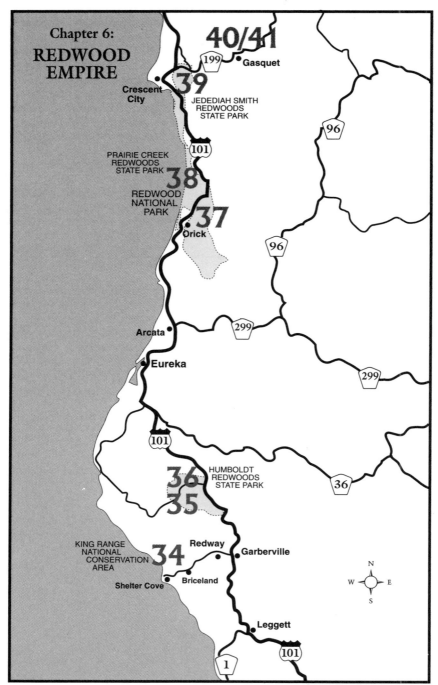

Chapter 6:

REDWOOD EMPIRE

40/41

199 • Gasquet

39
Crescent
City

JEDEDIAH SMITH
REDWOODS
STATE PARK

96

PRAIRIE CREEK
REDWOODS
STATE PARK
38

101

REDWOOD
NATIONAL
PARK **37**

• Orick

96

Arcata •

299

• Eureka

299

101

36
HUMBOLDT
REDWOODS
STATE PARK

35

36

KING RANGE
NATIONAL
CONSERVATION
AREA

34 Redway

• Garberville

• Briceland

Shelter Cove •

N
W ◆ E
S

• Leggett

1   101

CHAPTER 6

Redwood Empire

by Delaine Fragnoli

We could tell you that the redwoods are among the oldest and largest living things on earth. We could tell you that an old growth redwood forest is a rare and beautiful ecosystem. So rare and beautiful, in fact, that Redwood National Park and the surrounding California state parks have been declared a World Heritage Site and an International Biosphere Reserve by the United Nations.

We could pull out the overused superlatives that still don't convey the reality of these trees and forests. Words like majestic, towering, noble, venerable, awe-inspiring. Phrases such as "it's like being in a cathedral."

Fact is, even then we wouldn't come close to describing these marvels. The best we can do is urge you to go see them for yourself. See them on a mountain bike. Go and be awed.

While mountain bike opportunities in the national and state parks are limited (partly because of heavy use, partly because of unsuitable terrain and soil types, and partly because of politics), a mountain bike remains a great way to explore the redwoods. The biking you can do is both scenic and fun. Moist, tacky soil carpeted with pine needles provides great traction. Any hills you have to climb—they tend to be short and steep—are amply rewarded by forest views and ocean panoramas.

Along the fabled Humboldt coast, the best riding is in the King Range National Conservation Area, administered by the Bureau of Land Management. Just inland, Humboldt Redwoods State Park contains over 100 miles of trails, many of which are open to bikes. Access for both is off of Highway 101. The largest town in this area is Fortuna to the north, but several smaller communities dot the 101.

Redwood National Park, Prairie Creek Redwoods State Park, Del Norte Coast Redwoods State Park and Jedediah Smith Redwoods State Park form an emerald ribbon along California's northern-most coast. With the exception of Del Norte, each of these parks offers one substantial loop for mountain bikers.

Crescent City in the north and Eureka in the south are the largest jumping-off spots for exploring the area, although several smaller towns along

the coast offer services to travelers. Access is easy via Highway 101 and the Newton Drury Parkway, which bisects Redwood National and Prairie Creek parks.

Bordering the eastern side of Jedediah Smith State Park, the Smith River National Recreation Area offers longer backcountry trips on old logging roads and toll roads. Besides a rich mining history, the area is home to some of the eastern-most coastal redwoods as well as many other tree species, including four types of cedar.

As part of the Six Rivers National Forest, the area used to be managed primarily for logging, so you can see evidence of clear cutting in some spots. As a relatively new recreation area (it was established in 1990), the area is still developing its recreational potential. Plans for more campgrounds and efforts to map routes and trails are in the works, and NRA personnel are eager to help. Check with rangers for the latest trail information and road conditions.

Bisected by Highway 199, which parallels the Smith River and makes a lovely drive, the area is easily accessible from Crescent City. Services are available in Crescent City, Hiouchi and Gasquet. Smith River NRA headquarters are in Gasquet.

Trails Illustrated makes a Redwood National Park/North Coast State Parks/Smith River NRA topo map. This is the single map to get if you plan on exploring the whole area. To order, call (800) 962-1643. The map does not cover the Humboldt area.

34 King Range/Kings Peak

Distance: 10 miles for north ascent, 11 miles for south ascent, longer options possible
Difficulty: Strenuous, technical, exposure in some places
Elevation: 1,800' gain/loss
Ride Type: Out-and-back on singletrack and dirt roads
Season: April through October; tends to be wet in winter and spring, foggy in summer, best (warm and dry) in fall
Topo Maps: Shubrick Peak, Honeydew. (Call the BLM's Arcata office, 707-825-2300, for a very accurate map and brochure with trail mileages of the conservation area.)
Comments: There are several water sources in the area, but the water quality is questionable. Carry plenty of water or be prepared to treat any you find.

Overview: The beauty of this area is also its difficulty. Because of the very steep, rocky terrain, development has been impossible. The coast highway moves inland here, leaving a chunk of coastline to nature rather than to developers. Referred to as the Lost Coast, this is one of the few parcels of California coast where you can see an undisturbed meeting of land and sea. And what a dramatic meeting it is.

The rugged King Range slices through the area, its western slope dropping precipitously to the ocean shore. The slightly drier eastern slope, while still steep, is somewhat gentler as it descends into the Mattole River.

The pinnacle of the area, literally and in terms of views, is Kings Peak (4,088'). Actually, Kings Peak is the highest point along the whole California coast. The climb to this summit via the King Crest Trail is accompanied by incredible views, so try to pick a clear day to ride. You see the Pacific Ocean to the west (in April and May you may see whales breaching) and as far as the Yolla Bolly wilderness to the east. On perfect days it's said that you can actually make out Mt. Lassen in the east!

The price you pay for this privilege is a rough climb. The area, as I said above, is very rugged and rocky. Since it's a Wilderness Study Area, very little trail maintenance is done so the trails can get overgrown, especially in the spring. *Be prepared and self-sufficient.* While the area's terrain may intimidate some of you, it's not often that bikes are allowed in such wild and pristine places—and on singletrack, no less!

Getting There: The Conservation Area is about 60 miles south of Eureka, west of Garberville. There are two ways to do this ride. To get to either the north or south trailhead, start from Garberville on Highway 101 and follow the signs in the town for King Range. The road takes you through Redway. At this point, the road is called Briceland-Thorn Road.

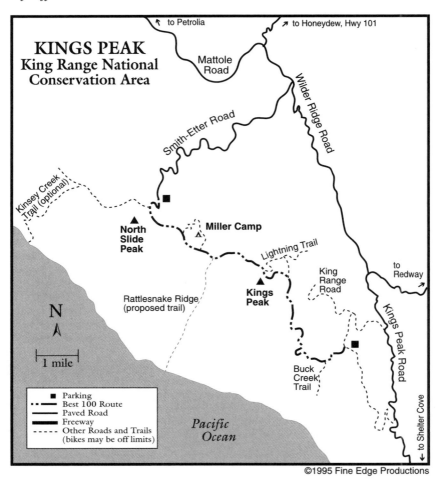

KINGS PEAK
King Range National Conservation Area

to Petrolia

to Honeydew, Hwy 101

Mattole Road

Wilder Ridge Road

Smith-Etter Road

Kinsey Creek Trail (optional)

North Slide Peak

Miller Camp

Lightning Trail

King Range Road

to Redway

Rattlesnake Ridge (proposed trail)

Kings Peak

Kings Peak Road

N

1 mile

Buck Creek Trail

■ Parking
∙∙■∙∙ Best 100 Route
─── Paved Road
━━━ Freeway
----- Other Roads and Trails
      (bikes may be off limits)

Pacific Ocean

to Shelter Cove

©1995 Fine Edge Productions

For the south trailhead, continue west on Briceland-Thorn, which becomes Shelter Cove Road, passing through the town of Briceland. At Kings Peak Road (signed)—called Horse Mountain Road on maps—turn north and drive about six miles to the junction with King Range Road, where you turn left. In about a mile, make a hard left on Horse Pasture Ridge Road (signed) and head south to the gate, where there is plenty of parking at the trailhead.

To get to the north trailhead, follow the directions to Briceland (given above). About three miles past Briceland, turn northwest on Wilder Ridge Road to Ettersburg. From Ettersburg, continue on Wilder Ridge Road north about 7.5 miles to Smith-Etter Road (signed), a 4WD road. Turn left (west) here, and continue all the way to the gate at the north trailhead—about six miles from the turnoff. There is limited parking in turnouts. *Do not park in the road.* Note that Smith-Etter Road is closed November through March.

Route: From Smith-Etter, the climb to Kings Peak is 5 miles; from Saddle Mountain it is 5.5 miles. Both routes climb the area's major ridge line to the peak. The southern route is tougher with more climbing. It starts out as a road grade and gets gradually narrower and steeper. The northern route has a little bit of descending mixed in with the climb, most of it at the beginning when you drop off the eastern flank of North Slide Peak.

Along its length, the King Crest Trail is narrow and rocky, making for some tough climbing. In places, it's actually cut into a cliff and there is potentially unnerving exposure. But the trail does flatten out in spots, particularly on the north route, and there are meadows. The trail can get overgrown. Trail maintenance is minimal and so are trail signs, so expect anything. In the spring, downed trees can block the trail. Check with BLM personnel for the latest trail conditions. Spurs jut off from the main route periodically and lead to vista points. To stay on track, keep climbing and keep on the ridge.

Just under halfway on the northern route, you pass a trail that takes off to your left. It leads to Miller Camp and loops back up to the main trail a little while later. Just past that, Rattlesnake Ridge trail drops to your right toward the beach. The BLM is working on extending it all the way to the beach. Eventually it will be 6 to 7 miles long.

As you approach to the peak, you come to a Y intersection with the Lightning Trail, which climbs up from your left. Go right for the shortest route to the top. (If you go left, the trail will eventually loop back to the peak, but you'll add some climbing.) Bear right at the next Y to get to the summit. The left fork skirts the top.

On the southern route, there isn't much to confuse you. Near the beginning, avoid the Buck Creek Trail, which plummets down to the beach on your left. Stay on the road bed. As you near the peak, the Lightning Trail takes off to your right. Go left for the shortest, easiest ascent. Bear left again at the next Y.

For both routes, return the way you came. Hardcore types could ride the entire trail out and back, but many people arrange a shuttle.

Also, if you absolutely must ride down to the beach, take either the Rattlesnake Ridge Trail (when it's completed) or the Kinsey Creek Trail. These are the "easiest" trails to come back up, although sea level to

3,400 feet in 7 miles, in the case of the Rattlesnake Trail and sea level to 2,400 feet in 3 miles, in the case of Kinsey Creek, don't exactly sound easy! Surprisingly, neither trail gets too sandy until the end.

Note that the Kinsey Creek Trail is shown but not named on any of the maps of the area. It is the singletrack that descends Kinsey Ridge, between Oat Creek and Kinsey Creek. To find it, from the northern King Crest trailhead, continue on Smith-Etter Road for about 2.5 miles. Right before you come to a gate across the road, look to your left for another road, which is also gated. This other road is the start of Kinsey Creek Trail.

35 Humboldt Redwoods State Park/ Grasshopper Peak

Distance: 17.5 miles
Difficulty: Very strenuous, mildly technical
Elevation: 3,100' gain/loss
Ride Type: Loop on dirt roads , little bit of pavement
Season: Year-round; tends to be wet in winter and spring, foggy in summer, best (warm and dry) in fall
Map: Park map available at Visitor Center for $1
Comments: Bikes are not allowed on hiking trails. Stay on fire roads. Consult the park map for details. Watch for poison oak. Humboldt Redwoods State Park can be reached at (707) 946-2409.

Overview: There are lots of reasons to visit Humboldt Redwoods State Park. It is home to the Rockefeller Forest, the largest tract of undisturbed old-growth coastal redwoods in the world. The grove also contains the Giant Tree, the world champion coast redwood. The world champion status is based upon the tree's height, circumference and crown size. Altogether, 17,000 of the park's 51,000 acres are old-growth.

The term *old-growth* refers not just to the size and age of the trees, but to the whole forest ecosystem. An old-growth forest houses young and old trees, snags, and a rich carpet of mosses and ferns.

The park also contains the entire Bull Creek watershed. Most of the available bike routes are in the Bull Creek area. Like much of the park, this area was acquired with financial support from the Save-the-Redwoods League. Founded in 1917, the League has been accumulating private funds and using them to purchase redwood forests since 1921.

Long before the League took an interest in the area, the Sinkyone Indians inhabited the land. Hunters and gatherers who lived on salmon and tanoak acorns, the Sinkyone used parts of the redwood trees for housing, basket-making and canoes.

Gold miners passed through the area during the nineteenth century until the Northwestern Pacific Railroad built the Redwood Highway in 1922. Then full-scale logging and tourism took over until the League intervened.

This particular loop, one of the best, highest, and most difficult climbs along the coast, takes you to Grasshopper Peak (3,379') and back along Bull Creek. The climb may be arduous but the descent is fun, and your surroundings are green and lush beyond imagining.

Getting There: The park is located 3 miles north of Garberville and 30 miles south of Eureka on Highway 101. The Bull Creek area is off of Mattole Road, about 10 miles north of the Visitor Center. The Grasshopper Peak trailhead is on the south side of Mattole, half a mile west of the Albee Creek Campground entrance. Note that Mattole Road is referred to as Bull Creek Flats Road

in some park publications.

Route: From the trailhead, head south and up on Grasshopper Road. Might as well put it in your granny gear from the get-go. This climb takes no prisoners as it ascends over 3,000 feet in 7 miles. Take it slow and enjoy your surroundings.

You have to go around a locked gate very early on. About 0.5 mile later, Squaw Creek Ridge Road takes off to your right. Stay on Grasshopper Road.

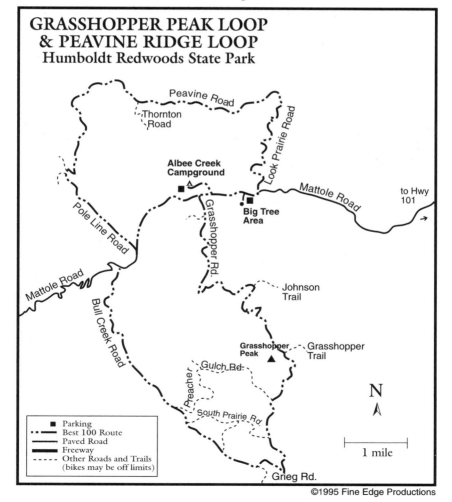

GRASSHOPPER PEAK LOOP & PEAVINE RIDGE LOOP
Humboldt Redwoods State Park

About halfway up, at a right-hand switchback, the Johnson Trail (no bikes) comes in from your left. This is a pretty spot to take a break, drink some water and rest your legs.

Just before 7 miles, when you approach Grasshopper Trail Camp on your left, your work is almost done. The Grasshopper Trail takes off from here, but it is closed to bikes. Grasshopper Peak itself and a fire lookout are on your right. The lookout reportedly makes a great sunset-watching spot for those of you with romantic notions in your heads and lights for your bikes. No matter what time of day, the views are great.

Now your work is over and you get to descend. Continue on Grasshopper Road down the backside of the peak. When you pass Preacher

Gulch Road at 8.5 miles, you will already have descended 800 feet. Drop 500 feet more to South Prairie Road, which you pass at 9.5 miles. At 10.5 miles Grasshopper Road ends at Grieg Road.

About 0.3 mile and 500 feet of elevation loss later, the steep Grieg Road dead ends at Bull Creek Road. Go right to continue your descent. Around 11.8 miles you pass South Prairie Road again. You pass Preacher Gulch Road and the Bull Creek Trail Camp at 12.8 miles.

From here, Bull Creek Road parallels Bull Creek for 3.5 miles, all the way back down to paved Mattole Road. A right turn onto the pavement takes you back to the trailhead and Albee Creek Campground.

36 Humboldt Redwoods State Park/ Peavine Ridge Road

Distance: 16.5 miles
Difficulty: Moderately strenuous, mildly technical
Elevation: 2,200' gain/loss
Ride Type: Loop on dirt roads and pavement
Season: Year-round; tends to be wet in winter and spring, foggy in summer, best (warm and dry) in fall
Map: Park map available at Visitor Center for $1
Comments: Bikes are not allowed on hiking trails. Stay on fire roads. Consult the park map for details. Watch for poison oak.

Overview: Although this ride starts with a steep climb, it is easier than the previous ride. The 7-mile stretch along Peavine Ridge is lovely and generally rolling terrain. The ride's greatest appeal, however, is that it takes you through plenty of old-growth forest.

Getting There: The turnoff for this ride, Mattole Road, is located 25 miles north of Garberville and 30 miles south of Eureka on Highway

101. The start of this ride, the Look Prairie Road trailhead, is a quarter mile east of the Big Tree Area on the north side of Mattole Road. Note that Mattole Road is referred to as Bull Creek Flats Road in some park publications.

Route: Head north and up Look Prairie Road. You have to go around a gate almost immediately. From here, you do most of your climbing in the first 4 miles. As you near the top of

the climb, you have to go around another gate. Soon after, Look Prairie ends at Peavine Ridge Road.

Head west, left. The road rolls along the ridge until it seems to end at Thornton Road, which drops off to your left. Go right to stay on Peavine. Soon the road begins to descend gradually on its way to Pole Line Road.

You have another gate to go around. Just after it, Pole Line Road takes off to your left (south), dropping 1,300 feet in 3 miles. Take Pole Line to its end at Mattole Road (there's another gate just before it reaches the pavement).

A left turn and 3 miles of easy spinning takes you back to the trailhead.

37 Redwood National Park/ Holter Ridge Loop

Distance: 19.5 miles
Difficulty: Moderate, not technical
Elevation: 2,100' gain/loss
Ride Type: Loop on dirt, gravel and paved roads
Season: Year-round; wet in winter and spring, crowded and foggy in summer, best (warm and dry) in fall
Maps: USGS Orick. (Redwood National Park puts out a brochure and trail map available at any Visitor Center; the Redwood Natural History Association produces a Trail Guide with map, suggested routes and mileages; Trails Illustrated Redwood National Park
Comments: Information and maps of the surrounding state parks can be obtained from the National Park's Visitor Information Center, (707) 464-6101. The Crescent City Chamber of Commerce can be reached at (707) 464-3174. The Redwood Natural History Association is another good resource, (707) 464-9150. State Park information can be had from the North Coast Redwoods District, (707) 445-6547.

Overview: This is the only legal mountain bike loop in Redwood National Park. The route climbs through old growth forest and second growth forest, crossing two streams on its way. While the old logging roads and pavement return do not require a lot of mountain biking skill, the climbing is steep in parts and the scenery is awe-inspiring. Riders without the endurance or desire to do the entire loop can do Lost Man Creek Trail as an out-and-back venture.

Getting There: The ride begins at the Lost Man Creek picnic area inside Redwood National Park. To get there, head north from the town of Orick for 3 miles on Highway 101. Turn right onto the gravel Lost Man Creek Road. (If you reach the Prairie Creek Visitor Center, you've gone too far.) Follow it for 2 miles to the picnic area.

From Crescent City, take Highway 101 south about 25 miles to the Newton B. Drury Scenic Parkway. Take the Parkway until it rejoins the highway. Continue 2 miles and go left on Lost Man Creek Road for 2 more miles to the picnic area.

Route: Begin by following lush, rock-studded Lost Man Creek. You cross two bridges in the first mile and another one soon after. The beauty of the creek and the climb that awaits you are enough to make even the heartiest rider want to linger.

Tear yourself away and prepare to sweat—you climb almost 1,000 feet in a mile! The grade eases just a bit, then climbs another 250 feet abruptly before mellowing out. You still go up, until, at just under 4.0 miles, you reach a trail junction.

Head right onto Holter Ridge Road, which follows the park's eastern boundary. Like most ridge routes, this is an up-and-down affair. You keep gaining altitude, but the climbing isn't steep or unpleasant. As you near the 9.5-mile mark, you top out at 2,250 feet and head down to paved Bald Hills Road.

A right onto Bald Hills (if you want you can go straight and head out to the Redwood Creek Overlook) takes you onto flat, even slightly descending terrain and gives your legs a chance to rest. Partway down, around 13.5 miles, look for the Lady Bird Johnson Grove (named for the former First Lady) on your right at the apex of a hairpin turn.

Park your bike in the parking area (bikes aren't allowed on the trail) and walk the self-guided Nature Loop Trail (informational pamphlets available at the trailhead) through mature redwood forest. From here, you also get a view of the Lost Man Creek drainage—the one you worked so hard to get out of!

Back on your bike, be prepared for a steep downhill (various sources estimate the grade at 15-17 percent!) as you plunge over 1,000 feet in less than 2 miles. Be careful as this section of road sees quite a bit of traffic from people venturing up and down from Lady Bird's Grove.

At 15.5 miles your descent ends at Newton Drury Parkway. Go right and pedal the pavement for just over 2.0 miles. A right onto Lost Man Creek Road and 2.0 more miles of spinning bring you back to your car.

38 Prairie Creek Redwoods State Park/Gold Bluffs Loop

Distance: 19 miles
Difficulty: Easy, mildly technical
Elevation: 900' gain/loss
Ride Type: Loop on dirt and gravel roads, singletrack, pavement
Season: Year-round; winter and spring are wet, summer is crowded and foggy, fall is best (warm and dry)
Maps: Redwood National Park puts out a brochure and trail map available at any Visitor Center; the Redwood Natural History Association produces a Trail Guide with map, suggested routes and mileages; Trails Illustrated Redwood National Park
Comments: Information and maps of Redwood National Park and the surrounding state parks can be obtained from the National Park's Visitor Information Center, (707) 464-6101. The Crescent City Chamber of Commerce can be reached at (707) 464-3174. The Redwood Natural History Association is another good resource, (707) 464-9150. State Park information can be had from the North Coast Redwoods District, (707) 445-6547.

Overview: The only legal mountain bike route in Prairie Creek Redwoods State Park, this lovely circuit begins on pavement but soon takes you into tall trees, through coastal prairies, past herds of Roosevelt elk, along pristine Gold Bluffs Beach and through second-growth forest. If that's not enough, you have several stream crossings, short sections of sand, and a few logs and rocks for a bit of technical challenge. This is probably the most enjoyable mountain biking in the redwood parks.

The loop can also be done in reverse; the only advantage to this is that you won't have to cross the park's main thoroughfare. The route is more fun the way it's described here. This way, most of the climbing is on pavement and most of the descending is on dirt.

Getting There: From Orick, go north on Highway 101 about 7 miles to the Prairie Creek Visitor Center, which is on your left (beach side). If you're coming from Crescent City, head south on Highway 101 for 25 miles. Take the Newton B. Drury Scenic

Parkway just over 8 miles to the Prairie Creek Visitor Center on your right (beach side). There is a $5 state park day-use fee. Additional parking can be found at the adjacent campground.

Route: Begin by going back out to the Drury Parkway. Cross it and head north (left turn). Be careful of the traffic! This is mostly uphill for just over 6.0 miles, but the climb is gradual and you do have a shoulder to ride on. Try to ignore the cars and enjoy your surroundings.

Be on the lookout for mileage marker 132.9. You're looking for the Ossagon Trail on your left across the parkway. The trail, which leads to Carruthers Cove Trail, Butler Creek, and the Coastal Trail, heads steeply up an embankment from the parkway. You'll probably lose all momentum crossing the parkway and, as a result, may have to walk your bike up this section.

Once over the embankment, a 0.5-mile downhill takes you into birch forest and to Ossagon Creek. Dismount and carry your bike on the stairs and across the bridge. On the other side, the trail remains level for awhile as it crosses a small prairie, a spot that the Yurok Indians used to call home.

Soon you head down steeply and back into the trees. Watch your speed here and stay in control. Some hikers have complained about bikers "flying" down this trail.

The trail crosses Ossagon Creek again and continues another 0.5 mile to a trail junction. Here, at about 8.0 miles, hang a left and head south. You're now on the Coastal Trail. Soon you splash through Butler Creek and then pass the Butler Creek Trail on your left.

The singletrack leads out of the woods and onto a wide expanse of beach and grass, called a coastal prairie. You soon come to a Y where one branch goes through the prairie and the other along the bluffs. Pick your trail; they soon rejoin. Then they split again. You may have to pick your trail according to where the elk are.

It seems that forests full of big trees demand at least one big mammal to inhabit them. This is a favorite area for the park's herd of Roosevelt elk, which feed in prairie areas but like the shade of the forest. The animals can grow to over 1,000 pounds and have impressive antlers that reach their largest proportions in the late summer and fall.

At 10.5 miles or so (depending on which trail you took through the prairie), the Coastal Trail crosses Fern Creek and arrives at Fern Canyon, complete with picnic area and off-limits-to-bikes Fern Canyon Trail. If you have the time, hike this beautiful trail; it's less than a mile and leads to a 50-foot deep canyon festooned with giant ferns and graced by a small waterfall.

Continuing the bike loop from Fern Canyon, the trail widens and turns into gravel Davidson Road. Be careful, Davidson is open to motor vehicles. It's easy riding along this relatively smooth road. You splash through two more creek crossings on your way to the Jogging Trail (yes, that's the official name).

At about 15.0 miles start looking for the Jogging Trail which takes off on your left. Originally a logging road, the 4-mile trail heads into second growth forest. They may be second growth, but these skyscraper trees still impress. The route is clearly marked with yellow signs with a jogger icon.

The trail crosses Wolf Creek

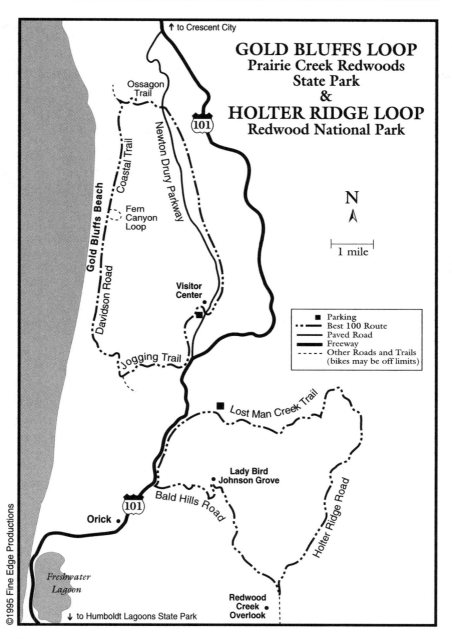

to Crescent City

GOLD BLUFFS LOOP
Prairie Creek Redwoods
State Park
&
HOLTER RIDGE LOOP
Redwood National Park

Ossagon Trail

Coastal Trail

Newton Drury Parkway

Gold Bluffs Beach

Fern Canyon Loop

Davidson Road

Jogging Trail

Visitor Center

N
A

1 mile

■ Parking
·—·— Best 100 Route
——— Paved Road
▅▅▅ Freeway
----- Other Roads and Trails
(bikes may be off limits)

Lost Man Creek Trail

Lady Bird Johnson Grove

Bald Hills Road

Holter Ridge Road

Orick

Freshwater Lagoon

to Humboldt Lagoons State Park

Redwood Creek Overlook

©1995 Fine Edge Productions

Bridge before emerging at campsite 48 in the Prairie Creek Campground. Make your way through the campground and back to your car at the Visitor Center, approximately 19.0 miles. *Note:* Park publications call this a 20-mile bicycle route, but actual mileage is closer to 19 miles.

39 Jedediah Smith Redwoods State Park/Howland Hill Road

Distance: 12.5 miles
Difficulty: Easy, not technical
Elevation: 750' gain/loss
Ride Type: Out-and-back on degenerating asphalt and gravel road
Season: Year-round; wet in winter and spring, crowded and foggy in summer, best (warm and dry) in fall
Maps: Redwood National Park puts out a brochure and trail map available at any Visitor Center; the Redwood Natural History Association produces a Trail Guide with map, suggested routes and mileages; Trails Illustrated Redwood National Park
Comments: Information and maps of Redwood National Park and the surrounding state parks can be obtained from the National Park's Visitor Information Center, (707) 464-6101. The Crescent City Chamber of Commerce can be reached at (707) 464-3174. The Redwood Natural History Association is another good resource, (707) 464-9150. State Park information can be had from the North Coast Redwoods District, (707) 445-6547.

Overview: In an area of limited mountain bike routes, Jedediah Smith Redwoods State Park is the most limited. The paved and gravel Howland Hill Road is virtually the only option for the fat-tire crowd. (You can ride unpaved Walker Road as well, but Howland Hills is the more scenic route.) While the mountain biking itself isn't challenging and the gawking tourists sharing the narrow road can be annoying, the route's virtue is its scenery—eye-popping, jaw-dropping scenery.

The road takes you through some incredibly large and old redwoods, depositing you at Stout Grove, home of the densest stand of redwoods on the coast. This old-growth grove was donated to the state by the Stout family, hence the name. The most spectacular specimen in the already spectacular grove is the Stout Tree, the largest redwood in the park.

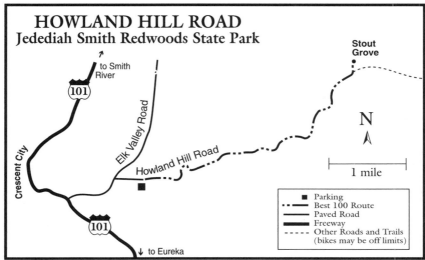

HOWLAND HILL ROAD
Jedediah Smith Redwoods State Park

Stout Grove

to Smith River

101

Elk Valley Road

Howland Hill Road

Crescent City

101

to Eureka

N

1 mile

■ Parking
∙∙∙∙∙ Best 100 Route
━━ Paved Road
▬▬ Freeway
---- Other Roads and Trails
(bikes may be off limits)

©1995 Fine Edge Productions

The route is of historical interest, too, as it was originally the Crescent City and Yreka Turnpike, a stage road that connected mining camps in California with their counterparts over the border in Oregon.

Getting There: From Crescent City, head south on Highway 101 to Elk Valley Road; turn left. Howland Hill Road is on your right, 1 mile up. Park along the road. This trip can easily be shortened by driving farther up the road and parking in any turnout.

Route: This is a very straightforward route, allowing you to concentrate on your surroundings rather than on trail directions. Simply head up Howland Hill Road. You get a nice, easy 0.8-mile warm-up before the road begins to climb. It enters the State Park and soon turns to dirt and gravel. Your climb is over at 1.8 miles.

Enjoy the level cruise from here to Stout Grove, as you pass through one magnificent grove after another. You may want to stop at Mill Creek bridge and enjoy the view. At 6.0 miles bear left onto the road to Stout Grove. Follow it to the parking area.

Leave your bike here and walk the half-mile Stout Grove Trail. Visit the Stout Tree and try to absorb its immensity—both its age and its size. Then turn your puny, insignificant self around and head back the way you came.

40 Smith River/ Old Gasquet Toll Road

Distance: 24.5-mile loop, 17 miles one way
Difficulty: Moderately strenuous, not technical
Elevation: 2,050' gain/loss for loop; 1,600' gain, 2,050' loss, net loss of 450' for one way
Ride Type: Loop on dirt, gravel and paved roads with singletrack option; or one way on dirt and gravel roads with singletrack option
Season: June through September, check snow conditions in May and October
Topo Map: Trails Illustrated Redwood National Park/North Coast State Parks/Smith River NRA
Comments: Call the Smith River NRA headquarters in Gasquet at (707) 457-3131 for information on camping and recreational opportunities.

Overview: One of the Smith River National Recreation Area's recommended "Backroads Discovery" tours, this route sees quite a bit of vehicle traffic during the summer months. But the good news is that the dirt roads are in relatively good condition.

That said, this trip features great vistas and several "interpretive stops" for those of you interested in learning more about the forest and the history of the area. Get a brochure at the ranger headquarters.

Plus the route offers a variety of options. Less-conditioned cyclists may prefer to do the one-way route, while stronger riders can do a full loop. Experienced mountain goats may choose a difficult hiking trail option on the return. Both the loop and the one-way trip could be done in the manner described or in reverse. Yet another strenuous all-dirt option, not described here, would involve going out the Old Gasquet Toll Road, up County Road 315 and back via the Elk Camp Ridge Trail.

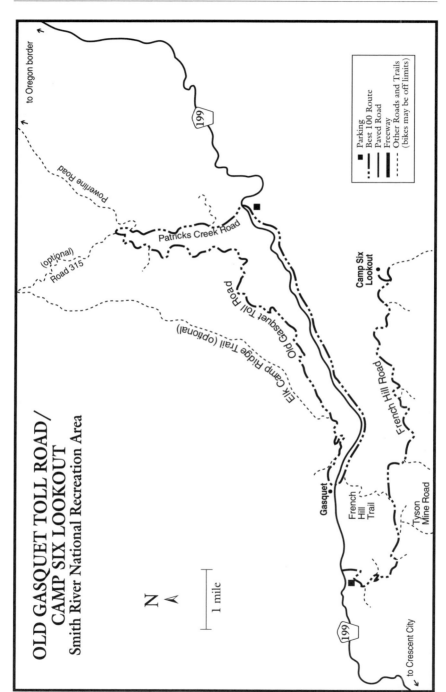

OLD GASQUET TOLL ROAD/
CAMP SIX LOOKOUT
Smith River National Recreation Area

to Oregon border

199

Powerline Road

Patricks Creek Road

(optional)
Road 315

Old Gasquet Toll Road

Elk Camp Ridge Trail (optional)

Camp Six
Lookout

French Hill Road

Gasquet

French
Hill
Trail

Tyson
Mine Road

199

to Crescent City

N

1 mile

Parking
Best 100 Route
Paved Road
Freeway
Other Roads and Trails
(bikes may be off limits)

©1995 Fine Edge Productions

As the ride's name implies, the route follows the Old Gasquet Toll Road. Built in 1887 by Horace Gasquet, the road ran from Crescent City, California to Waldo, Oregon. Gasquet charged $1 for a man and a horse to use the road. Don't worry, the only toll mountain bikers have to pay is in sweat!

Getting There: Smith River NRA headquarters are in the town of Gasquet, 19 miles east of Crescent City on Highway 199. You can do this ride one way by leaving one car in the town of Gasquet and driving a second car to the trailhead at the junction of Highway 199 and Patrick Creek Road. To do the full loop, park in the town of Gasquet.

Route: From Gasquet, head east on Highway 199. This generally flat route follows the North Fork of the Smith River. It's 7.5 miles to Patricks Creek Road (numbered as County Road 316). The highway begins a gradual climb as you near Patricks Creek Road.

Those of you doing the one-way route drive to this point. Park off the side of the road or in the Patrick Creek campground. You will need to subtract 7.5 miles from the following mileages.

Hang a left onto dirt Patricks Creek Road. About 0.5 mile up, you come to three spurs on your left. If you're interested in the interpretive stops, turn up the middle spur to get to the first stop. Pass a large boulder and continue down the old road to the creek. Here you can see a weir that was built to create pools for fish.

Backtrack to the main road and continue to follow it as it parallels Patrick Creek. At about 8.4 miles you pass a landslide area. When the road

comes to a T, bear left onto the Old Gasquet Toll Road. Patricks Creek Road goes to the right and turns into Powerline Road. It continues another 7 miles to the Oregon border. Our route, however, is to the left.

Soon you cross Patrick Creek and reach a fork in the road. County Road 315 takes off to the right. The Old Gasquet Toll Road (County Road 314) continues to the left.

If you are interested in the strenuous singletrack option, head up Road 315. You climb about 2,000 feet to the top of the ridge to the Elk Camp Ridge trailhead. The Elk Camp Ridge Trail (2E04) is a rolling 9.5-mile singletrack which eventually deposits you at the ranger headquarters.

Meanwhile, back at the junction of Roads 315 and 314, those of us with more modest ambitions turn left to stay on the Old Gasquet Toll Road and begin a climb of our own. The first part is the steepest. Once out of the creek bottom, the road contours along a mountainside.

You pass a succession of interpretive stops. At 11.1 miles you come to the Old Patrick Creek Lodge, built in the late 1800s as a stage coach stop for passengers and horses traveling the Toll Road. Continue for 3.1 miles to your next interpretive stop, a view of High Dome (3,821'). You reach prospector Melderson's grave at 14.7 miles. Around the 17.8-mile mark you pass Danger Point, so named because it was hazardous for stage coaches to pass one another here. Be careful of oncoming traffic yourself!

You cross Eighteen-Mile Creek 1 mile later. The name stems from the fact that the creek is roughly 18 miles from the Oregon border. Creeks you passed earlier were named Twelve-Mile Creek, Eleven-Mile Creek and Ten-Mile Creek respectively.

The last and final stop is at a vista point for French Hill and Signal Peak, 21.1 miles. From here it's 1.7 miles to the next junction, where you go left, downhill. The road turns to pavement and forks at 23.3 miles. Go left toward the recreation area headquarters, keeping left to get back out to Highway 199 and your car.

41 Smith River/ Camp Six Lookout

Distance: 22.6 miles
Difficulty: Moderately strenuous, not technical
Elevation: 3,200' gain/loss
Ride Type: Out-and-back on dirt and gravel roads, singletrack option
Season: June through September, check snow conditions in May and October
Maps: Trails Illustrated Redwood National Park/North Coast State Parks/Smith River NRA
Comments: Call the Smith River NRA headquarters in Gasquet at (707) 457-3131 for information on camping and recreational opportunities.

Overview: Here's your chance to engage in one of the favorite pastimes of Northern California mountain bikers—climbing to lookout towers. The climb starts out steeply, levels off and then begins a gradual ascent before growing steeper again as you approach the Camp Six lookout. Along the way you'll pass stands of some of the highest and most eastern coastal redwoods. Here they mix with other trees such as Douglas fir, tanoak, alder, knobcone pine and sugar pine. And, of course, you get the payback of a great view from the top of the lookout!

Getting There: From Gasquet, go west on Highway 199 to French Hill Road. It's 2.2 miles from the Gasquet Ranger Station, across the street from the Wagon Wheel motel and cafe on your left. You can drive or ride to this point. The mileages in the route description are from the beginning of French Hill Road.

Route: Head up French Hill Road (County Road 411/Forest Service Road 17N04); it begins to climb right away. At the first Y, head left. At the next junction, go right and continue climbing. In these first couple of miles you can see a 10-year-old clear-cut that has been replanted. This area of the forest is no longer being logged.

The climb begins to ease as you

come up to a third road junction. Go left again. You are now traveling due east, paralleling Highway 199 below you. At 3.4 miles, you pass Tyson Mine Road which branches to the right. Stay on French Hill Road.

You pass French Hill Trail on your left. There's a grove of coastal redwoods on your right at 5.6 miles. On the coast, redwoods seldom share space with other trees, but in this transitional zone they mix with conifers.

Several roads jut off to your right along here. Ignore them and stay on French Hill heading east and upward. The climb gets steeper until, at 8.8 miles, you pass a turnout on your left. From the turnout you can see the Gasquet Toll Road (see the previous ride) across the canyon.

A road goes to your left at 10.2 miles, but you continue straight—and up. Just under a mile later, 11.1 miles total, you reach Forest Road 17N71. You're almost to the lookout now, just 0.2 mile up 17N71.

Built by the Civilian Conservation Corps in the 1930s, the lookout shares space with radio and TV antennas. Climb to the top of the lookout (3,725') if it's open, or up the first flight of stairs if it's closed, and take a well-deserved break. Enjoy the view. Notice the "pygmy" forest directly below you. These 200-year-old lodgepole pines are "only" 30-feet tall, a result of the area's poor soil and harsh weather.

When you're rested and ready for a fun, high-speed downhill, head back the way you came up. After you pass the redwood grove on the way down, about 19.2 miles, those who want some challenging singletrack should be on the alert for the French Hill Trail (2E25) off to your right. The trail twists steeply down to the highway, dropping about 1,600 feet in 2.7 miles. It deposits you on the south side of the highway right across from the ranger station. A left turn takes you back to Gasquet. Those too faint of heart to try the singletrack can simply retrace their tire treads back to the French Hill Road/Highway 199 intersection.

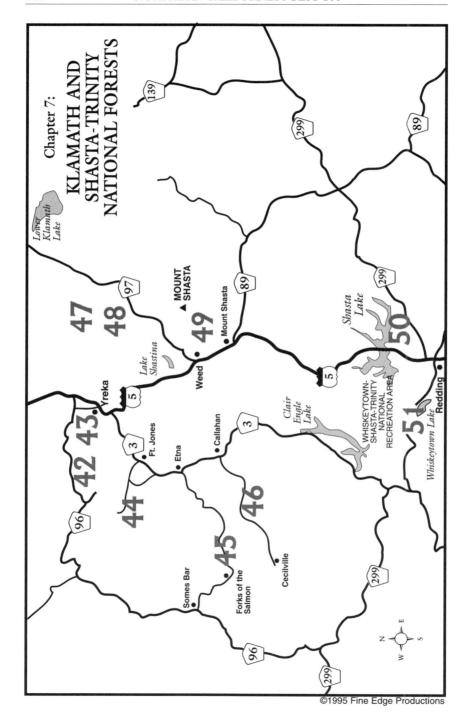

Chapter 7:
KLAMATH AND
SHASTA-TRINITY
NATIONAL FORESTS

Klamath and Shasta-Trinity National Forests

by Robin Stuart

Located between the coast ranges and the Cascades, the Klamath National Forest houses the Marble, Salmon, Scott Bar and Siskiyou mountain ranges. The forest's four National Wild and Scenic Rivers are among the largest in the state. These rivers and steep, high mountain ranges provide unparalleled recreational opportunities: awesome white-water rafting, over 1000 miles of trails, picnicking and camping, and outstanding fishing and hunting.

The Forest has been quick to pick up on and promote mountain biking. A few years ago, rangers published *A Cyclist's Guide to Great Mountain Biking Routes on the Klamath National Forest,* which outlines 17 rides. You may still be able to get a Xerox copy at one of the ranger stations.

The area's five ranger districts are remote and uncrowded. That means *no trail conflicts!* Visitors and locals alike are friendly and relaxed—it's amazing what happens when you have elbow room! Local mountain bikers retain the sport's original ethos; they're laidback and not as interested in shredding gnarly singletrack as they are in exploring beautiful areas by bike. They behave more like backpackers who cover more ground with a bike. Not that they dislike singletrack, but there's not that much around, except the off-limits-to-bikes Pacific Crest Trail.

Most of the riding is on fire roads (some 3,000 miles worth) that climb to vista points and fire lookouts. Other roads parallel several of the major waterways, so cool swimming holes are never far away. A few legal singletracks and rough doubletracks provide technical challenges for the more advanced rider. The only hazards you need watch out for are logging trucks and hunters during hunting season.

When you visit Klamath, you ride among pines, Douglas firs, Port Orford cedars and big-leaf maples. Look for wild huckleberries and blackberries, too. When you're riding near water, you're likely to see muskrats, river otters, mergansers and great blue herons. The Goosenest District in particular is great

for birdwatching. The Pacific flyway crosses the area and literally millions of migratory birds rest here in spring and fall.

Access to Klamath is fairly easy via Interstate 5, which intersects the Forest. Higher elevations are usually clear of snow from June or July to October. Bordering on the south is Shasta-Trinity National Forest, which contains the Whiskeytown-Shasta-Trinity National Recreation Area along with the Chappie-Shasta OHV area, administered by the BLM's Redding Resource Area.

The natural landmark of this area is, of course, Mt. Shasta (14,162'). Although you can't ride on the mountain, you can ride all around it. Recreational opportunities in the NRA center around four lakes: Trinity, Lewiston, Shasta and Whiskeytown. Hiking trails around these lakes provide great fun for families and those not up for backcountry riding. Home to the 10-year-old Lemurian-Shasta Classic mountain bike race, the OHV area offers rough, difficult and technical riding.

Major towns in the area with full services include Redding, Yreka and Weed. For additional information, contact Klamath National Forest at (916) 842-6131. Shasta-Trinity National Forest can be reached at (916) 246-5222. For a map of the Chappie-Shasta OHV area, call the BLM's Redding Resource Office at (916) 224-2100.

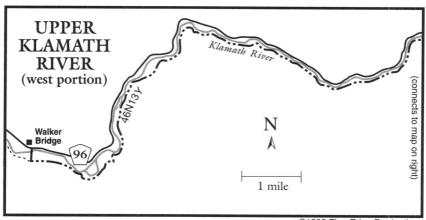

UPPER KLAMATH RIVER (west portion)

Klamath River

46N13Y

Walker Bridge

96

N

1 mile

(connects to map on right)

42 Upper Klamath River

Distance: 19 miles
Difficulty: Easy, not technical
Elevation: Rolling with a net gain of 200'
Ride Type: One way on dirt road with car shuttle; strong riders can ride out-and-back
Season: Year-round; spring brings wildflowers and fall brings color
Topo Maps: Badger Mountain, McKinley Mountain, Hawkinsville
Comments: The town of Klamath River has a gas station and convenience store. There are also several lodges in the area.

Overview: On this ride you parallel the upper reaches of the Klamath River and Highway 96. You can see remnants of the area's past in the form of old dredger piles and abandoned cabins. You're also likely to catch sight of deer, muskrats, turtles, eagles, osprey and great blue herons. Make this an all-day affair. Bring along a picnic lunch—there are many suitable spots to stop and kick back.

Getting There: From Yreka (pronounced Y-reka), head north on Highway 263 for 10 miles to Highway 96 (right after you cross the Klamath River) and go left (west). About 2 miles later you come to the Ash Creek Bridge. This is where you start your ride. But first you need to

drop your return vehicle at Walker Bridge, 18 miles farther down Highway 96. Park off the road.

Route: Cross the Klamath River on Ash Creek Bridge and hang a right onto 46N13Y. This graded, well-maintained dirt road parallels the Klamath River as it makes its way downstream. Although open to vehicles, most auto tourists take Highway 96, so you won't encounter much traffic. The river itself sees a lot of traffic from rafters and fishermen.

The road rolls along, but never steeply and never uphill or downhill for long as it follows the river's undulating course. At times you ride right beside the river, and at times you climb briefly onto bluffs for more of

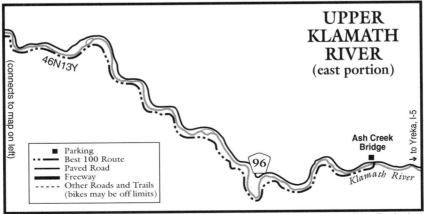

©1995 Fine Edge Productions

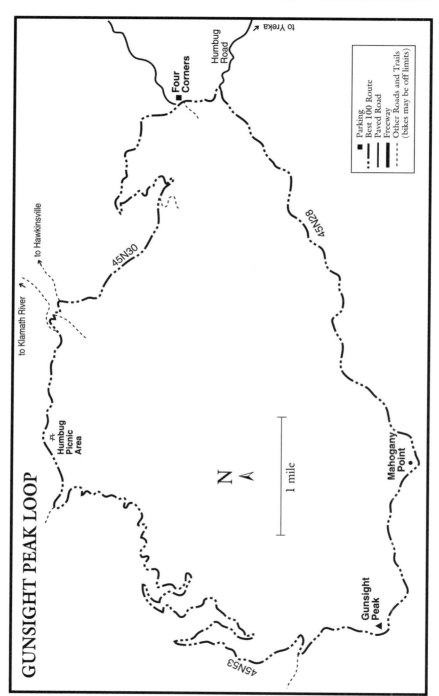

GUNSIGHT PEAK LOOP

to Yreka

Humbug
Road

Four
Corners

to Hawkinsville

45N30

45N28

to Klamath River

Humbug
Picnic
Area

N

1 mile

Mahogany
Point

Gunsight
Peak

4SN53

Parking
Best 100 Route
Paved Road
Freeway
Other Roads and Trails
(bikes may be off limits)

an overview of the area. But you're never far from the sight and sound of the river.

Stay hugging the river and you can't get lost. You know you're near the end when you pass the Eagle Nest Golf Course. Although the road continues to follow the river downstream, your route ends at 19 miles at Walker Bridge. Cross the bridge to get back to Highway 96.

43 Gunsight Peak Loop

Distance: 20 miles
Difficulty: Moderately strenuous, somewhat technical
Elevation: 3,300' gain/loss, 6,100' high point
Ride Type: Loop on dirt roads and rough doubletrack
Season: Spring, summer, fall
Topo Maps: Badger Mountain, McKinley Mountain, Indian Creek Baldy, Yreka
Comments: Nearest services are in Yreka, 3 miles away. Carry plenty of water.

Overview: Yeah, so you have to climb some on this ride. It's worth it. On the way up you get fine views to the south, including Mount Shasta, and the climb is broken up. You have to climb some at the beginning of the ride and some at the end. Once you top out at Gunsight Peak you get *10 miles* of downhill nirvana, including 7 miles of fun and challenging doubletrack. This is gold country as well, and the area is dotted with mine sites.

It's also the site of the Humbug Hurry-Up, an annual race that attracts over 400 competitors. The event is so popular that it has gained sponsorship from Coors Light. If you're here in July, give Dave Rawlings and Team One Speed a call for more information, (916) 842-6988. But be prepared to really climb—the long course features a 13-mile hill! Because of the wealth of riding in the area, Rawlings has considered organizing a 100-mile ride, which he would name the Humbug Hurry On and On and On!

Getting There: From the town of Yreka, head west on either Miner or North streets. At Humbug Road go right. Follow Humbug for 3 miles (it turns into a dirt road) to the Four Corners saddle. Park off the road here. Note that strong climbers who want to add another 1,800-foot climb to the ride can pedal from Yreka.

Route: From the intersection, head southwest on Road 45N28. Get into a comfortable gear for the long but very manageable climb. The road is a graded, maintained road so traction isn't a problem as you gain about 1,700 feet in the next 6 miles.

Take in the views to the south. Along here you can see Yreka behind you, Shasta Valley and Mount Shasta to the south, and the Humbug Creek drainage to the north.

You ride along the flank of several peaks in these first 6 miles, some of which have radio facilities on them. When you reach Mahogany Point with its radio towers, it's worth stopping to soak in the view. From here it's roughly another 2 miles to Gunsight Peak.

At Gunsight Peak, the road swings north and starts to descend. After a mile, you reach an intersec-

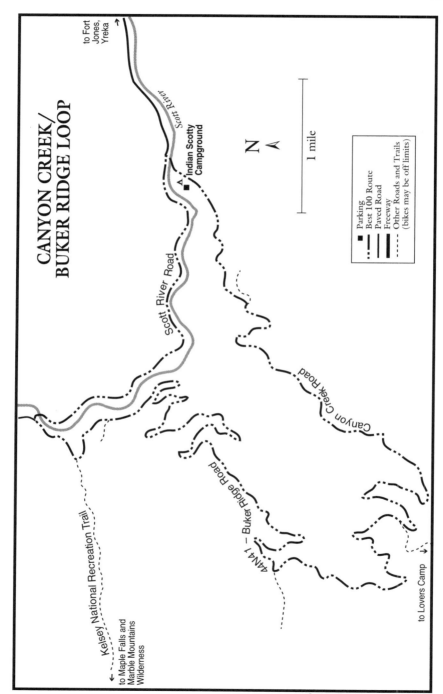

CANYON CREEK/
BUKER RIDGE LOOP

to Fort
Jones,
Yreka

Scott River

Indian Scotty
Campground

Scott River Road

N

1 mile

Parking
Best 100 Route
Paved Road
Freeway
Other Roads and Trails
(bikes may be off limits)

Canyon Creek Road

4N41 — Buker Ridge Road

Kelsey National Recreation Trail

to Maple Falls and
Marble Mountains
Wilderness

to Lovers Camp

tion with 45N53. Go right onto 45N53. This is Sucker Creek Road. Don't worry, you won't be a sucker for taking this route.

This rough doubletrack is blocked to 4WD vehicles, so you don't have to watch out for motorized traffic. It's easy to get up speed here (you drop almost 3,300 feet in 7 miles), so be careful. Loose rocks and steep dropoffs are the main hazards and can send you sliding and cartwheeling.

Once you're down to Humbug Creek, you cross the creek and go right. The doubletrack turns into a

graded road here and follows the creek for a couple of miles past Humbug picnic area. This is easy pedaling until you reach a bridge. Just beyond the bridge, make a sharp right onto Road 45N30.

This is where things get painful. Now you have to climb out of the creek drainage and back up to the Four Corners intersection. Get in your granny gear and suffer up a 1,500-foot climb (in about 4 miles). Hey, that downhill was fun, wasn't it? Keep telling yourself that and you'll be back to your car before you know it.

44 Canyon Creek/ Buker Ridge Loop

Distance: 18 miles
Difficulty: Moderate, not technical; singletrack option is more technical
Elevation: Gain/loss 2,200', singletrack adds 1,000' gain/loss
Ride Type: Loop on dirt roads and pavement, singletrack option
Season: Spring, summer, fall
Topo Maps: Scott Bar, Boulder Peak, Marble Mountain, Grider Valley
Comments: Nearest services are in Fort Jones, which has stores, restaurants and accommodations. Several campgrounds in the area make good base camps. Water is available at Indian Scotty campground.

Overview: Part of this ride follows the Scott River, one of the Klamath National Forest's major waterways and a designated Wild and Scenic River. Side creeks as well as the river offer great swimming holes en route. On the way out, the route also takes you near the Marble Mountain Wilderness. On the way back, you get views into the dramatic Scott River Canyon. The ride even includes a singletrack option that passes a lovely waterfall and on its way to the wilderness boundary.

In addition, you pass spawning and rearing ponds for salmon and steelhead, complete with interpretive

displays. You may also want to explore the old Kelsey Creek Guard Station above the Scott River Bridge.

Getting There: Fort Jones is about 16.5 miles southwest of Yreka on Highway 3. From the town of Fort Jones, take the Scott River Road (it parallels the Scott River) west for 12 miles to the turnoff for Indian Scotty Campground. Turn left and cross the concrete bridge. Park at the campground.

Route: You begin your ride amid moss-draped Douglas fir at Indian Scotty. From the campground, go back out to the main road you came in on and go right. This is Canyon Creek Road, a well-maintained, graded dirt road. Like most good loops, this one gets the climbing over with early so you can finish on a downhill.

You climb away from the Scott River gradually. At 4 miles you cross a bridge. Just upstream from here is a good swimming hole if you're hot and ready for a break. The climb is about half over at this point. You cross several creeks as you continue climbing. The Marble Mountain Wilderness lies to the south, and your route skirts the boundary here.

When you pass the signed turn-off for Lovers Camp, a lovely campsite very near the wilderness boundary, you have about 2 miles of climbing left. At the intersection at 8 miles, turn right onto Buker Ridge Road (44N41). The climb is over now and you can relax for an easy, speedy 6-mile downhill to Kelsey Creek and the Scott River. (At Kelsey Creek, a side channel has interpretive signs explaining the salmon ponds there.)

When 44N41 crosses the creek, bear right toward the Scott River to finish the loop. You drop down to Scott River Road and go right for 3.5 miles of easy pavement spinning back to your car.

If you still have energy and you're interested in a challenging singletrack, try out the Kelsey National Recreational Trail. Instead of going right after you cross the creek, go left up Kelsey Creek Road for 0.5 mile to the trailhead.

At one time the Kelsey Trail ran for 200 miles between Crescent City and Fort Jones. Built as a mule train route by Chinese laborers in the 1800s, it now sees mostly backpackers. This is one of the sections of the trail open to mountain bikes.

The singletrack climbs about 1,000 feet in 3 miles as it makes its way along Kelsey Creek to the Marble Mountains Wilderness boundary. The ride is wet and wild, and is even more fun on the way back when you're headed downhill! About a half mile from the wilderness area, you come to Maple Falls. Some people feel it is the prettiest waterfall in the region, and you'll see why.

Tempting though it is, do not enter the wilderness area; bikes are prohibited. This out-and-back sidetrip adds about 7 miles to your ride total.

45 Forks of the Salmon/ Sawyers Bar Loop

Distance: 40 miles
Difficulty: Strenuous
Elevation: 3,600' gain/loss
Ride Type: Loop on dirt roads and pavement
Season: Spring, summer, fall
Topo Maps: Forks of Salmon, Sawyers Bar, Tanners Peak
Comments: You can find telephones as well as general stores in Forks of Salmon or Sawyers Bar. Two campgrounds, Little North Fork and Red Bank, are located between the two towns. Note that neither campground has piped water.

Overview: Views of the North Fork of the Salmon River and of the Salmon-Trinity Alps highlight this ride. Forks of the Salmon is a rather literal name as you will see. The town is located at the junction of the North and South Forks of the Salmon River. This ride begins by climbing the spine between the two forks and is a good way to familiarize yourself with the area's rugged topography.

After this hard climb, you ride through near-virgin stands of old-growth Douglas fir before descending to the quaint old mining town of Sawyers Bar. Throughout the ride you're within sight and sound of the Salmon River, yet another of Klamath National Forest's Wild and Scenic Rivers. As with most waterways in the Forest, the Salmon has seen a lot of mining. You pass several mine sites and dredge tailings on your route.

Getting There: From Yreka, take Highway 3 to Etna, then turn west onto North Fork Road—which parallels the North Fork of the Salmon. Continue southwest about 40 miles to Forks of the Salmon. (From the west, Forks is 18 miles southeast of Somes Bar.) Park at the USFS station on the south side of North Fork Road, near the North Fork bridge.

Route: Start by crossing the bridge and heading east on 39N28. Another road soon veers south over the South Fork of the Salmon. You want to stay on 39N28, which follows the north bank of the South Fork. You parallel the South Fork for a couple of miles before the road swings north, then east, and starts to climb.

You climb steadily up Blue Ridge through an area burned by the wildfires of 1987. One advantage of the fires is that you have fine views of the Salmon-Trinity Alps to the south. The ascent levels somewhat as you approach Picayune Lake on your left. Just past the lake, the grade resumes a steeper pitch as you continue your march up the ridge line.

When 39N28 sweeps south in a large switchback, you need to hang a sharp, hairpin left onto 39N27. Road 39N27 heads north on up the ridge. The bad news is that you gain 400 feet in two switchbacks; the good news is that the climb is almost over.

Next you pass Jones Lake and intermittent Mud Lake on your left. Then you begin the final climb to the 4,800-foot mark. The top of Blue Ridge with its lookout tower rises steeply to your right. You then contour around its northern flank and finally begin the much-anticipated descent to Eddy Gulch.

When you reach Eddy Gulch, a lefthand switchback sweeps you northward. Soon after a road forks to

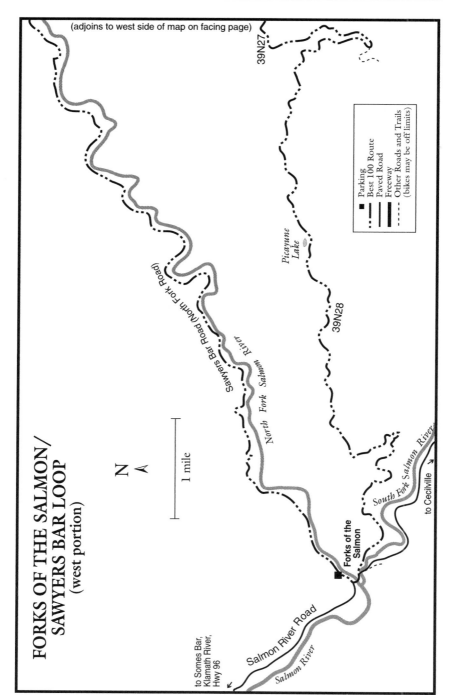

(adjoins to west side of map on facing page)

39N27

Parking
Best 100 Route
Paved Road
Freeway
Other Roads and Trails
(bikes may be off limits)

Picayune Lake

39N28

Sawyers Bar Road (North Fork Road)

North Fork Salmon River

South Fork Salmon River

to Cecilville

Forks of the Salmon

FORKS OF THE SALMON/
SAWYERS BAR LOOP
(west portion)

N

1 mile

Salmon River Road

to Somes Bar,
Klamath River,
Hwy 96

Salmon River

© 1995 Fine Edge Productions

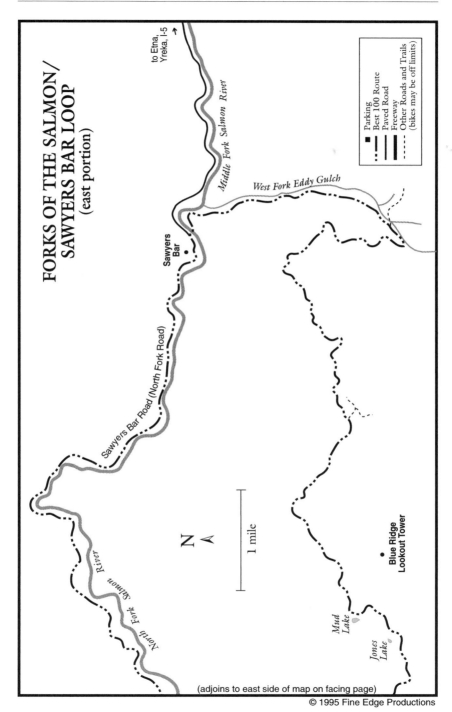

FORKS OF THE SALMON/
SAWYERS BAR LOOP
(east portion)

to Etna,
Yreka, I-5

Middle Fork Salmon River

West Fork Eddy Gulch

Sawyers
Bar

Sawyers Bar Road (North Fork Road)

North Fork Salmon River

N

1 mile

Blue Ridge
Lookout Tower

Mud
Lake

Jones
Lake

■	Parking
	Best 100 Route
	Paved Road
	Freeway
	Other Roads and Trails (bikes may be off limits)

(adjoins to east side of map on facing page)

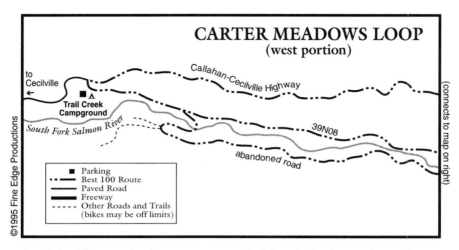

the right. This spur leads to numerous tunnels and mines if you feel like exploring. Otherwise, ignore it and continue heading north, paralleling the stream. You can see dredge tailings here along the creek.

Near the 25-mile mark you approach the North Fork of the Salmon. Turn left onto paved North Fork Road. You have 15 easy, downhill miles back to your car at Forks of the Salmon. Along the way, you pass reminders of the area's mining past, including several mines, a couple of cemeteries, Bestville townsite and more dredge tailings. The North Fork of the Salmon keeps you company the whole way back.

46 Carter Meadows Loop

Distance: 11 miles
Difficulty: Moderate, somewhat technical
Elevation: Gain/loss 1,600', high point 6,200'
Ride Type: Loop on dirt roads, singletrack and pavement
Season: Spring, summer, fall
Topo Map: Deadman Peak
Comments: Nearest services are in Callahan and Cecilville. You can camp at Trail Creek campground. Water is available at the campground.

Overview: Among the prettiest areas of the Klamath National Forest, Carter Meadows is crisscrossed by old logging roads and trails. Like most meadows, it's nicest in spring when the wildflowers bloom. It's also wettest in spring! In the summer it's relatively cool. It's quiet and beautiful no matter when you visit.

This route circles Carter Meadows, following the South Fork of the Salmon River—which isn't much more than a stream at this point— much of the way. A section of singletrack and an old logging road offer some technical challenge, too.

Trail Creek campground makes a good base camp for checking out the area. It's worth spending a weekend here, as there are miles of roads

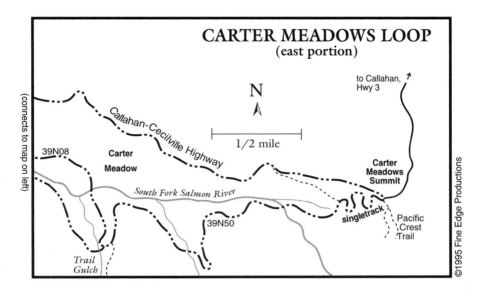

CARTER MEADOWS LOOP
(east portion)

N

to Callahan, Hwy 3

1/2 mile

Callahan-Cecilville Highway

39N08

Carter Meadow

Carter Meadows Summit

South Fork Salmon River

39N50

singletrack

Pacific Crest Trail

Trail Gulch

(connects to map on left)

©1995 Fine Edge Productions

and trails to explore by foot or by knobby.

Getting There: From Callahan, take the Callahan-Cecilville highway west for 12 miles to the Carter Meadows Summit. You can park here at the crest, but I prefer to park at Trail Creek campground, 5 miles farther down the highway on the south side of the road. This way you get the 5-mile pavement climb over with at the beginning of the ride.

Route: Leave the campground and head back out to the highway. Turn right (east) and begin the 1,300-foot climb to the summit. As pavement climbs go, this one isn't too bad since traffic is minimal and the grade isn't too steep. Look on it as a good way to warm up and to earn the singletrack that's coming up.

At 5 miles you reach the summit. Look for a trailhead right at the crest on your right. (The closed-to-bikes Pacific Crest Trail passes through here, too. Don't get on it by mistake.) The singletrack drops

steeply through the trees to Carter Meadow. After a mile, it runs into a dirt road (39N50). Soon you cross a creek and drop some more to another creek crossing.

Just before a third stream crossing at the trailhead at Trail Gulch, you have a decision to make. You can swing right onto 39N08 and continue on ungraded dirt or you can pick up an old abandoned road on the other side of Trail Gulch. Although a bit tougher, mainly because the trail surface is rougher, this abandoned route is more secluded. Road 39N08 follows the north side of the South Fork and the abandoned road follows the south side.

Either way you have about 3 miles back to Trail Creek campground. Road 39N08 leads directly back to the campground. If you take the old "put-to-bed" road (about 10 miles), you join another old road. Make a hard right, cross the South Fork and rejoin 39N08. If you start heading south and climbing, you have missed the turn.

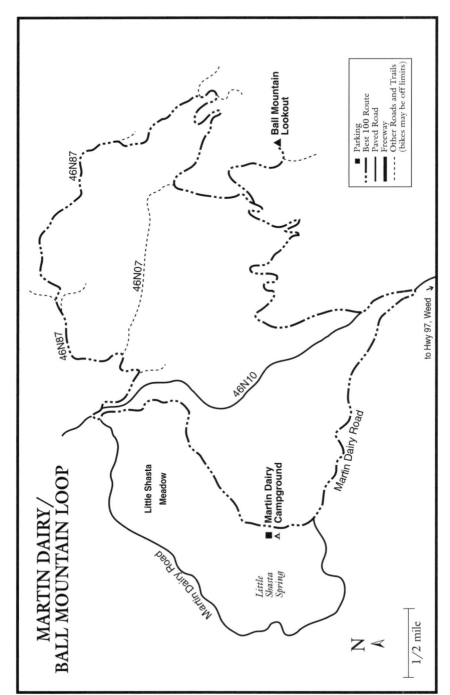

MARTIN DAIRY/
BALL MOUNTAIN LOOP

Ball Mountain
Lookout

Parking
Best 100 Route
Paved Road
Freeway
Other Roads and Trails
(bikes may be off limits)

46N87

46N07

46N87

46N10

to Hwy 97, Weed

Martin Dairy Road

Little Shasta
Meadow

Martin Dairy
Campground

Little
Shasta
Spring

Martin Dairy Road

N

1/2 mile

47 Martin Dairy/ Ball Mountain Loop

Distance: 15 miles
Difficulty: Moderate, mildly technical
Elevation: 1,900' gain/loss, 7,780' high point
Ride Type: Loop on dirt roads and pavement
Season: Spring, summer, fall; check snow levels as late as June
Topo Map: Panther Rock
Comments: Nearest services are in Dorris or Weed. The closest town, MacDoel, has a small store. Martin Dairy and Juanita Lake are beautiful places to camp. Water is available at both campgrounds.

Overview: Located in the Goosenest District, Martin Dairy is a peaceful, high mountain campground on the Little Shasta River. The lush meadow is shaded by pines and separated from private property on one side by a quaint split-rail fence.

The Goosenest District is quickly becoming *the* area for mountain biking in the Klamath National Forest. Somewhat flatter than other districts, the Goosenest features miles of roads and trails suitable for fat-tire bikes, and several new trails are in the works. In the winter, snowmobiling and cross-country skiing are popular here. Deer Mountain and Four Corners feature marked snowmobile routes that turn into fun mountain bike trails in the summer months.

The particular ride described here starts in the meadows and aspens around Martin Dairy campground (a great weekend camping spot), then ascends Ball Mountain, where you get good views of the Shasta Valley and Mount Shasta as well as the Butte Valley.

The route is mostly on an unmaintained dirt road that is closed to 4WD traffic, so expect lots of peace and quiet. Also expect to see wildlife—deer, bear and eagles—as you pass through high-elevation old-growth fir forests.

Getting There: From Weed, drive approximately 25 miles northeast on Highway 97 to Forest Service Road 46N10 near Mt. Hebron Summit. Take 46N10 north to the campground. If you are coming from the Goosenest Ranger Station, take Prather Ranch Road west and follow signs to the campground. Park at the campground.

Route: Head north on the paved road you took to the campground. Take it out to 46N10 and go right. Shortly after that, when the road forks, go left onto a gated dirt road. At the next intersection, go left on 46N07 and left again at the following intersection onto 46N87. Yet another intersection comes up almost immediately. Go right here.

Less than a mile later a spur takes off to your right and another soon takes off to your left. Stay on 46N87. You climb through stands of fir and lodgepole pine as you make your way around the north flank of Ball Mountain. You have about 7 miles of climbing on this remote, unmaintained road.

When you start switchbacking up the east side of Ball Mountain, two roads veer to your left in quick succession. Ignore them and stay on 46N87. At the T with 46N07, go left and keep climbing. You pass a spur on your right, and then you come to another intersection. Go left for the final steep ascent of Ball Mountain. You climb about 400 feet in this last push to the top.

At the top, visit the Ball Moun- tain lookout. From here you have tremendous views, especially toward Mount Shasta in the south. Try to catch your breath—you're at 7,780 feet here—before you begin your descent.

Now you backtrack down to

the last intersection you passed on the way up. Go left to drop off the west face of Ball Mountain. (You have about a 5.5-mile downhill run on dirt road and pavement back to Martin Dairy campground.)

The dirt descent is steep, dropping almost 1,000 feet in about 3 miles. When the dirt road ends at paved 46N10, go left. Soon after that, make a hard right onto Martin Dairy Road to complete your loop.

48 Herd Peak Lookout Loop

Distance: 21 miles
Difficulty: Moderately strenuous, mildly technical, optional doubletrack descent is more technical
Elevation: 2,300' gain/loss, 7,071' high point
Ride Type: Loop on dirt roads
Season: Spring, summer, fall; check snow levels in spring
Topo Maps: Grass Lake, The Whaleback, Solomons Temple
Comments: Nearest services are in Weed. CalTrans has a rest stop 2 miles north of the starting point on Highway 97 with restrooms and a phone. A beautiful campground at Juanita Lake is a 30-minute drive north. Water is available at Juanita Lake.

Overview: In an area with great lookouts and wonderful views, Herd Peak may offer the most spectacular vista. One Forest Service publication gushes that the panorama from Herd Peak lookout is a "visual feast. . . one of the finest vista points in Siskiyou County." It's hard to believe such hyperbole, so you'll just have to make the climb and see for yourself.

Two cautions: one, much of this route is open to vehicle traffic, so be careful. Second, the terrain is very rocky, and even on the maintained dirt roads you will find big rocks half buried. The rocks are easily seen when you're climbing slowly, but watch your speed on the downhill portion of the loop or you will take some hard hits. It's enough to make you want a suspension fork if you don't already have one.

Getting There: From Weed, take Highway 97 northeast for about 20 miles. Park at the Mount Shasta overlook just south of Grass Lake Summit.

Route: Cross to the north side of the highway and head north on 45N24. You come to an intersection almost immediately. Go right. At the next intersection, go left to stay on 45N24 as it turns southward. Soon thereafter, a rough doubletrack comes in on your right. This road is the optional return route. For right now stay on 45N24.

The first 6 miles contour along the west side of Miller Mountain, offering sweeping views into Shasta Valley. Most of the climb is pretty moderate, but there are several brutally steep, but thankfully short, pitches that you may have to walk.

Stay on 45N24 as it climbs northward, then turns east. At the T with 44N39Y, go right for the final grunt to the top of Herd Peak. You pass a couple of roads on your right. Keep on 44N39Y as it skirts the east flank of Miller Mountain. When you come to a small saddle, you're almost done climbing. The grade levels briefly here before you grind to a halt on top of Herd Peak.

The lookout is manned in the summer months and you're welcome to visit from 9:30 a.m. to 6:00 p.m. Rest, relax and enjoy the views. You can see Mount Shasta, Shasta Valley, the Eddy peaks, Butte Valley, and more. The only direction you don't have a view is behind you to the north.

When you're ready to leave, you can head down 44N39Y the way you came to where it ends. Go right on 45N22 and take it back to the highway. This is a fast, fun down-hill—watch for those rocks!

For a more demanding descent, look for a very rough doubletrack dropping off the east face of Herd Peak just before you get to the small saddle. At the top it's closer to a singletrack than a doubletrack. Steep and bumpy, it descends in a series of switchbacks to 45N24. Several other roads traverse the eastern flank of Herd Peak. Stay on the one that pitches downward.

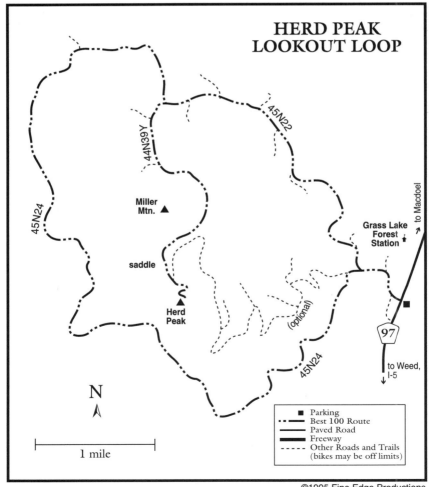

HERD PEAK
LOOKOUT LOOP

45N22

44N39Y

45N24

Miller
Mtn. ▲

to Macdoel

Grass Lake
Forest
Station

saddle

(optional)

▲
Herd
Peak

97

45N24

to Weed,
I-5

N
∧

1 mile

■   Parking
▪▪▪▪ Best 100 Route
——   Paved Road
▬▬▬ Freeway
---- Other Roads and Trails
      (bikes may be off limits)

©1995 Fine Edge Productions

49 Mount Shasta Loop

Distance: 65 miles
Difficulty: Strenuous, mildly technical
Elevation: 3,200' gain/loss
Ride Type: Loop on pavement, dirt roads and gravel
Season: May through October; can be hot in mid-summer
Topo Maps: City of Mount Shasta, McCloud, Elk Springs, Ash Creek Butte, Mount Shasta, The Whaleback, Juniper Flat, Hotlum
Comments: Best done as a two-day venture, the route can be completed in one long day by strong riders. Less conditioned riders may cut the route short by devising a shuttle. Nearest services are in the towns of Mount Shasta and McCloud. You must be self-sufficient on this ride. I highly recommend getting all 8 necessary topo maps. Treat all water taken from streams.

Overview: Since 14,162-foot Mount Shasta is a designated wilderness area, you cannot bike on the mountain itself. This route, however, will get you close to the mountain and allow you a good look at the area's fascinating geology.

Mount Shasta's network of logging roads offers lots of possibilities, although much of the surrounding forest has been logged extensively (expect logging trucks on this ride). The area's hiking trails tend to be very sandy and, therefore, not a heck of a lot of fun to ride.

This ride requires some preparation. You must be self-sufficient. Take plenty of clothing as temperatures and weather conditions can change a lot throughout the day, no matter what time of year you ride. Pack a good supply of food and water, and don't forget your tools.

You'll see a great variety of terrain and vegetation as you make your way around monolithic Mount Shasta. The mountain's east side has several streams and is wetter. As you head north, you move into high desert sage and juniper. At the ride's summit at Military Pass, you have views of the enormous rock formation, The Whaleback, to the north. On the north

side you pass through a volcanic landscape of lava flows. Here, to the south, you can see the mountain's glaciated north faces. Two distinct formations, Cinder Cone and Black Butte, mark the route's western side.

Spring is a good time to ride since you'll be treated to wildflowers. Although the route can be a little muddy, that's better than the sand you get by the end of the summer. Most of the year, expect gravel, sand and washboard.

Getting There: Start in the town of Mount Shasta.

Route: Make your way to Mount Shasta Boulevard and head south. Go left on Old McCloud Road. You begin with a climb—in fact, the first 10 to 12 miles are among the ride's steepest. At 8 miles (mileage will vary depending on where you start in Mount Shasta), turn left on Ski Park Highway. About 0.3 mile later continue straight onto a dirt road. You are now on Forest Service Road 31.

Continue climbing for another 5 miles. You pass several roads that lead to the north and several to the south. Stay on the main graded dirt road, heading east. About 15 miles into your ride, you start passing springs. A nice 2-mile downhill leads to Mud Creek Dam. At roughly 17 miles you cross Mud Creek. (Yes, it can be muddy here in the spring!)

Past this stream crossing you begin to climb again. Stay on Road 31 as it begins to swing northward. You cross a second large stream, Ash Creek, at about 20 miles. *Note: you should refill your water bottles at Mud Creek and/or Ash Creek because there's no more dependable water sources along* *the way. Treat all water.* From here, the climb eases off and you have pretty level going to about the 26-mile mark.

Once again, there are numerous spur roads. Stay on the main graded road until it ends at a T with Forest Road 19, also called Military Pass Road. Go left. Just over 2 miles later, Road 19 continues due north. Go left (northwest) and make the gradual climb to Military Pass (6,000'). It can get sandy along here,

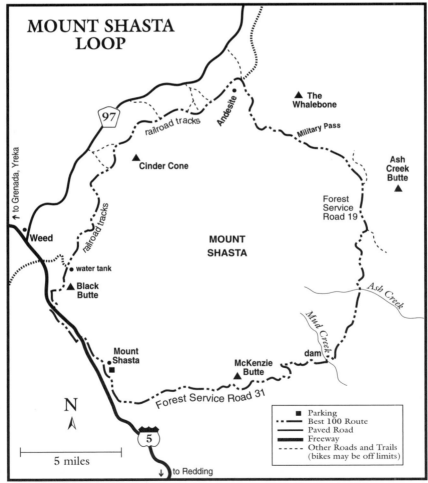

MOUNT SHASTA
LOOP

© 1995 Fine Edge Productions

but persevere—the sandy sections don't last forever.

Continue on the road you're on and enjoy the ensuing downhill. You lose nearly 1,000 feet of elevation before the descent begins to level off. At 37 miles turn left onto Andesite Road. A mile later go right at the Y intersection for a fun, swoopy downhill.

Stay on the main graded road until it crosses the railroad tracks at 42 miles. If you don't mind a lot of pavement, you can continue straight out to Highway 97 and take it toward Weed (left turn). This could also serve as a possible shuttle stop for those of you not up for the whole ride.

More adventurous spirits can turn left and follow the railroad tracks. There is no established road here so you ride on gravel—for almost 15 miles. It's not as bad as it sounds! Plus, you don't have to worry about vehicle traffic! There are several bailout points—dirt access roads that take you out to Highway 97 if you decide you've had enough.

At 47 miles you come to a railroad trestle. Cross it. This may be disconcerting for some of you and you may elect to ride down into the valley and back up.

Continue to follow the tracks as they loop southward. As you near the 57-mile point, be on the lookout for a big black water tank on the opposite side of the tracks. (This is at the Black Butte siding yard.) Cross the tracks here. Soon you see a dirt road on the left. Take it and make the first right onto a graded dirt road. This road leads to pavement. Go left.

Take the pavement along the west flank of Black Butte. This road takes you under Interstate 5. After crossing under the highway, turn left onto Summit Drive. Go left on Abrams Lake Road and cross I-5 again. Abrams Lake Road ends in a T at Spring Hill Drive. Go right and follow Spring Hill Road to Mount Shasta Boulevard. Turn left and head into the town of Mount Shasta.

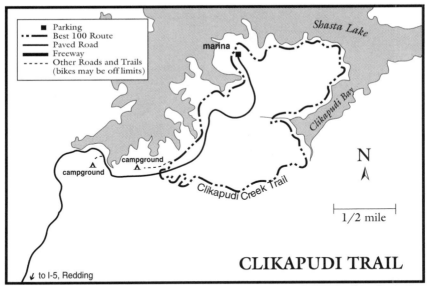

CLIKAPUDI TRAIL

©1995 Fine Edge Productions

50 Clikapudi Trail

Distance: 8 miles
Difficulty: Moderate, somewhat technical
Elevation: Rolling, there are no major climbs
Ride Type: Loop on singletrack
Season: Year-round; summer can be crowded
Topo Map: Bella Vista (trail not shown)
Comments: Nearest services are in Redding, 15 miles away. Restrooms and water are available at the Jones Valley boat ramp. Watch for poison oak along the creek.

Overview: Of the three hiking trails in the Shasta Lake area that are open to mountain bikes, this one is the longest and most interesting. (The other two trails, Bailey Cove and Packers Bay, barely amount to 6 miles together.) Besides being almost all singletrack, the loop features some steep downhills with tight switchback corners. Along the way, you follow the shore of Shasta Lake and Clikapudi Creek (the route can be muddy in spring) as you make your way through oak, madrone and Douglas fir. You're likely to see squirrels,

deer and lots of birds, including robins, blue herons, grouse, quail, ospreys, woodpeckers and chickadees.

You also pass an archeological site where a Wintu Indian village is being excavated. In fact, "Clikapudi" comes from the Wintu word "Klukapusa," which means "to kill." No, this ride won't kill you! The name comes from a battle between the Wintus and some local traders. Remember not to disturb the site.

Getting There: From Redding, take Interstate 5 north and follow the signs to Jones Valley. Proceed to the end of the road and park in the Jones Valley Marina lot.

Route: Although it is possible to ride this loop in the opposite direction, this clockwise version lets you go down the steepest stuff and, thus, tests your downhill abilities.

Look for the trailhead at the north end of the parking lot. Several hiker signs and Clikapudi signs mark various parts of the trail. The trail's first 4 miles are pretty level with a few short downhills as you begin by following the shoreline of Shasta Lake as it curves into Clikapudi Bay.

As you near the end of Clikapudi Bay you cross a small stream. The singletrack continues straight across on the other side. Soon you come to an intersection with an access road that leads to the Wintu village site.

Stay right and continue on the trail.

The trail follows Clikapudi Creek for a while before heading upward. At least the trail surface is smooth! On the other side of this hill, that nice little series of switchbacks awaits you. Don't dab in the corners! I warned you that they were coming up!

The switchbacks deposit you on a paved road. Go right and look for the trail, which continues on the other side of the road just a few yards away. Head down to a T in the road. The left fork goes to the lower Jones Valley campground. Make the sharp switchback right to stay on the main singletrack.

For the next mile, the trail contours along the lakeside at a gentle grade. Follow the trail to its end at the southwest corner of the parking lot.

51 Boulder Creek

Distance: 8.3 miles
Difficulty: Moderate, mildly technical
Elevation: 1,000' gain/loss
Ride Type: Loop on pavement, gravel roads and singletrack
Season: Year-round
Topo Maps: French Gulch, Whiskeytown

Overview: Along with Shasta Lake, Whiskeytown Lake is a focal point for recreational activities in the Whiskeytown-Shasta National Recreation Area. Plenty of campgrounds, water sports, abandoned mines, and miles of dirt roads and trails make Whiskeytown a great vacation spot for a weekend or a week.

Just one of several available mountain bike routes, this ride along Boulder Creek offers something for both beginning and more advanced riders. The ride is highlighted by half a dozen stream crossings and a 3-mile section of singletrack. The proximity to water makes it a cool ride in the summer months. Be sure to keep your bike in control and your speed in check since these trails see a lot of use, particularly in the summer months.

Getting There: From Redding, go west on Highway 299 to the west end of Whiskeytown Lake, about 15 miles. Follow the sign for the Judge Francis Carr Powerhouse (a left turn). Take this road, South Shore Drive, to the picnic area and park.

Route: You can ride this loop in either direction. The climb is more gradual the way it's described here. Stronger climbers may want to reverse directions and do a shorter but much steeper climb.

From the picnic area, continue east on paved South Shore Drive. You start out paralleling the lake but soon climb a little bit away from it. Just after the road turns south you come to a dirt crossroad. This is Boulder Creek Road. Go right around the gate and get ready for some single-track fun!

The road narrows into Boulder Creek Trail. You begin to follow Boulder Creek and soon you cross it for the first time, followed in quick succession by four more stream crossings. Although the overall trend is upward, the terrain here is rolling as you go in and out of the streambed. These crossing aren't technical, but you do need to watch for rocks. Not long after the fifth stream crossing, bear right to avoid a spur road. (If you ride in the late summer, one of these crossings may be dried up.)

After 3 miles of fun, the trail begins to widen as you climb toward the ride's high point. At about the 6-mile point, Mill Creek Road takes off to your left. Continue straight. It's worth taking a break here to

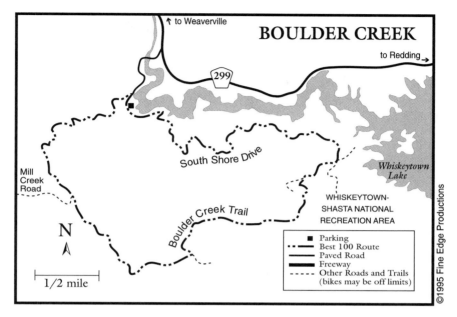

enjoy the views.

From here you have about 2 miles of downhill through a forest of madrone, oak, maple and pine. As you can imagine, the color here is nice in the fall. The descent is steep, but the wide gravel road gives you plenty of room to maneuver. As you near the lake, a road leads to the right. It goes to some penstocks. Stay left and head to the pavement. A right turn takes you to the picnic area.

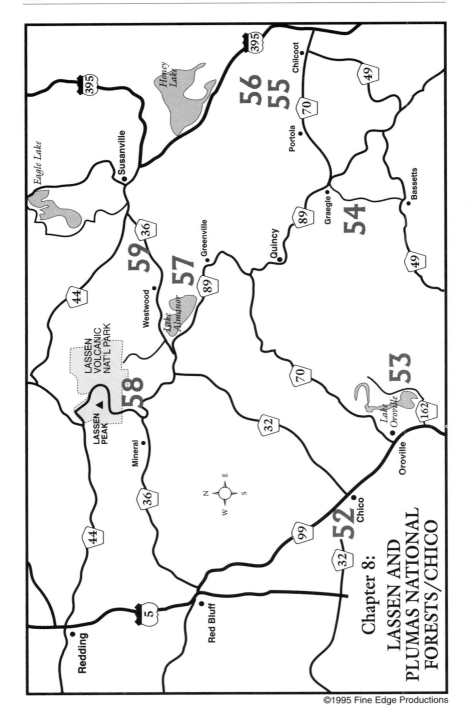

Chapter 8:

LASSEN AND
PLUMAS NATIONAL
FORESTS/CHICO

Lassen and Plumas National Forests/Chico

by Delaine Fragnoli

Located in the middle of the great Sacramento Valley, Chico makes a great jumping-off spot for exploring the northern reaches of the Sierra Nevada. Chico itself is a laid-back town with an aura of Northern California hipness. It's also home to several fringe-of-the bike-industry types (that's said as a compliment). Jeff Lindsay, maker of Mountain Goat bicycles, Bob Seals of Cool Tool, and the self-proclaimed retro-grouches of Retro Tec all call Chico home. Pleasant most of the year, the area can get sweltering hot in the summer months. That's when local cyclists head to the hills.

Rising to the northeast of Chico, Plumas National Forest encompasses the Feather River drainage, the Middle Fork of which is a National Wild and Scenic River. The dramatic terrain features knife-blade-thin ridge lines, dramatic canyons cut by rivers and streams, and several waterfalls, including the impressive Feather Falls. While parts of the forest have been logged, much of the area's 1,146,000 acres remains carpeted with Douglas fir, Ponderosa pine, white fir, red fir and sugar pine.

Climate is temperate (except at higher elevations) and Highways 70 and 395 provide year-round access to most areas. Much of the forest lies around 5,000 to 6,000 feet. The area has been inhabited for over 8,000 years. The Washo and Paiute Indians were followed by the Hudson Bay Company in the 1830s and by gold seekers in the 1850s. Lots of old mine sites and abandoned homesteads dot the area. Timber and agricultural interests took hold after that.

These days the Forest is primarily managed for recreation. There are dozens of campsites (call 1-800-280-CAMP for reservations) and all kinds of recreational possibilities, from rafting and fishing to hiking and backpacking—and, of course, mountain biking.

Virtually all of the area's roads and trails are open to bikes, with the exceptions of the Pacific Crest Trail, the Bucks Lake Wilderness, and a few other assorted trails. The Forest Service prints a series of route sheets (available from

ranger stations) describing recommended mountain bike rides. Several of these
are included in this chapter.

Currently, the Forest Service is in the process of analyzing the effects of
mountain biking on many of the trails. Thus, most of the recommended routes
follow maintained and unmaintained dirt roads, with a few sections of singletrack.

Route-finding is relatively easy as the Forest's roads are generally well
marked. Yellow or unpainted aluminum K-tags in the trees can help you find
your way, too, when used in conjunction with a Plumas National Forest map,
available at ranger stations.

The Lassen National Forest borders Plumas on the north. Straddling the
northern reaches of the Sierra Nevada and the southern flanks of the Cascade
Mountains, its varied topography includes volcanic lava flows (Lassen Volcanic
National Park sits in the middle of the Forest), dry oak-covered hills in the east,
and high peaks and deep canyons in the south.

Excellent fishing and birdwatching, as well as the National Park, bring
visitors to the Forest. It's home to raptors such as eagles, red-tail hawks, rough-
legged hawks and osprey. Although the area is just now turning on to mountain
biking, mountain bikers have free reign of the Forest's logging roads.

Two snowmobile areas, one at Fredonyer Pass and another at Swain
Mountain also offer good mountain biking opportunities. About the only place
bikes are prohibited are in Lassen National Park and on the Pacific Crest Trail.
In the National Park, bikes are restricted to the narrow, shoulderless, paved
main road into the Park.

At present, a Lassen County task force is working on a trails masterplan.
The task force has sought input from local cyclists and the plan will contain
mountain biking trails. Many of the popular routes in the area cross private land
and the county has been reluctant to obtain easements. Because of this
questionable legal status, those routes have not been included in this book and
may not be included in the masterplan. Check with rangers for the latest
information.

I have tried to cover a large area with this chapter, and the following
routes are a very small sampling of the possibilities. There are innumerable long-
distance bike-touring options in these parts.

More conditioned cyclists are encouraged to check out Butte Meadows,
one hour northeast (40 miles) of Chico off of Highway 32. Starting at Cherry
Hill campground you can fashion a roughly 50-mile loop up and over Humbug
Summit (6,700'), followed by a fun, screaming downhill, and a climb over
Humboldt Summit (6,610').

Those interested in overnight touring should consider the Ponderosa
Way, which runs from the town of Manton to Jarboe Gap on Highway 70 just
north of Lake Oroville. The route can be shortened by accessing it from the
towns of Red Bluff, Cohasset, Forest Ranch or Paradise. (Yes, you can say you
rode in paradise!) Rolling in and out of virtually every drainage in Butte County,
the route has lots of climbing and descending—and scenic views.

Check with Campus Cycles in Chico, (916) 345-2081, and outfit
yourself with a Lassen National Forest map, a Plumas National Forest map and
the AAA Feather River/Yuba River map. Both these routes can get very hot
in summer.

52 Upper Bidwell Park

Distance: 8 miles
Difficulty: Moderate, somewhat technical
Elevation: 900' gain/loss
Ride Type: Loop on dirt road and singletrack
Season: Year-round; can get hot in summer
Topo Maps: Richardson Springs, Paradise West. Trail map of Chico and Bidwell Park can be obtained by calling the City of Chico at (916) 895-4972.
Comments: Helmets are required in the Upper Park except on pavement (?!). Bicycles are prohibited in the Caper Acres area. Do not ride right after a rain.

Overview: A very bike-friendly city, Chico has plenty of bike paths. The easily accessible Bidwell Park is the town's mountain biking center, particularly Upper Bidwell Park. Centered around Chico Creek, Lower Bidwell Park has a maze of mostly unmarked trails which are fun to explore. But most riders head up Upper

Bidwell's North Rim Trail, which gives you great views of the Central Valley. To the east, you can see the Sierra Nevada. In the spring and summer you may find swimming holes along the Lower Rim Trail.

You can extend this ride by biking from Chico to the park or by dropping into Lower Bidwell on the

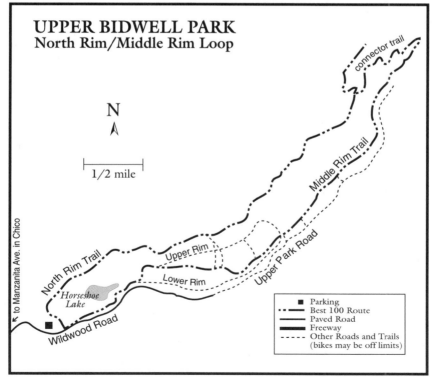

UPPER BIDWELL PARK
North Rim/Middle Rim Loop

©1995 Fine Edge Productions

way out or back. The route can be done by going out the North Rim Trail and back the Middle Rim Trail, or vice versa.

The 2,400-acre park gets its name from Annie Bidwell, widow of General John Bidwell, Chico's founder. Annie Bidwell donated the land to the city but, ironically, died destitute. The whole park is about 10 miles long and contains swimming pools, picnic areas and a variety of other recreational facilities. It's a great place to spend a leisurely day, or to get a quick and rewarding workout.

Getting There: From the town of Chico, ride your bike or drive northeast on South Park Drive. Bear left at the Y onto Centennial Avenue and quickly hang a left onto Manzanita Avenue. Take the first right, Wildwood Road, for 1 mile. There's a trail sign for North Rim on the left side of the road. Park in the turnoffs on either side of the road.

Route: Many options are possible here. A series of parallel trails with connectors are open to bikes: North Rim Trail, Upper Rim Trail, Middle Rim Trail, Lower Rim Trail and the Upper Park Road. The following is just one possibility. If you're not sure if a trail is open to bikes, watch for trail symbols painted on rocks.

From the parking area, follow the trail signs for the North Rim Trail. At first the wide trail is rough, having been cut from volcanic basalt, as it climbs up the ridge. Climbing on this rough, rocky stuff is what earns this ride its moderately strenuous rating. The fire road smoothes out as you ascend into a pine forest and later it begins to narrow. The climb is moderate as you make your way to the park's northeastern corner.

At about 3.0 miles, a connector

trail drops off to your right, but keep on North Rim to its end on a plateau. From here you have those views I mentioned earlier. Gawk for awhile before backtracking to the connector trail. Take this singletrack down to the Middle Rim Trail. The trail is somewhat technical as it traverses several gullies. Erosion can be a bit of a problem along here so be careful, especially in the switchbacks. The singletrack dumps you directly onto the Middle Rim Trail.

Several trails take off from the Middle Rim. Most of the ones which take off to your left connect with the Lower Rim Trail, while the ones which go to your right lead up to the Upper Rim Trail.

Stay on the Middle Rim Trail all the way back to where it intersects the North Rim Trail past Horseshoe Lake. Should you accidentally get on the Lower Rim or Upper Rim trails, they all rejoin near Horseshoe Lake. You can go around either the north or the south side of the lake to reconnect with the North Rim Trail. Backtrack along North Rim the way you came in to get back to your car.

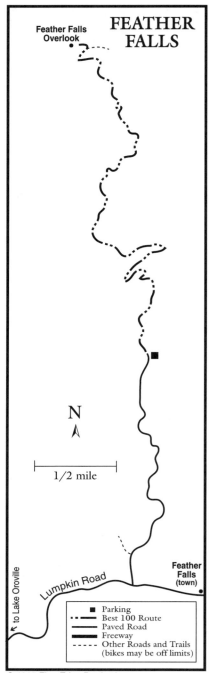

FEATHER
FALLS

© 1995 Fine Edge Productions

53 Feather Falls

Distance: 7 miles; you can add 4 miles by riding from the town of Feather Falls
Difficulty: Moderate, somewhat technical
Elevation: 2,400' gain/loss
Ride Type: Out-and-back on singletrack; a new trail will soon allow for a single-track loop
Season: April through October; the falls are most spectacular in spring
Topo Maps: Brush Creek, Forbestown
Comments: Nearest services are in Oroville. The town of Feather Falls has a restaurant and a store. No water is available en route—bring all you will need.

Overview: One of the biggest attractions in Plumas National Forest, Feather Falls is the nation's sixth-tallest waterfall, dropping 640 feet. The Feather Falls Trail leads to a dramatic overlook; the materials for the observation platform had to be helicoptered in! You can definitely get vertigo up here! The falls cascade into the middle fork of the Feather River, this portion of which is a protected Wild and Scenic River. One of the first such designated rivers, the Middle Fork makes its way from near Beckwourth down into Lake Oroville.

While you're in the Lake Oroville area, check with the rangers at the Lake Oroville State Recreation Area, (916) 538-2200. At presstime, the area had about 18 miles of trails that a ranger described as "hit and miss." However, a 33-mile trail was in the process of being finished. An additional 5 miles of singletrack was in the planning stage. The trails may be open by the time you read this!

Getting There: Take State Route 162 east from Oroville to Forbestown Road, about 8 miles. Go right on Forbestown. Six miles later, take a left onto Lumpkin Road toward the town of Feather Falls. On the outskirts of town, there's a sign for Feather Falls, directing you to go north on a dirt road. The road ends at the trailhead.

Route: The trail is very straightforward; there are no tricky intersections or turns. The trail rolls along before dropping to the viewing platform. Most of the route is in the trees until you come to the surprising and breathtaking overlook. Narrow and rocky, the trail gets steep in spots, particularly near the end where it gets very step-like. Many of you may want to walk the last section; locals have been known to play around on this section for an hour trying to clean it!

You have to earn your pleasure on the climb back out. The last mile in particular is steep. It's a grunt but it's doable. At presstime, the Forest Service was completing a connector trail which loops from near the beginning of the existing trail to the viewing platform. The new trail will provide an easier way back to the trailhead and parking area. Going down to the falls on the older, steeper trail and back up to the trailhead on the new trail is still about a 7-mile loop, but it's an easier 7 miles.

In the spring, expect things to get a little muddy. No matter when you visit, control your bike on the steep stuff. This trail sees a lot of use, particularly in the summer months.

54 Mills Peak Lookout

Distance: 12 miles
Difficulty: Moderately strenuous, not technical
Elevation: 850' gain/loss, start/end 6,500', high point 7,340'
Ride Type: Out-and-back on dirt roads
Season: Spring, summer, fall
Topo Maps: Gold Lake, Clio
Comments: Nearest services are in Graeagle and Bassett Station. Several lodges and campgrounds dot the Gold Lake Highway.

Overview: From Mills Peak Lookout you can enjoy views of eastern Plumas County. You can also stop at an easy half-mile signed nature trail, Red Fir Nature Trail, on the way up or back.

The climb itself is not that hard—although it gets steeper as you go—but you may feel the altitude. The road surface is mostly graded dirt with some gravel.

While you're in the area, you may want to stop at Frazier Falls. You pass the well-signed trailhead off of the Gold Lake Highway on your way to and from the Mills Peak ride. An easy half-mile hike takes you to the

100-foot waterfall. Late spring or early summer is the best time—wildflowers are out and the falls are full. No bikes allowed on this trail.

Lots of lakes and several campgrounds in the area make this a great place to spend a weekend.

Getting There: From Highway 89 just southeast of the town of Graeagle, take the Gold Lake Highway, signed as County Road 519, south to the junction with Mills Peak Road (County Roads 721/822). The intersection will be on your left.

Or, from Highway 49, go north on Gold Lake Highway for 8 miles to

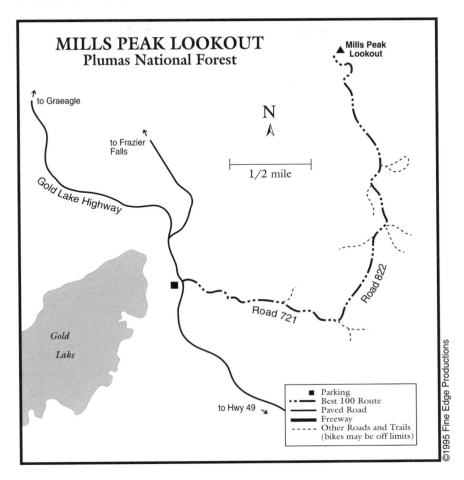

MILLS PEAK LOOKOUT
Plumas National Forest

▲ Mills Peak Lookout

to Graeagle

to Frazier Falls

N

1/2 mile

Gold Lake Highway

Road 721

Road 822

Gold Lake

to Hwy 49

■ Parking
Best 100 Route
Paved Road
Freeway
Other Roads and Trails
(bikes may be off limits)

©1995 Fine Edge Productions

Mills Peak Road. Park across from the intersection in the turnout.

Route: Head up Mills Peak Road (County Road 721) for 1.5 miles. Along the way you pass one spur road on your left. Stay on Road 721. At 1.5 miles turn left (due north) onto County Road 822.

Less than a mile later, the road begins to climb a bit more steeply. You pass several spur roads (I counted three) in succession. Continue north on Road 822.

Past a spring and a fourth spur road, you come to the Red Fir Nature Trail on your right. This 0.5-mile trail through a stand of ancient red firs has interpretive signs for you to follow, and makes a great excuse to stop climbing and to catch your breath before the final push to the lookout.

Back on 822, you reach Mills Peak Lookout at 6 miles. During the summer months, Forest Service personnel may be on duty and are usually full of information. Enjoy the views of Plumas County, and of the Middle Fork of the Feather River to the north. Return the way you came.

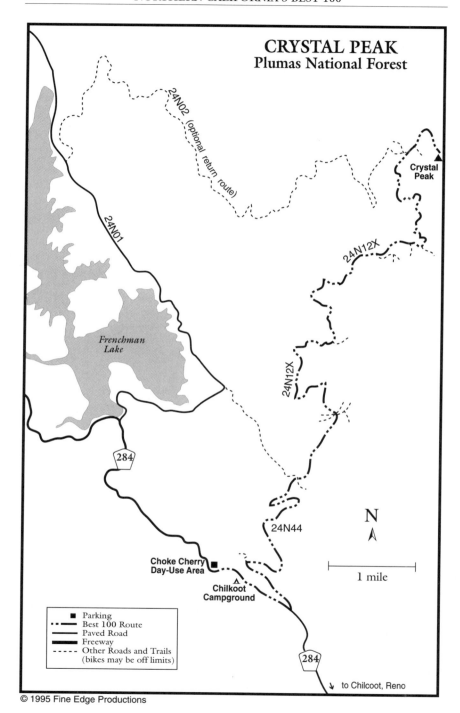

CRYSTAL PEAK
Plumas National Forest

24N02 (optional return route)

24N01

Crystal Peak

24N12X

Frenchman Lake

24N12X

N

1 mile

24N44

Choke Cherry
Day-Use Area

Chilkoot
Campground

284

■ Parking
•–•–• Best 100 Route
—— Paved Road
▬▬ Freeway
- - - Other Roads and Trails
        (bikes may be off limits)

284

↘ to Chilcoot, Reno

55 Crystal Peak

Distance: 23 miles
Difficulty: Moderately strenuous, not technical
Elevation: 2,700' gain/loss, 7,780' high point
Ride Type: Out-and-back on dirt roads, loop option possible
Season: Spring, summer, fall
Topo Maps: Frenchman Lake, Constantia
Comments: You can find gas, lodging and food in Chilcoot. Nearby campgrounds include one just north of Chilcoot and four at Frenchman Lake.

Overview: This route is east of Frenchman Lake, the recreational focal point of the Milford Ranger District. The view from Crystal Peak is the highlight of this ride in the Diamond Mountains, the northernmost range of the Sierra Nevada. Along the way you travel past old mine workings and abandoned cabins, relics of the area's mining past.

Just the drive itself to the trailhead is interesting since the road from Chilcoot travels through a canyon of bizarre and wonderfully weird volcanic mud formations. Called lahar, these formations are the result of volcanic ash mixing with water to make a mud flow.

Getting There: From the town of Chilcoot on Highway 70, take Highway 285 about 5 miles, past the Chilcoot Campground and over the one-lane bridge. Park in the Choke Cherry Day-Use Area on your right.

Route: From the day-use area, head back along the highway past the campground for about a mile. Look for Forest Service Road 24N44 on your left. It is a hard left, almost a U-turn. You climb about 900 feet in the next couple of miles as 24N44 switchbacks its way up a ridge before leveling out at a saddle. Ignore the crossroads at the saddle and keep heading north-

east on 24N44.

A mile past this saddle you pass a road off to your right, followed quickly by two roads leading to the left and another leading to the right. Continue north onto the middle route straight in front of you, 24N12X. This road contours along a hillside, gaining elevation all the while.

At the next Y, veer left (due north) to stay on 24N12X. A few other roads take off to your right as you climb toward Crystal Peak. Stay on 24N12X.

At milepost 9.8 (your mileage will be about 10.8), a jeep trail leads to the left. Go right and continue climbing. Your lungs will probably be noticing the altitude as you are up around 7,600 feet at this point. Hang in there, you have less than a mile now to the top. The road peters out at the summit (7,780').

From the top you can see the spine of the Diamond Mountains stretching to the northwest (you're literally looking at the north end of the Sierra Nevada) and the southeast. To the northeast you have views into Long Valley and the Fort Sage Mountains. Frenchman Lake and Dixie Mountain (see the following ride) lie to the west.

Return the way you came for a fast and fun downhill. That's one thing about long climbs—the more you go up, the more you get to come down! One option for a loop would be to descend to the jeep road (24N02) back at milepost 9.8.

Rougher than the route up, it drops 7.0 miles, depositing you on 24N01. Head left and follow the Frenchman Lake shore to return to your car.

56 Dixie Mountain Loop

Distance: 16.2 miles
Difficulty: Strenuous, somewhat technical
Elevation: 2,700' gain/loss, 8,327' high point
Ride Type: Loop on dirt roads and singletrack
Season: Spring, summer, fall
Topo Maps: Dixie Mountain, Frenchman Lake
Comments: Chilcoot has gas stations, motels and restaurants. Treat all water taken from streams or lakes.

Overview: This ride is on the opposite side of Frenchman Lake from the previous ride, and gives you a look at some of the same terrain from a different perspective. Like virtually every ride that ends at a lookout, this one requires climbing, some of it steep; however, the spectacular views (I'm not exaggerating) from Dixie Mountain Lookout (8,327') are worth the work. The steep climb and the high elevation make this a rather

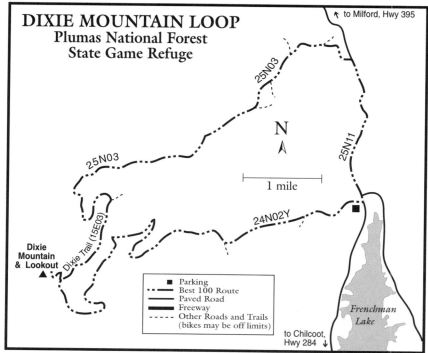

DIXIE MOUNTAIN LOOP
Plumas National Forest
State Game Refuge

↑ to Milford, Hwy 395

25N03

N

25N11

1 mile

25N03

24N02Y

Dixie Mountain & Lookout ▲

Dixie Trail (15E03)

Frenchman Lake

Parking
Best 100 Route
Paved Road
Freeway
Other Roads and Trails
(bikes may be off limits)

to Chilcoot, Hwy 284 ↓

©1995 Fine Edge Productions

strenuous ride.

The route is actually in the Dixie Mountain State Game Refuge. Here you're likely to see some large specimens of the area's mule deer herd on your ride, especially near the several springs and streams you pass. Four nice campgrounds around Frenchman Lake make this a good place to spend a weekend.

Getting There: From the town of Chilcoot, located on Highway 70, head north on Highway 284 (Frenchman Lake Road) to Frenchman Dam, about 8 miles. Go straight on Forest Road 25N11 for 6 miles to Forest Road 24N02Y. It is on your left and it is signed "Dixie Mountain Lookout." Park off the road.

Route: From the 25N11/24N02Y junction, go west on 24N02Y. It starts climbing right away. Enjoy the first 2 miles because it gets steeper and the air gets thinner. You climb 1,600 feet in the next 4.5 miles. There are few switchbacks as the road marches seemingly straight up the Grigsby Creek drainage. Thankfully it's a graded dirt road so the trail surface is good. Along the way you parallel the creek and pass two streams before a switchback takes you over

the creek and away from it.

At 6.5 miles you come to a junction with the Dixie Mountain Trail (15E03). Veer left and climb the final 500 feet or so to Dixie Mountain and the lookout, which you reach at 6.8 miles. The air is really thin at this point, and you will probably be ready for a break. Enjoy the panoramic views. To the west you can see the Dixie Valley; to the east you can see Frenchman Lake and the Diamond Mountains. Can you pick out Crystal Peak, the previous ride's summit?

When you've recovered from the climb, backtrack to the Dixie Mountain Trail, at 7.1 miles, and head northeast on it. Yee-hah! The singletrack drops steeply for just over a mile before merging into 25N03 at about 8.2 miles.

On 25N03, a sweeping left-hand switchback is followed by a right-hand one just as you cross Lookout Creek. From here you have 6 miles of downhill bliss on an ungraded dirt road. Stay on 25N03 all the way back to 25N11, which you reach at approximately 14.2 miles. Go right on 25N11 for 2.0 miles back to your starting point. Be careful of vehicle traffic on 25N11.

57 Three Lakes

Distance: 28 miles
Difficulty: Moderately strenuous, mildly technical
Elevation: 2,700' gain/loss, high of 6,400'
Ride Type: Out-and-back on dirt roads and singletrack
Season: Spring, summer, fall
Topo Map: Greenville NW
Comments: You can find all services in Greenville. There's a campground a mile north of town. Treat all water taken from lakes.

Overview: On the boundary of Lassen and Plumas National Forests, this route travels to three tiny high-altitude lakes. Trapped in rock formations following volcanic eruptions, these cold water lakes sit nestled atop

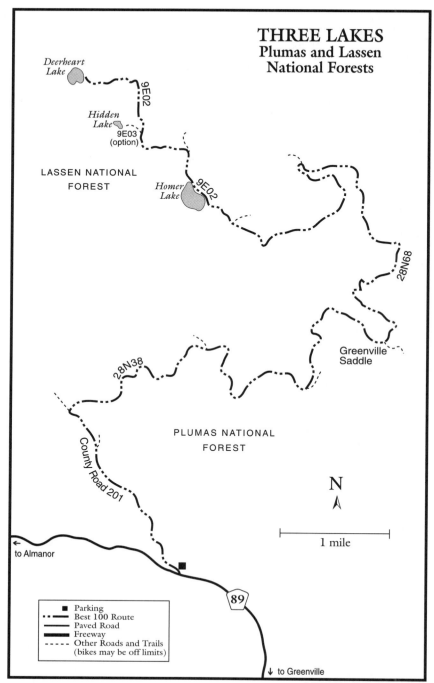

THREE LAKES
Plumas and Lassen
National Forests

Deerheart
Lake

9E02

Hidden
Lake
9E03
(option)

LASSEN NATIONAL
FOREST

Homer
Lake
9E02

28N68

28N38

Greenville
Saddle

PLUMAS NATIONAL
FOREST

County Road 201

N

1 mile

to Almanor

89

Parking
Best 100 Route
Paved Road
Freeway
Other Roads and Trails
(bikes may be off limits)

↓ to Greenville

©1995 Fine Edge Productions

Keddie Ridge. Rugged and spectacular, they are well worth the climb.

The trip's distance and the altitude, which you may feel on the steeper parts of the climb, earn it the moderately strenuous rating.

Getting There: From the town of Greenville, take Highway 89 north for 2 miles to County Road 201, which heads north from the right side of the highway. There's a sign for Hauns Meadow on the right side of the highway. Park off the highway at this road junction.

Route: Go up gravel road 201 for 2.0 miles. Turn right onto Forest Service Road 28N38. After a flat section, it begins to climb in earnest toward the Greenville Saddle. You ascend almost 1,400 feet in 5 miles, but don't worry—the grade is moderate and the road surface is good.

You reach Greenville Saddle at the halfway point, 7 miles. The saddle also marks the boundary between Plumas National Forest and Lassen National Forest. When you come to a Y at the saddle, head north (left) onto Road 28N68. (Road 28N38

contines east.)

Most of the climbing is over at this point. The grade eases until it's almost level, but the road gets a little rougher. Unlike 28N38, this road is not graded. At the road junction at 10 miles, turn left onto the road for Homer Lake. Just under 12 miles, the road degenerates into a trail (9E02) as it starts to climb to Homer Lake. You reach the south end of Homer Lake, the largest of the three lakes, at 12 miles. Those too pooped to pedal any farther can stop here.

For some singletrack fun, continue on the trail as it skirts the northeast shore of the lake. You climb a tad bit more on the way to Hidden Lake which is...er, um...hidden. About a mile past Homer Lake a trail (9E03) climbs steeply to your left. Take it if you want to ascend 300 feet to Hidden Lake, which is the smallest of the three lakes.

Continuing on 9E02 it's less than a mile to Deerheart Lake. The singletrack ends at the lake at 14 miles. Enjoy the solitude before retracing your steps. The return route is almost all downhill!

58 Spencer Meadow Trail

Distance: 10 miles
Difficulty: Moderate, somewhat technical
Elevation: 1,800' gain/loss
Ride Type: Out-and-back on singletrack
Season: Spring through fall
Topo Maps: Childs Meadow, Reading Peak
Comments: Do not cross the boundary into Lassen National Park!

Overview: This may be the closest you'll ever get to Mount Lassen on a mountain bike, since bikes are prohibited in Lassen National Park. An interesting side note: Before there were any "no bikes allowed" signs years ago, a group of Chico cyclists rode and pushed their bikes to the top of Mt. Lassen. It may have been the one and only ascent by bike ever.

Park personnel reportedly weren't too thrilled with the escapade.

Lassen National Forest, however, will let you ride most trails, including the Spencer Meadow National Recreation Trail, which leads due north toward Lassen and the national park boundary. Besides the views toward Lassen, you can enjoy an alpine meadow (carpeted with

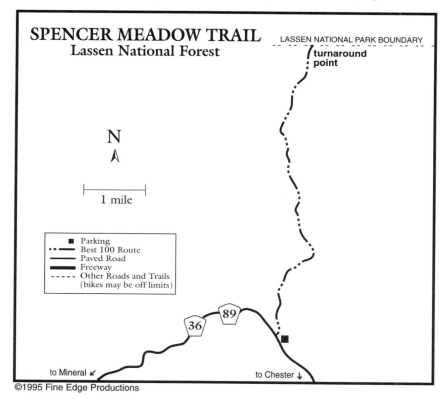

SPENCER MEADOW TRAIL
Lassen National Forest

LASSEN NATIONAL PARK BOUNDARY

turnaround point

N

1 mile

■ Parking
∙∙—∙ Best 100 Route
—— Paved Road
━━ Freeway
- - - - Other Roads and Trails
  (bikes may be off limits)

89
36

to Mineral ↙

to Chester ↓

wildflowers in the spring) and Mill Creek Spring, which is the source of Mill Creek, one of the Sacramento River's tributaries. And, in an area in which most of the moutain biking is on logging roads, it's nice to get on some singletrack.

Getting There: From the town of Red Bluff on Interstate 5, take Highway 36 east for 43 miles to the town of Mineral. Continue on Highway 36 for another 7 miles, past the Highway 89 turnoff, which heads north to Lassen National Park. The trailhead is on the north side of the highway. There is parking available at the trailhead.

Route: Beginning in a forest of black oaks, incense cedar and ponderosa pine, the route climbs moderately for the first half mile. After this it grows steeper for about a mile. After you pass a spring and cross a stream, near 1.5 miles, your work is almost done.

The trail continues to gain elevation gently. You begin to see Jeffrey pine, lodgepole pine and red fir. Several faint spurs take off to your left and lead to fishing spots. Stay on the main trail. You may stop at Spencer Meadow or follow the trail along the east side of the meadow to the National Park boundary, which is signed. Do not enter the National Park.

Enjoy the downhill return. Watch your speed on the last steep 1.5 miles.

59 Bizz Johnson Trail

Distance: 25.4 miles, 29.9 miles if you ride from the town of Westwood
Difficulty: Easy, not technical
Elevation: Begin 5,500', end 4,200'
Ride Type: One way on dirt roads and trail, some pavement; can be done as an overnight trip; can be shortened by accessing the trail at any of six trailheads; all options require a car shuttle unless you want to ride out-and-back
Season: May to September; check snow levels in April and October
Map: The route is very well signed with numbered interpretive stops along the way. Get a free brochure, trail map and interpretive guide from the BLM office in Susanville, (916) 257-0456 or the Lassen National Forest, Eagle Lake Ranger District, (916) 257-2151.
Comments: If you want to make this a multi-day trip, there is a 3-day limit between trailheads. You must camp at least 1 mile from trailheads. You need a campfire permit; seasonal fire restrictions apply.

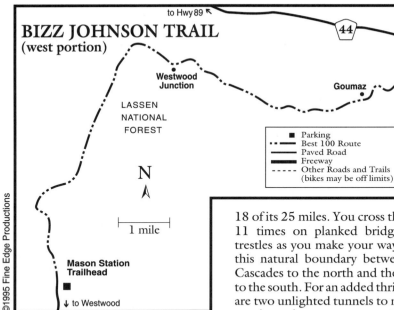

BIZZ JOHNSON TRAIL
(west portion)

to Hwy 89

Westwood Junction

Goumaz

LASSEN NATIONAL FOREST

N

■ Parking
·-·— Best 100 Route
—— Paved Road
▬▬ Freeway
- - - Other Roads and Trails
(bikes may be off limits)

1 mile

Mason Station Trailhead
■
↓ to Westwood

©1995 Fine Edge Productions

(connects to map on right)

18 of its 25 miles. You cross the river 11 times on planked bridges and trestles as you make your way along this natural boundary between the Cascades to the north and the Sierra to the south. For an added thrill there are two unlighted tunnels to maneuver through.

Overview: The Bizz Johnson Trail is a poster child for the Rails-To-Trails Conservancy and the Bureau of Land Management. The first successful rails-to-trails conversion on BLM lands, the route is co-managed with the Lassen National Forest (16 miles of the trail are on National Forest lands). Named for the congressman who helped secure the right-of-way, the trail follows the old Fernley and Lassen line of the Southern Pacific Railroad.

The mellow 3-percent grade means you can ride the trail from Westwood to Susanville or vice versa. Riding it west to east (i.e. starting in Westwood) allows for a virtually all-downhill ride—and that's the route described below! Along the way you drop from ponderosa pine forest to high desert landscape.

In addition to the route's historic interest, it travels the beautiful and rugged Susan River Canyon for

Getting There: Leave one car at the Hobo Camp trailhead and picnic area just outside the town of Susanville (at the end of South Street) or in Susanville itself. (If you're riding from Susanville, you can access the trail at the south end of Lassen Street or Miller Road.)

From Susanville, drive the second car west on Highway 36 toward Westwood. Turn right on County Road A-21 just before you reach Westwood. Go 3 miles to County Road 101 and turn right again. The trailhead at Mason Station is half a mile down Road 101 on your left.

If you're staying in Westwood you can ride from town to the trailhead by taking Ash Street north to County Road A-21. From there follow the above directions to the Mason Station trailhead. The route is signed. This will add 4.5 miles to your total.

Route: From the back of Mason Station parking area, take the connector

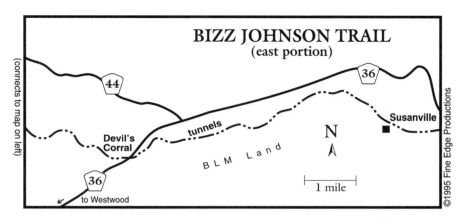

trail 0.25 mile to the Bizz Johnson trail. Go right. That's about all the trail directions you need to follow this well-signed route. There are some 32 signed interpretive stops along the way. Be sure to get a copy of the "I remember when" brochure from the BLM or Lassen National Forest so you know what you're looking at.

It's 7.5 miles to Westwood Junction, the next trailhead. Along the way you'll ride through pine forests, which include some old-growth pines, and catch views of Pegleg Mountain to the northeast. You have nice views of the Susan River as you make your way to Goumaz Station,

located 12.7 miles into the ride.

The scenery gets more and more beautiful as you continue. You can see the Diamond Range, the northernmost range of the Sierra Nevada. You cross a trestle before reaching Devil's Corral at 18.9 miles. From here, it's 6.5 miles into Susanville. This last segment is where you find the tunnels. If you find riding through the darkness disconcerting, there are trails which skirt each tunnel.

This trail should be taken at a leisurely pace. Pack a picnic lunch to enjoy along the way. Those of you who like to fish or swim may do so in the Susan River.

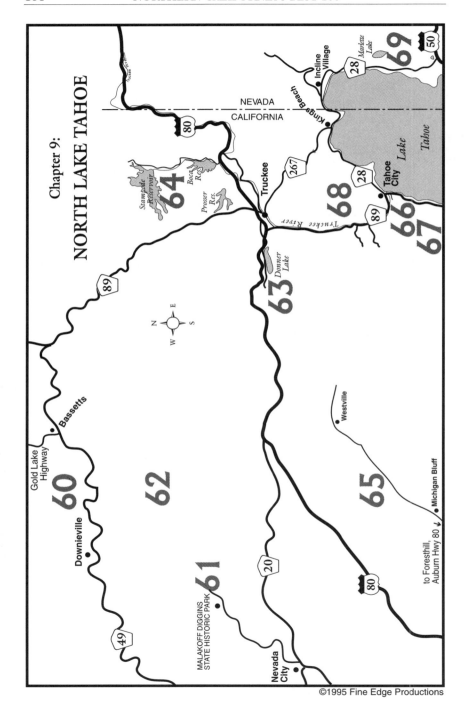

Chapter 9:
NORTH LAKE TAHOE

CHAPTER 9

North Lake Tahoe

by R. W. Miskimins and Carol Bonser

Among Northern California's rightly celebrated landscapes, none is more spectacular than Lake Tahoe. Surrounded by the granite ruggedness of the Sierra Nevada, Lake Tahoe beckons, a turquoise jewel. While the lake itself is the focal point for much of the area's recreation, it's not the only place for awesome mountain biking.

The surrounding foothills and mountains are filled with alpine lakes and meadows, pine forests and aspen groves. You'll also find remnants of Tahoe's rich mining past as well as historic routes such as the Old Emigrant Trail (traversed by the ill-fated Donner party).

The riding is rigorous for its elevation (2,000' to 10,000'), elevation gain, and sometimes technical terrain. But whatever sweat you pour out, your efforts will be well rewarded—often with epic panoramic views. Don't worry, we've included some easier rides, too!

This chapter includes such world-famous rides as The Great Flume Ride and the Downieville Downhill. The rides traverse the Tahoe National Forest (916-265-4531), parts of the Toiyabe National Forest (702-882-2766), and the northern portion of the Lake Tahoe Basin Management Unit (916-573-2600). The area is dotted with campgrounds (information on them is available from the above mentioned land agencies), while Tahoe itself has a wide of range of hotels, restaurants and services for those of you planning an extended vacation.

If you enjoy the rides in this chapter—and we're sure you will—you'll also want to check out Chapters 10 and 11, South Tahoe and Reno.

60 Downieville Downhill

Distance: 16 miles
Difficulty: Strenuous, technical
Elevation: 6,407' to 7,000' to 2,899'
Ride Type: One way downhill on dirt roads and trails
Season: June through October
Topo Maps: Gold Lake, Sierra City and Downieville (7.5 min.), or Sierra City and Downieville (15 min.)
Comments: Requires a car shuttle. You'll lose over 4,000 feet of elevation on this ride, so make sure you have good brakes!

Overview: A visit to the Sierra Buttes area should appear on every mountain bike rider's "must do" list! The Sierra Buttes are gigantic, jagged, rocky pinnacles that push straight up over 2,000 feet from the surrounding forest lands. They can be seen from miles away and form a strong contrast to the more gentle northern Sierra Nevada. The forest land below the Buttes, known as the Lakes Basin Recreation Area, has an incredible amount of area to explore by mountain bike. Nearby lakes provide swimming, fishing, windsurfing and water skiing and there are many places to camp. Sardine and Salmon Creek are full-service USFS campgrounds with water, tables, fire rings and vault toilets. There are also five undeveloped camping areas.

Getting There: Sierra Buttes and the Lakes Basin are located on the Gold Lake Highway, named after Gold Lake, the largest lake in the area. From the Bay Area or Sacramento, take Interstate 80 east to Auburn and go north on Highway 49. Highway 49 travels through the Gold Country and then begins to climb back into the Sierra Nevada. About 16 miles east of Downieville, at the small town of Bassetts, turn north on the Gold Lake Highway. Follow Gold Lake Highway to Gold Lake Campground on your left.

From Lake Tahoe, go north on Highway 89 to Sierraville. Turn left, staying on Highway 89 (49 and 89 at this point), and follow the signs toward Quincy. Five miles farther, turn left on Highway 49 and follow the signs to Downieville. You drive over Yuba Pass before dropping down the west side to get your first glimpse of the Sierra Buttes. When you reach Bassetts, turn right (north) on the Gold Lake Highway and take it to Gold Lake Campground on your left.

You need to arrange a shuttle or leave a car somewhere near the town of Downieville. There is limited parking in Downieville, so you might find it easier to have someone meet you just outside of town along Highway 49. (There are good swimming holes on the North Fork of the Yuba River.)

Route: From Gold Lake camping area, turn right (south) onto Gold Lake Highway. At 0.8 mile turn right on the gravel road that goes to the Pack Station and boat launching area. Ride past the turnoff to the stable and the boat ramp at 1.2 miles and continue to the end of the gravel road. Look to your left for a sign: *Squaw Lake 1 mile—Little Gold Lake*

2 miles—Summit Lake 3 miles. From here on the road gets rough as you head for Summit Lake. Some sections are quite rocky and look like streambeds, but never for very long. Be on the lookout for horses, because the Pack Station runs five trips a day on busy weekends. The horses seem accustomed to mountain bikes, but don't forget that the riders may have very little experience. If you see a group of horseback riders, slow down to a snail's pace or dismount until they pass.

You reach the turnoff to Squaw Lake at 2.0 miles. It's about 0.5 mile uphill (250 feet elevation gain). De-

tour up to the lake if you like. (The following mileages do not include any detours.) After 2.7 miles you pass the turnoff to Little Gold Lake on your left. You can see the lake through the trees. At 3.0 miles ride southeast to the far end of Gold Lake to some great campsites. Continue until you reach the *Private Land* sign and the cable across the road. Take a left turn, and begin the uphill part of the ride. (No one promised it would be *all* downhill!) The next section winds up and away from Gold Lake, passing a cabin, then crossing the Pacific Crest Trail (closed to bikes). Stay on the main road to the top of the ridge—

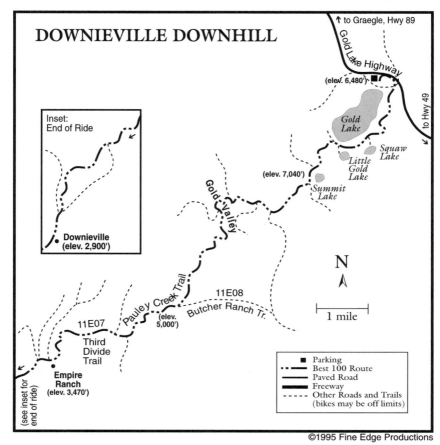

DOWNIEVILLE DOWNHILL

↑ to Graegle, Hwy 89

Gold Lake Highway

(elev. 6,480')

to Hwy 49

Gold Lake

Inset: End of Ride

Squaw Lake

Little Gold Lake

(elev. 7,040')

Summit Lake

Downieville (elev. 2,900')

Gold Valley

N

11E08

Butcher Ranch Tr.

1 mile

Pauley Creek Trail

(elev. 5,000')

11E07

Third Divide Trail

Empire Ranch (elev. 3,470')

(see inset for end of ride)

■ Parking
∙—∙—∙ Best 100 Route
——— Paved Road
▬▬▬ Freeway
- - - - Other Roads and Trails
(bikes may be off limits)

©1995 Fine Edge Productions

a good climb.

If you tire or have to push your bike, just remember that it is only 1 mile to the top. After you crest the ridge, the road goes downhill to Summit Lake. At 4.0 miles you reach a major OHV trail intersection. Continue on the main OHV trail that goes straight ahead. Follow the signs to Gold Valley and Pauley Creek Trail. (On some maps this road is called the Summit Lake Trail.) As you drop down the west side of the ridge, it's an all downhill ride into Gold Valley 1,100 feet below. You ride past several intersections, many of them leading to old mines. Stay on the main road and keep following the signs to Gold Valley and Pauley Creek Trail.

When you enter Gold Valley, 7.2 miles, the road turns south down the valley. After crossing Pauley Creek, you arrive at an intersection with the road going to Smith Lake, which is located 0.7 mile west of this point. Continue to the southern end of Gold Valley on the Pauley Creek Trail. At 7.7 miles, as you leave the valley, the trail descends quickly into Pauley Creek Canyon. Stay on the trail as it follows the creek downstream.

Pauley Creek Trail intersects with Butcher Ranch Trail (11E08) at 9.4 miles. Stay to the right and continue to follow Pauley Creek. You have now lost over 2,000 feet in elevation since you left Summit Lake, and the canyon walls are getting quite steep. Continue on the main trail that goes downhill. Stay to the right on the Third Divide Trail (11E07) at 11.4 miles. Ride through the divide and continue downhill to Lavezzola Creek and Empire Ranch. Stay left on the main road that follows Lavezzola Creek, crosses it, and goes through the Second Divide back to Pauley Creek.

From here just stay on the main road and follow all the signs to Downieville. Eventually you will be on road S514. When the dirt road ends after 14.8 miles, continue straight ahead on the paved road that takes you into Downieville. At 15.6 miles turn left onto Highway 49, where either your car or a friend's is waiting for you!

61 Relief Hill Loop

Distance: 13 miles, 29 miles with Washington detour
Difficulty: Moderate, nontechnical; option to Washington is difficult
Elevation: Begin/end 3,300'; 4,600' high point; the optional ride to Washington goes down to 2,600 feet to the South Yuba River and you will have to climb back out.
Ride Type: Loop on dirt roads
Season: Year-round; possibility of low-elevation snow storms in winter
Topo Maps: Pike, Washington, North Bloomfield, Alleghany (7.5), or Alleghany (15)
Comments: A small campground is located at Malakoff State Park, with a small lake nearby for swimming and fishing. You can find water within the campground and at several locations throughout the park.

Overview: Located on the western edge of Tahoe National Forest is Malakoff Diggins State Historic Park. Every trip to the northern Gold Country should include a visit to Malakoff Diggins to see the effect of large scale hydraulic mining done throughout the foothills of the Sierra Nevada. Within the Park is the site of the largest hydraulic gold mine in the world (operated 1866-1884). Although the mining tore away nearly half a mountain, the destruction resulted in the creation of cliff walls similar to the sandstone spires and natural formations found in Utah.

You can view this site by mountain bike from the roads. But to get a closer look you have to walk—all hiking trails within the Park are closed to mountain bikes. The State Park is on the edge of the National Forest, so finding a place to ride is not a problem. The Relief Hill Loop ride takes you out of the State Park into the National Forest with an option of riding farther out to the historic town of Washington where you can see several old restored buildings.

Getting There: To get to Malakoff Diggins, take Interstate 80 to Auburn; go north on Highway 49 through Grass Valley and Nevada City. Twelve miles north of Nevada City, turn right on Tyler Foote Crossing Road and continue to the Park.

Route: From the Park campground, turn left on the main road that climbs back up to the ridge. When the road splits at the grammar school at 0.8 mile, stay right and ride past the school. The road through here is gravel and dirt with oiled sections. At 4.0 miles continue straight ahead at the 4-way intersection, staying on the gravel road. At 5.8 miles turn right on the dirt road signed *Snowtent Rd./ Relief Hill*. Your uphill is over and now it is time to start back down into the canyon.

A road takes off to the left at 6.9 miles. Continue down the hill following the signs to Relief Hill. At 8.4 miles the road to the left goes to Washington, 8 miles farther, an historic town you might want to visit by bike. To finish the loop, stay to the right following the signs to North Bloomfield. Soon you pass by some old cabins and new homes. Continue until 11.2 miles when the road ends. Turn right. The road to the left goes to the town of Relief. After 12 miles you are back in the Park in the historic town of North Bloomfield. Turn right, ride past the museum, and stay on this road back to the campground.

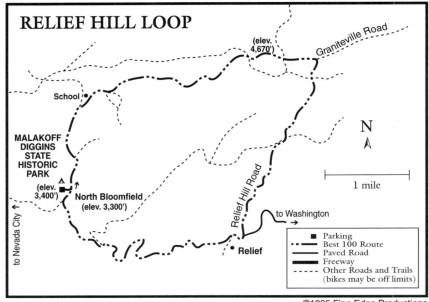

RELIEF HILL LOOP

(elev. 4,670')

Graniteville Road

School

MALAKOFF DIGGINS STATE HISTORIC PARK
(elev. 3,400')

North Bloomfield (elev. 3,300')

to Nevada City

Relief

to Washington

N

1 mile

Relief Hill Road

■ Parking
∙∙−∙∙− Best 100 Route
——— Paved Road
▬▬▬ Freeway
− − − − Other Roads and Trails
(bikes may be off limits)

©1995 Fine Edge Productions

62 Shotgun Lake

Distance: 10 miles, 11 miles with Penner Lake option
Difficulty: Easy, nontechnical; optional Penner Lake loop is very technical
Elevation: Begin/end 6,600'; 7,100' high point
Ride Type: Out-and-back on singletrack
Season: Late May through October
Topo Maps: English Mountain and Graniteville (7.5), or Emigrant Gap (15)

Overview: The Bowman Lake Area is located 40 miles east of Auburn, north of Interstate 80, at elevations between 5,500 and 7,500 feet. The fun about riding here is that there are so many lakes so close together that you can ride to several in one day! This is a wonderful spot to visit if you enjoy canoeing, swimming and fishing in addition to mountain biking. Trails and roads are very well marked. You will be riding in and out of private and public lands, so always remember to respect the private property signs. There are several devel-

oped and undeveloped U.S. Forest Service campgrounds in the area should you choose to camp.

Getting There: The ride begins at Carr Lake. From Auburn, drive east on Interstate 80 and take the Highway 20 off-ramp (1 mile east of the Yuba Gap turnoff), following the signs to Nevada City. Go west on Highway 20 for 3.5 miles to Bowman Lake Road (Forest Road 18). Drive 8.5 miles out Forest Road 18 and turn right on Forest Road 17. Follow the signs to Carr and Feely Lakes, 4 miles

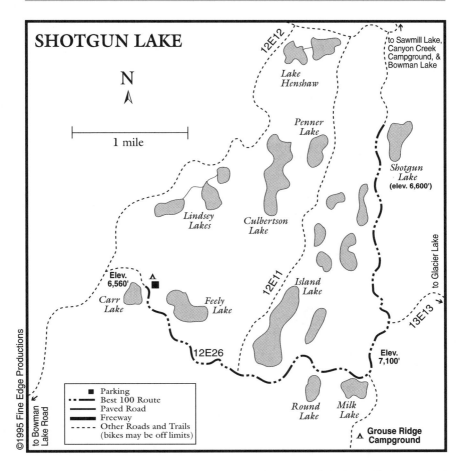

farther. Forest Road 17 is dirt, so if you have a new car you may choose to start riding from Forest Road 18, which lengthens the ride by 8 miles (4 miles each way).

Route: From Carr Lake, turn left on the road just before the outhouses in the campground. Ride uphill to Feely Lake. At 0.1 mile you arrive at Feely Lake and the Round Lake Trailhead (12E26) for Island Lake, Milk Lake and Grouse Ridge Campground. Continue on the Round Lake Trail. About 1.0 mile into the ride you pass a pond and a small lake, and the trail

forks. The left fork is called Crooked Lake Trail, 12E11. Stay to the right, ride up over the ridge, and you come to Island Lake.

Continue on the main trail at 1.5 miles. (The fork that leads to the right goes to Round Lake.) At 1.6 miles turn right on the main trail. Turn left at 1.7 miles, following the sign to Milk Lake. At 2.2 miles you reach the top of a small hill and another intersection. The trail straight ahead goes to Grouse Ridge Campground. Off to the right is Milk Lake. Take the Grouse Ridge Trail to the left, following the sign to Glacier

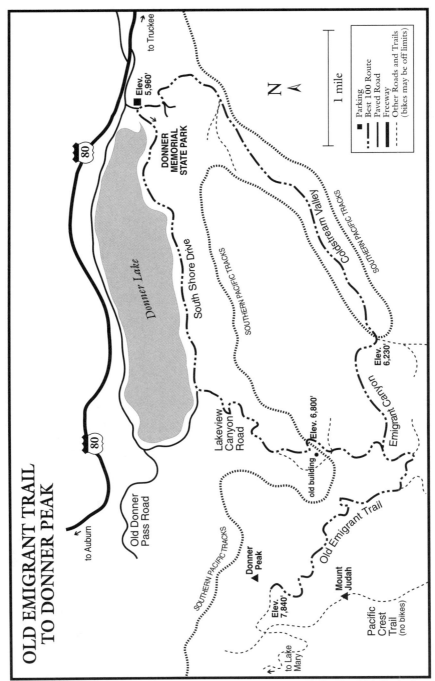

OLD EMIGRANT TRAIL
TO DONNER PEAK

to Auburn

80

80

to Truckee

Elev.
5,960'

DONNER
MEMORIAL
STATE PARK

Donner Lake

South Shore Drive

SOUTHERN PACIFIC TRACKS

Coldstream Valley

SOUTHERN PACIFIC TRACKS

Elev.
6,230'

Emigrant Canyon

Lakeview
Canyon
Road

old building

Elev. 6,800'

Old Emigrant Trail

SOUTHERN PACIFIC TRACKS

Donner
Peak

Elev.
7,840'

Mount
Judah

Pacific
Crest
Trail
(no bikes)

to Lake
Mary

N

1 mile

■ Parking
·-··-·· Best 100 Route
———— Paved Road
———— Freeway
········· Other Roads and Trails
          (bikes may be off limits)

© 1995 Fine Edge Productions

Lake and Sawmill Lake.

At another intersection at 3.0 miles, stay to the left on the Grouse Ridge Trail. (The road to the right goes to Glacier Lake Trail, 13E13.) You reach Middle Lake around 4.3 miles, which is on its way to becoming Middle Meadow. Continue on the main trail. At 4.7 miles you reach a large meadow and a new section of trail that keeps you up on the rocks and out of the wet meadow. Five miles of riding brings you to Shotgun Lake, which is also almost a meadow. When you are ready, follow your tracks back to Carr Lake for a total of 10 miles.

If you would like a slightly longer and much more technical ride, you can continue north from Carr Lake for another 0.8 mile. At the edge of the canyon, turn left on the trail signed *Bull Pen Trail 12E12, Rock Lake 1 mile*. After 1.0 mile (near Rock Lake), stay left and follow the signs to Penner Lake. At 7.5 miles from where you began at Carr Lake, stay on the trail that goes along the east shore of Penner Lake. After passing Crooked Lakes and Island Lake, 9.5 miles, you are back at the intersection of trail 12E26 to Grouse Ridge. Turn right to return to Carr Lake.

63 Old Emigrant Trail to Donner Peak

Distance: 18.5 miles
Difficulty: Strenuous, technical
Elevation: 5,940' to 7,840'
Ride Type: Out-and-back on jeep roads and singletrack
Season: June through October; fall is particularly scenic
Topo Maps: Norden and Truckee (7.5), or Donner Pass and Truckee (15)
Comments: Water is available at Donner Memorial State Park. Late in the summer you may not reach water again for 12 miles (Cold Creek). Be sure to filter or treat all water you take from streams.

Overview: A scenic high-country ride, this route features a fun downhill on singletrack and old jeep roads. Some people may have to walk a few short sections of the uphill, but never for very long. A good ride for enjoying fall colors, this route follows a section of the Old Emigrant Trail, which was first marked in 1924.

The whole Donner Summit area is rich in California history. Everywhere you ride, you will be reminded of the early pioneers who traveled through here on their journeys to the west. Monuments are dedicated to the tragic journey of the Donner

Party, which tried to cross the Sierra during the winter of 1846–47, and to the amazing tunnel dug by hand through the mountains to complete the Central Pacific Railroad. If you enjoy history, be sure to visit the museum at the entrance to Donner Memorial State Park.

Like much of the area along Interstate 80, there is a great deal of private land in the vicinity. New gates, *No Trespassing* signs and *No mountain bikes* signs have begun to show up, closing off routes to the public. The Pacific Crest Trail also crosses through this area, and it is closed to mountain bikes. This ride goes through private land, but it is open to the public.

The most popular place to stay here is Donner Memorial State Park, which is open June through September. Make reservations by calling MISTIX at 1-800-444-7275 or the State Park at (916) 587-3841. Three USFS campgrounds—Silver Creek, Goose Meadows and Granite Flat— are located nearby on Highway 89 between Truckee and Tahoe City.

Getting There: This ride starts and ends at Donner Memorial State Park located just off Interstate 80 on the shore of Donner Lake. From Tahoe City, go north on Highway 89 to Interstate 80. Head left (west) on 80 to the Park on your left.

Route: From Donner Memorial State Park, ride west through the park along the shore. At 1.4 miles go around the two gates that mark the western boundary of the Park, and continue riding west on South Shore Drive. Turn left on Lakeview Canyon Road at 2.7 miles. It is hard to find, but if you look carefully you can see a brown Forest Service sign, *Lakeview Canyon*, almost hidden in a patch of overgrown bushes. The road starts off steep, then eases up the rest of the way into the canyon. Stay right at 3.4 miles on the main road and continue climbing. At 3.8 miles go left and finish the climb up to the railroad tracks. (The right turn also goes to the tracks, but the left is more direct.)

When you reach the railroad tracks, 4.2 miles, turn right on the road that follows along the tracks. At 4.8 miles, as the

railroad tracks begin to curve into Lakeview Canyon, look across the tracks for the power lines. Ride a short distance past the lines and then carefully cross the tracks. Look for a trail that goes up the hill next to the remains of an old building. Follow this trail to the top of the saddle. (It becomes a road on the way up.) After 5.0 miles you reach the top, from which you can see Squaw Peak and the mountains of Granite Chief Wilderness to the south.

Turn right on Old Emigrant Trail at 5.4 miles. The road is very rocky at first but smooths out as you begin the climb up Emigrant Canyon. Old Emigrant Trail is very well marked with a variety of older and newer signs. At 6.2 miles, when you reach a small round meadow on your right, the road forks in several directions. Take the road that goes straight ahead, just to the left of the meadow. It turns into a trail, and you should

still be following the old trail signs. In the next section there may be short uphills that some people will walk, but if the traction is good, the uphill is all rideable.

You reach a saddle at the base of Mount Judah at 7.6 miles and the trail again becomes a narrow road. The steep parts of the climb are over, and the road gradually climbs the rest of the way to Donner Peak. At 8.9 miles, Old Emigrant Trail reaches the saddle behind Donner Peak. Look for the monument with a sign: *Emigrant Trail Truckee River Route— Highest Point on the Truckee Route— Elevation 7,850 ft.* From here there is a trail to the top of Donner Peak (8,019'). Hike up to the top, enjoy the view, and prepare for the fun downhill ahead! When you are rested, follow your tracks back down to the intersection where you first got onto Old Emigrant Trail.

At 12.4 miles, when you reach the intersection, continue straight ahead on Old Emigrant Trail. Stay right at 13.4 miles and ride across Emigrant Creek. When the road ends at just 14 miles, turn left and ride up to the railroad tracks. Cross when it is safe and continue on the main road through Coldstream Valley. Stay to the left when you reach the ponds. After you leave Coldstream Valley, 17.4 miles, you arrive at a gate that may be open or closed. Go around the gate and continue. If you are staying in the Park, you can enter the campground on the trail next to the split rail fence ahead. If you parked at the entrance, continue riding out the paved road, turn left by the gas stations on Donner Pass Road, and ride back to your car.

64 Sardine Peak Lookout Loop

Distance: 31 miles
Difficulty: Strenuous, mildly technical
Elevation: 6,000' to 8,135'; over 2,000' of climbing
Ride Type: Out-and-back with a loop on dirt roads
Season: May through October or until the first major snowstorm; the best time to visit is in spring, when the meadows are bright green and full of wildflowers; also nice in the fall when the aspen and cottonwood leaves change color; can get very warm here in the middle of the summer.
Topo Maps: Boca, Sardine Peak, Dog Valley and Hobart Mills (7.5), or Truckee and Loyalton (15)
Comments: Water is available at Logger Campground and at several creeks along the way. Be sure to filter or treat all water you take from mountain streams.

Overview: The Stampede/Sardine Peak area is located to the north of Truckee and east of Highway 89 at the edge of the Tahoe and Toiyabe National Forests. It features miles of dirt roads winding through large aspen groves, past giant juniper trees, and through meadows and small valleys following numerous creeks. This is a place for those who enjoy long rides on good dirt roads with few rocky sections. The road system is well signed, which should give most mountain bikers the confidence to

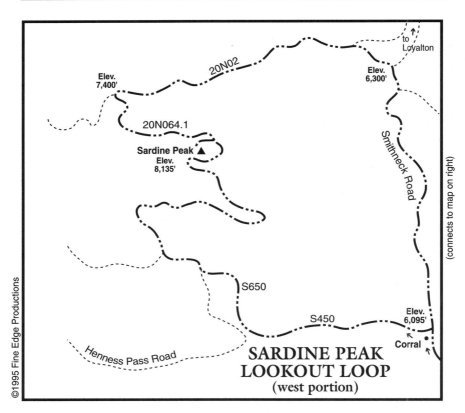

SARDINE PEAK LOOKOUT LOOP
(west portion)

explore on their own beyond the ride described here. (All County Roads are marked with road numbers on white paddle markers.)

Getting There: This ride begins and ends at Logger Campground along the south shore of Stampede Reservoir. The ride can also be done from any of the campgrounds within the area by riding to the end of the pavement on County Road 270.

To reach Stampede Reservoir from 80 in the town of Truckee, go east a few miles to the Boca Reservoir area. Go north on either Stampede Meadows Road or Boca Road/Dog Valley Road, following the signs to Stampede Reservoir and then to Logger Campground.

Route: From Logger Campground, turn left on S261. Ride across the dam and continue to County Road S270. At 2.0 miles turn left on S270. Ride through Hoke Valley to the far end of Stampede Reservoir. At 4.0 miles turn left at the end of the pavement on Henness Pass Road (County Road S860). A right on Henness Pass Road leads to Dog Valley (and into the state of Nevada near Reno), another area with many dirt roads to explore by mountain bike. Stay right on the main road at 4.6 miles.

When you reach Sardine Valley, 5.6 miles, turn left and stay on the main road. At 6.3 miles, at a triangular intersection, continue straight ahead on the main road which heads west and then turns north along the

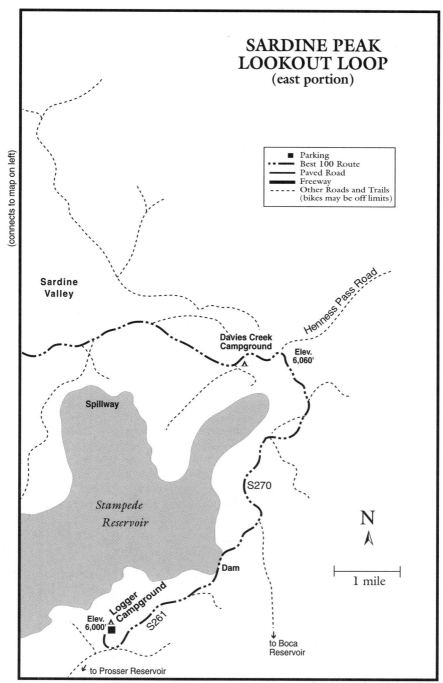

SARDINE PEAK
LOOKOUT LOOP
(east portion)

(connects to map on left)

■ Parking
Best 100 Route
Paved Road
Freeway
Other Roads and Trails
(bikes may be off limits)

Sardine
Valley

Henness Pass Road

Davies Creek
Campground

Elev.
6,060'

Spillway

S270

Stampede
Reservoir

N
∧

1 mile

Dam

Logger Campground

Elev.
6,000'

S261

to Boca
Reservoir

to Prosser Reservoir

© 1995 Fine Edge Productions

edge of Sardine Valley. Turn left at 7.3 miles on County Road S450 which begins to climb as you enter Davis Canyon. At 9.1 miles turn right on Lemon Canyon Road (County Road 650). (The road to the left goes to Highway 89, 8 miles away.) At 10.5 miles turn right at the sign: *Sardine Lookout 4 miles.* The next 4 miles are a steady climb, and you gain 1,500 feet up to the top of the ridge. At 14.2 miles turn left and continue the last short climb to the lookout tower.

From the top, 14.5 miles, you can see your starting point, Stampede Reservoir, with Boca Reservoir in the distance, Sardine Valley below. To the southwest are Donner Lake and the higher peaks of the Sierra Nevada. To the northwest are the jagged Sierra Buttes. When you are through enjoying the view, ride back down to the last intersection. At 14.8 miles turn left on Road 20N64.1. (You came up the road that is to your right.) Turn right on 20N02 at 16.4 miles and get ready for some downhill fun.

As you descend, be on the lookout for two huge western juniper trees 0.5 mile down the road. The one on the right has a sign stating that it is one of the largest specimens living today. Continue downhill into Trosi Canyon, which is full

of aspen and cottonwood trees. This section is spectacular in the fall when all the leaves are yellow, orange and gold! At 18.8 miles continue past the gate. Please be sure to leave it as you found it (open if it was open and closed if it was closed).

Stay to the right on the main road at 18.9 miles. When you reach Sardine Valley, 19.7 miles, turn right on Smithneck Road, following the signs to Stampede Reservoir. The road forks at 19.7 miles as you reach the north end of Sardine Valley. Either fork takes you back to Stampede Reservoir. (These directions take you to the right on Smithneck Road.) At 23 miles, County Road S450 takes off to your right. Here you are back at the 7.3-mile point. Follow your tracks back to Logger Campground.

65 El Dorado Canyon Loop

Distance: 31 miles
Difficulty: Strenuous, technical; *do not try this ride alone*
Elevation: Begin/end 3,500' feet; 5,400' high point; 1,800' low point; 3,600' of climbing
Ride Type: Loop on dirt roads and singletrack
Season: Mid-May through October; spring and fall (after the first rains) are the best times to do this ride; avoid the middle of summer when the canyon is very hot and dry
Topo Maps: Michigan Bluff and Westville (7.5), or Duncan Peak (15)
Comments: Watch out for rattlesnakes in the canyon and poison oak all along the trail section. No water is available at the start of the ride, so be sure your bottles are full when you leave Forest Hill. The only water on the ride is at the 27-mile point in El Dorado Canyon. Be sure to filter or treat all water taken from mountain streams.

Overview: The Forest Hill area, located 18 miles east of Auburn, covers a wide variety of terrain from steep, rocky river canyons lined with oak trees to the high country of Granite Chief Wilderness Area. The Forest Hill area, now sparsely populated, was once full of booming gold mining towns. You ride on old trails with colorful names like "Last Chance," trails that were at one time toll roads. Everywhere you look there are signs of mining that took place here in the 1850s.

A very challenging ride, the El Dorado Canyon Loop follows part of the route of the Western States 100 Endurance Race, one of the best known ultra-marathon running events in the country. To qualify as a finisher you must run the entire 100 miles, with 17,000 feet of elevation gain and over 21,000 feet of elevation loss, in under 30 hours. Much of the Western States 100 Trail lies within Tahoe National Forest, and much of it is open to mountain bikes (except for the portion which goes through Granite Chief Wilderness Area). The rest of the trail is marked on the Tahoe National Forest Map. If you enjoy the El Dorado Canyon section you may want to try some others.

Getting There: From Sacramento, drive east on Interstate 80 to Auburn. Take the Foresthill exit and continue to Foresthill. At the eastern edge of town where the road forks, stay left on Forest Hill Divide Road for 4.5 miles to Baker Ranch. Turn right on the road to Michigan Bluff. At 2.9 miles farther you reach the gold rush town of Michigan Bluff. Limited parking is available in front of the homes here. To conserve parking space, please park straight in rather than parallel.

Route: From Michigan Bluff, ride back up the paved road on which you came in. At 0.6 mile turn right on Chicken Hawk Road, which starts off as a paved road. Several roads head off to the left and right; just stay on the main road that goes northeast out the ridge. At 1.2 miles, stay right on Chicken Hawk Road which becomes a dirt road. The road continues to climb back up on the ridge. If you look off in the distance to the right, you can see the Crystal Range of the Sierra Nevada. Chicken Hawk Road ends at wide, paved Forest Hill Divide Road at 5.5 miles. Turn right.

For the next 10 miles you ride along the paved road. It is steady, but never steep, as you gain 1,200 feet

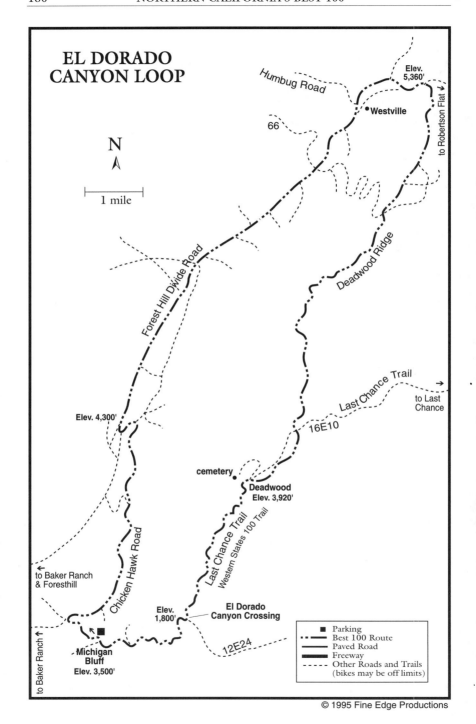

EL DORADO CANYON LOOP

N

1 mile

Humbug Road

Elev. 5,360'

•Westville

66

to Robertson Flat

Forest Hill Divide Road

Deadwood Ridge

Last Chance Trail

to Last Chance

16E10

Elev. 4,300'

cemetery

Deadwood
Elev. 3,920'

Last Chance Trail

Western States 100 Trail

Chicken Hawk Road

to Baker Ranch & Foresthill

Elev. 1,800'

El Dorado Canyon Crossing

12E24

to Baker Ranch

Michigan Bluff
Elev. 3,500'

■	Parking
·—·—	Best 100 Route
——	Paved Road
▬▬	Freeway
- - -	Other Roads and Trails (bikes may be off limits)

© 1995 Fine Edge Productions

before going slightly downhill to Deadwood Ridge. This part of the ride is scenic and not difficult, but many may prefer to do a shuttle option to avoid riding 10 miles of pavement. (Leave one car at Michigan Bluff and one at Deadwood Road. To get to the beginning of the ride from Foresthill, take Forest Hill Divide Road 17 miles to Deadwood Road.)

Turn right on Deadwood Road at 15.3 miles. Take a break in the shade and prepare for the downhill! First the road takes you gradually down Deadwood Ridge, but it gets steeper and your speed increases. At 21.6 miles continue on Deadwood Road, passing the Western States 100 Trail that goes east to Devils Thumb. Go left on the Western States 100 Trail at 23.3 miles. Deadwood Road heads to the right and ends up at the same place, but the trail is more fun to ride. The Western States 100 Trail and Deadwood Road meet again at the Deadwood Cemetery at 24.2 miles. This old cemetery from the gold rush days is all that is left of a town.

From here the loop continues down the trail to the left. Please read the warning posted on the trail sign! The trail is not well maintained from this point on; it is very steep and narrow, and it is open to motorcycles, hikers and horseback riders. *Caution:* If you are tired, do not proceed! Once you ride down into the canyon the only way out is by bicycle or by foot. If someone is injured it will be up to your group to get help or manage the rescue alone.

The trail—historically known as the "Last Chance Trail"—quickly begins to drop off into El Dorado Canyon. If you try this ride in the fall after the first rain, the big leaf maple trees will be yellow and the air will be filled with the strong scent of bay trees that line the trail. This is a fun, technical section, and all your efforts will be concentrated on negotiating the route. Plan to stop occasionally to shake out your hands and enjoy the view! *Watch out for poison oak the entire way down, and beware rattlesnakes the closer you get to the river!*

Cross the bridge over El Dorado Canyon at 27.7 miles. Below the bridge there is a good swimming hole and a nice place to take a break in the shade. If you are out of water, be sure to resupply here. *(Filter or treat all water taken from the river.)* Don't be fooled by the map and assume you are almost back to the car—it's a 3,500-foot climb and a thirsty 3.5 miles away. For many this still won't sound too tough, but the trail winds its way out onto south-facing slopes with very little shade.

When you are rested, start up the trail. There is an old jeep road here too, but it is steeper than the trail, so most people prefer to follow the Western States 100 Trail. If you haven't yet gained a new respect for long distance runners, this next section of trail may convince you! The first part of the climb is the steepest, but the worst part is when the trail heads out into the sunny spots on the south-facing slopes. If you start to feel tired, just think a moment about the runners making their way up out of the canyon. This is the 60-mile point in the race and the lead runners get here after running 10 to 11 hours!

Everyone will push in spots on this climb. Just remember it is only 3.5 miles to your car. Once the trail crosses the creek in Poor Mans Canyon, it becomes more rideable. When it merges with the road it's an easy ride the rest of the way back to your car. Gasp!

66 Ward Creek Loop

Distance: 15.5 miles
Difficulty: Intermediate
Elevation: Start, 6,240'; low point, 6,185'; high point, 7,280'
Ride Type: Loop on pavement and dirt
Season: June through October
Topo Maps: USGS 7.5 min. Tahoe City; Fine Edge North Lake Tahoe Basin Recreation Topo Map

Overview: This ride is well-suited to intermediate riders or better. It is only moderately strenuous and not very technical, with about two-thirds of the route on pavement. Beginners with strength and endurance can also do well on this ride.

Getting There: From the Y in Tahoe City (Highways 89 and 28) drive south about a quarter of a mile. Turn right and park at the Truckee River Access Bike Trail Parking. This is a large parking lot to accommodate the hundreds of cyclists who ride in this area every day all summer.

Route: From where you parked, ride your bike out of the parking area (retrace the route you drove in). At just under a quarter of a mile, just before Highway 89, turn right onto the paved bicycle trail that runs alongside the highway. Ride south, past William Kent Campground.

At 2.25 miles, turn right onto Pineland Drive (look for two large poles with "Pineland" carved into them). About a half-mile later turn left onto Twin Peaks Drive. A sign at this turn points to Ward Valley. Stay on the main road as the name changes to Ward Creek Boulevard, and later to Courchevel Road (5 miles from where you started).

Turn right onto Chamonix Street at 5.25 miles. When the pave-

ment ends (just over 5.5 miles) take the dirt road directly ahead. Ride up a short hill, then go right on the main road marked 16N48. At 6.75 miles, after crossing a creek bed, stay on the main trail to the left. After 8 miles of cycling, you can catch some views of the Truckee River below and Lake Tahoe behind you for about a half mile. The road then swings west through an abandoned ski area. After a brief view down into Alpine Meadows, the descent begins!

The dirt road you've been following ends at a Forest Service gate, 10.25 miles from where you started the ride. Continue down the paved road (Snow Crest). At just over 10.5 miles turn right onto Alpine Meadows Road. When you reach Highway 89 (11.5 miles), turn right and pick up the paved trail along the south side of the road. Follow this trail back to the Y, turn right, and cycle back to the parking lot for a total mileage of 15.5 miles.

Options: A popular option for the Ward Creek Loop that makes it shorter, easier (eliminates most of the climbing), and less of a pavement ride, requires shuttling cyclists to the start of the dirt at the end of Chamonix Street. This eliminates about 5.5 miles, reducing the total ride mileage to 10 miles. For a second variation giving an easier and shorter ride (11

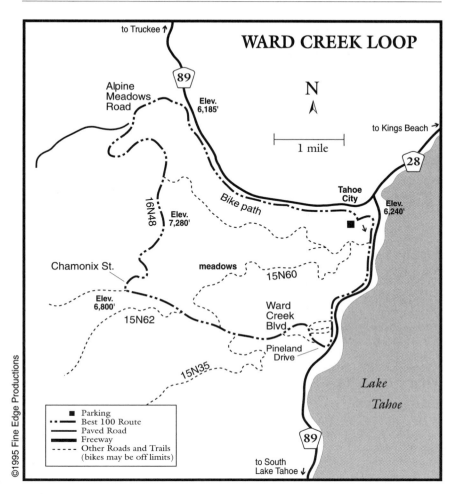

WARD CREEK LOOP

to Truckee ↑

89

Alpine
Meadows
Road

Elev.
6,185'

N

to Kings Beach →

1 mile

28

16N48

Bike path

Tahoe
City

Elev.
7,280'

Elev.
6,240'

Chamonix St.

meadows

15N60

Elev.
6,800'

15N62

Ward
Creek
Blvd.

Pineland
Drive

15N35

Lake
Tahoe

■ Parking
·─·─ Best 100 Route
──── Paved Road
━━━━ Freeway
- - - - Other Roads and Trails
      (bikes may be off limits)

89

to South
Lake Tahoe ↓

©1995 Fine Edge Productions

miles total), 1.5 miles after you turn left onto Twin Peaks Road, watch for a left turn onto a dirt road called Upper Ward Creek. Follow the main road (there are several turns available for exploration) until the road ends, then turn around and ride back to where you started.

Another popular option to the Ward Creek Loop is to add a loop past Paige Meadow, or to ride it as a separate, short (about 10 miles) beginner route. Pick up this loop between the Truckee River Access park-

ing lot and William Kent Campground. Follow the signs to Granlibakken Ski Resort (the turn is about one mile south of the Tahoe City Y). Just before the resort, turn left on Rawhide and stay on it as it turns to dirt. At about 4 miles from the highway you come to Paige Meadow (a group of several large meadows). Go west through the meadows and head southwest to connect with Ward Creek Boulevard. A left turn takes you back to where you started in Tahoe City.

67 Miller Lake Loop

Distance: 14 miles
Difficulty: Advanced
Elevation: Start, 6,230'; low point, 6,230'; high point, 7,320'
Ride Type: Loop on pavement, dirt road, and singletrack
Season: June through October
Topo Maps: USGS 7.5 min. Meeks Bay, Homewood; Fine Edge North Lake Tahoe Basin Recreation Topo Map

Overview: Miller Lake Loop is best suited to advanced riders. It has about as much variability in riding surface as you will find on any regularly ridden route in the Lake Tahoe Basin. You'll ride on highways, residential streets, wide dirt thoroughfares, narrow, boulder-strewn 4WD roads, well-groomed, smooth singletrack, and treacherous, rocky, 18-inch-wide paths. Only a little over 3 miles of the ride is on pavement, and most of it is deep in the Sierra forest. This ride is a challenging and scenic mountain bikers getaway!

Getting There: Start at General Creek Campground just south of Tahoma, off Highway 89 on the west side of Lake Tahoe. For a small fee, you can park your vehicle in one of the day use areas.

Route: From the entrance to General Creek Campground, ride through the campground in a northwesterly direction, following the signs to camp spaces 149 and 151. Between these two spaces, about three-quarters of a mile from the entrance, ride onto the dirt road headed west. You are on a loop from the campground that is very popular for cyclists and hikers, and, when the snow falls, for cross-country skiers as well.

At just over one mile, you come to a large sign reading "Meadows in the Tahoe Basin" where you con-

tinue west on the main road. At just over 2.25 miles the main trail turns left to loop back to the campground. You continue straight ahead onto singletrack. A sign at this point indicates that Lily Pond and Lost Lake lie ahead.

Ride and walk the narrow, sometimes technical, singletrack until a turn at 3 miles. The trail straight ahead goes to Lily Pond and bicycles are not allowed. Turn left, following the signs directing you toward Lost Lake. At 5 miles the trail crosses General Creek. One-half mile later your trail ends at a jeep road T, where you turn right (the left is a dead-end road going to Duck Lake and Lost Lake).

After your right turn at 5.5 miles, you cross the creek again and climb up the ridge. At nearly 6.5 miles, you crest the ridge and start downhill to reach Miller Lake. At 7.25 miles (next to Miller Lake) you come to another T, where you turn right on the Rubicon Jeep Trail. Be warned that the Rubicon road has areas of boulders that can give novice cyclists problems. Jeep traffic has packed them tightly together, so most of the boulder fields are rideable if you don't slow down too much.

Ride east and northeast, past Miller, Lily and McKinney lakes, all on your right. At about 10 miles, just after a brief and tricky rocky down-

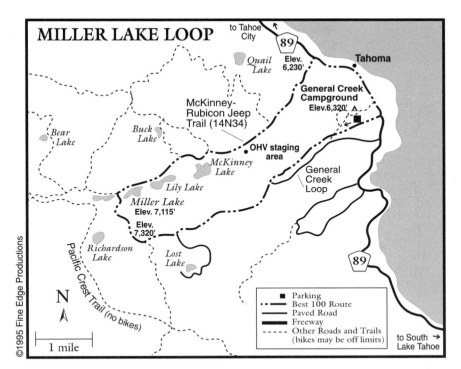

MILLER LAKE LOOP

to Tahoe City

89

Quail Lake

Elev. 6,230'

Tahoma

General Creek Campground
Elev.6,320' △

McKinney-Rubicon Jeep Trail (14N34)

Bear Lake

Buck Lake

OHV staging area

McKinney Lake

General Creek Loop

Lily Lake

Miller Lake
Elev. 7,115'

Elev. 7,320'

Pacific Crest Trail (no bikes)

Richardson Lake

Lost Lake

89

N

1 mile

■ Parking
∙—∙—∙ Best 100 Route
——— Paved Road
▬▬▬ Freeway
- - - - Other Roads and Trails
     (bikes may be off limits)

to South →
Lake Tahoe

© 1995 Fine Edge Productions

hill, you pass an OHV staging area on your right (with restrooms). At 10.75 miles, you pass a road going across a bridge left (to Quail Lake). Continue ahead on the Rubicon Jeep Trail until you reach pavement at 11.5 miles.

Once on pavement in a residential neighborhood, follow the signs to Highway 89 (Springs Road, Bellevue, McKinney-Rubicon Springs Road). Reaching Highway 89, you've ridden 12.5 miles. Go right (south) through Tahoma. Most of this part of your ride is on a paved bicycle trail paralleling the highway. At 13.75 miles turn into General Creek Campground and head for your car in the parking lot. Arriving back at your car, your total ride without sidetrips has been 14 miles.

Options: An extremely popular ride for beginning mountain bike enthu-

siasts is the General Creek Campground Loop. Starting from the day-use parking area, ride the route described above until the point where you go onto singletrack (2.25 miles). Instead of going ahead toward Lost Lake, stay on the main trail swinging left and across the bridge. Consider riding on the long wooden ramp just for fun. At 2.5 miles swing left back onto wide trail across the bridge. At 3.75 miles turn left, crossing the creek on a big bridge, to end the loop part of this ride at just over 4 miles (at the sign about meadows). Go right to return to your car. When you reach the parking lot, you've completed a total ride of about 5.25 miles. This loop, all on relatively smooth roads and trails, is suited to riders of all levels, with the total elevation gain of only 200 feet.

There are numerous other op-

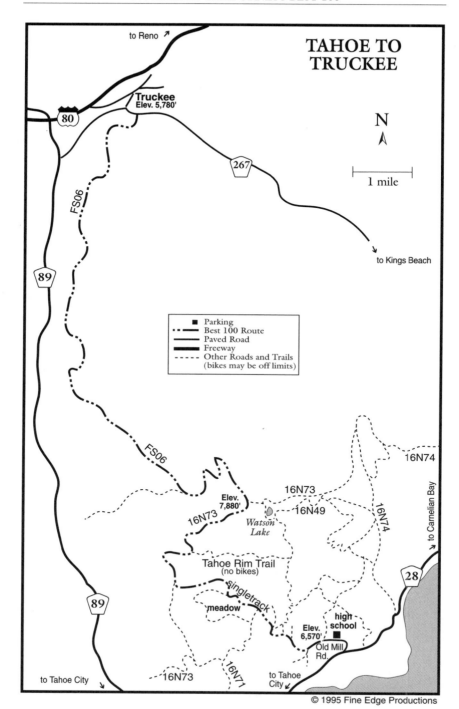

TAHOE TO TRUCKEE

to Reno

Truckee
Elev. 5,780'

80

267

FS06

89

1 mile

to Kings Beach

■ Parking
Best 100 Route
Paved Road
Freeway
Other Roads and Trails
(bikes may be off limits)

FS06

16N74

16N73

Elev.
7,880'

16N49

16N73

to Carnelian Bay

Watson
Lake

16N74

Tahoe Rim Trail
(no bikes)

singletrack

28

89

meadow

high
school

Elev.
6,570'

Old Mill
Rd.

to Tahoe City

16N73

16N71

to Tahoe
City

© 1995 Fine Edge Productions

tions related to the Miller Lake Loop. Consider sidetrips from the basic route to Lost Lake, Richardson Lake (southwest of Miller Lake), Quail Lake, and so on. For the hardy, once you encounter the Rubicon Jeep Trail, there are dozens of miles of narrow, rough roads available for exploration. When you get to the Rubicon, you can access the Barker Pass area by following Miller Creek to the left and then heading north to follow either North Miller Creek or Barker Creek. There is enough riding all around here to tire even the strongest of cyclists—and enough Sierra Nevada scenery to satisfy your needs for a dramatic mountain backdrop for your exhaustion!

68 Tahoe to Truckee

Distance: 17.25 miles (or up to 22.5 miles)
Difficulty: Advanced
Elevation: Start, 6,570'; low point, 5,780'; high point, 7,880'
Ride Type: Shuttle with varied riding on pavement, dirt road, and singletrack
Season: June through October
Topo Maps: USGS 7.5 min. Kings Beach, Tahoe City, Truckee;
Fine Edge North Lake Tahoe Basin Recreation Topo Map

Overview: Sometimes called the TNT, this is one of the most popular rides in the Lake Tahoe area—due, in part, to its great variety. There are long sections of climbing, flat riding, and descending. Although it is entirely on dirt, the surface ranges from wide, well-groomed road to narrow (but not very technical) singletrack to rocky, non-maintained jeep trail. Due to its length, the climbing involved, and a few rough spots here and there, the Tahoe to Truckee route is best suited to advanced riders, but strong intermediates also enjoy the one-way run on this great ride.

Getting There: Start at North Lake Tahoe High School in Tahoe City. Please note that locals start this ride from various locations. (The starting point at Highlands Community Center features a new singletrack.) The simplest route, however, begins at the high school. From the Highway 28/89 junction in Tahoe City, drive or cycle north on Highway 28 (through town). At Old Mill Road (about 2.5 miles), turn left. At 2.75 miles turn left on Polaris Road. Go just past the high school to start this ride (park your vehicle there). If you ride your bike to this point, you've added a little over 3 miles to the one-way Tahoe to Truckee mileage.

For a shuttle, leave a car at the north end of the dirt road (FS06). Drive south on Highway 267, turn right on Palisades Road (one-half mile), turn right on Silver Fir Drive (1.5 miles) after Palisades became Ponderosa, then turn left onto Thelin Drive (1.75 miles) and find the green gate for Forest Service Road 06 (2 miles). Park the shuttle vehicle here.

Route: Most often ridden one-way after shuttling a vehicle, this ride offers a delightful tour of the Sierra from Lake Tahoe to the town of Truckee. Beginning just past the

pavement at North Lake Tahoe High School, continue ahead on dirt. At just under a quarter of a mile you pass a sign for Burton Creek State Park. A few hundred feet later (just under a third of a mile), turn right and start up the hill (straight swings left and down through a creek bed).

Just past a yellow sign reading *California State Park Property* (at 0.75 mile), go left at the fork. At just under 1.25 mile swing left at a sloppy four-way intersection. (A right turn here can get you back to Highway 28, a few miles east of Old Mill Road.) Continue on the main road about 2.75 miles (just past Antone Meadows on your left), and make a right turn here. You pass the back of a yellow sign on your left and soon start climbing on a delightful singletrack. *Caution:* Traffic on this singletrack is two-way. Watch for oncoming, downhilling cyclists!

At 3.75 miles, the singletrack ends at Forest Road 16N73, which turns sharply as you encounter it. Turn right and proceed up the forest road. (A left turn here can loop you back to Tahoe City.) At 4.5 miles, the Tahoe Rim Trail crosses the road you're riding on—continue ahead. At 6.75 miles you arrive at an intersection with another main road, Forest Service Road 06. If you bear right and uphill you will follow Mt. Watson Road (73) and come out on State Highway 267 at Brockway Summit. To complete the Tahoe to Truckee run, however, bear left and begin descending—its mostly downhill the rest of the ride! Stay on the main road (wide and not technical) all the way to Truckee.

At 11 miles there is a large covered sign on your left for the Robie Equestrian Park—no bikes allowed. Continue ahead on the main road. Forest Service Road 06 ends in Truckee at Thelin Drive, 17.25 miles from North Lake Tahoe High School. Downtown Truckee is two miles away. If you are cycling all the way to Truckee (19.25 miles from North Lake Tahoe High School), follow in reverse the shuttle parking directions in the "Getting There" section. The total distance of the Tahoe to Truckee Ride, if you cycle from downtown Tahoe City to downtown Truckee, is 22.5 miles.

Options: There are numerous options on the southern portion of this ride and virtually none as you get close to Truckee. For a short ride, when you reach the "sloppy four-way intersection" at 1.25 miles, turn right and head northeast. To get back to Highway 28 you need to take one of the roads or trails headed south or southwest.

A popular loop from Tahoe City and back requires a left turn, instead of a right, when you finish the singletrack. This puts you on 16N73 headed south. You come to a left onto 16N71 (at about 5.5 miles), and either road will take you back to Tahoe City, coming out of the forest near the golf course. Road 16N71 is a little shorter and is more popular with local mountain bikers.

Other options for routes in this area include looping around Antone Meadows and back to North Lake Tahoe High School (instead of the right turn onto the singletrack at 2.75 miles), and a right turn (actually, almost straight ahead) at Forest Service Road 06 (6.75 miles), followed very shortly by another right turn to get to Watson Lake. Many cyclists from the Tahoe City area ride from the high school to Watson Lake as an afternoon's out-and-back (15.5 miles total). There are numerous roads in the Watson Lake area, so you might consider taking along a map and exploring some of them.

Finally, be aware that some of the hardiest mountain bikers approach the Tahoe to Truckee Ride as an out-and-back, with a total distance of between 35 and 45 miles, depending on where they start and end and where they turn around. With between 4,000 and 5,000 culmulative feet of climbing, they certainly get plenty of riding for one day!

69 The Great Flume Ride

Distance: 13.75 miles
Difficulty: Intermediate
Elevation: Start, 6,990'; low point, 6,295'; high point, 8,150'
Ride Type: Usually a shuttle; mostly dirt road and singletrack
Season: June through October
Topo Maps: USGS 7.5 min. Glenbrook, Marlette Lake; Fine Edge North Lake Tahoe Basin Recreation Topo Map

Overview: This ride is not technically difficult, but does require basic mountain biking skills to assure safety. If you are a beginner or are afraid of heights, do not attempt the second portion of this ride (the Flume Trail itself), where you must cycle a narrow trail, sometimes alongside a steep dropoff, for over four miles. The first

portion of the ride is the climb to Marlette Lake, an elevation gain of 1,200 feet. This part also is best suited to intermediate or advanced riders.

The Great Flume Ride is the only mountain bike ride in the Tahoe area that has been featured in the sport's most popular magazines. It has received considerable national

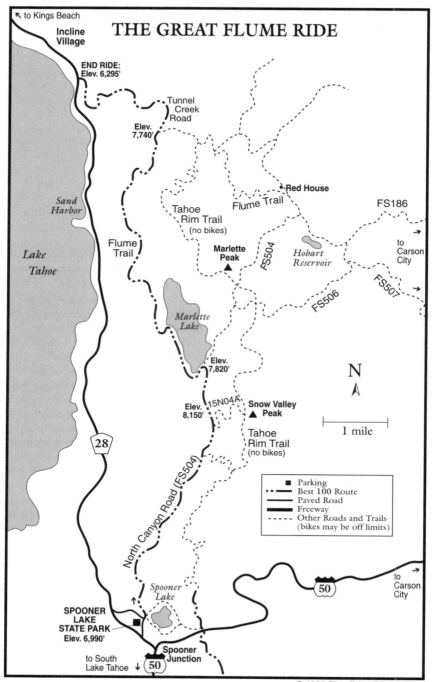

THE GREAT FLUME RIDE

to Kings Beach

Incline Village

END RIDE: Elev. 6,295'

Tunnel Creek Road

Elev. 7,740'

Sand Harbor

Red House

Flume Trail

FS186

Tahoe Rim Trail (no bikes)

Flume Trail

Lake Tahoe

Marlette Peak ▲

FS504

Hobart Reservoir

to Carson City

FS506

FS507

Marlette Lake

Elev. 7,820'

N

Elev. 8,150'   15N04A

Snow Valley ▲ Peak

1 mile

Tahoe Rim Trail (no bikes)

28

North Canyon Road (FS504)

■ Parking
▪▪▪ Best 100 Route
——— Paved Road
━━ Freeway
- - - Other Roads and Trails
(bikes may be off limits)

Spooner Lake

50

to Carson City

SPOONER LAKE STATE PARK
Elev. 6,990'

Spooner Junction

to South Lake Tahoe ↓   50

© 1995 Fine Edge Productions

attention and was labeled one of Western America's Top Ten routes! It certainly ranks as the most popular off-pavement ride among the hundreds of possibilities in the Lake Tahoe area.

Getting There: From Incline Village, take Highway 28 south to just north of its junction with Highway 50. Turn left into Spooner Lake State Park. For a small charge you can leave your car there all day.

Depending on enthusiasm, stamina, skill, and vehicle availability, there are different ways to approach this ride. Described below is the basic Spooner to Sand Harbor route (via Highway 28). This route follows Service Road 504 (North Canyon Road) from Spooner Lake to Marlette Lake, then the Flume Trail from Marlette Lake to Tunnel Creek Road, and finishes by descending Tunnel Creek Road back down to Highway 28 between Sand Harbor and Incline Village. This approach to the Great Flume Ride involves leaving a car in the Sand Harbor area to shuttle people and bikes back to Spooner Lake State Park.

Route: Begin the Great Flume Ride by cycling from the parking lot to the northeast corner of Spooner Lake and picking up North Canyon Road headed north to Marlette Lake (follow the signs). You then begin the long climb to the ridge just before Marlette Lake, an elevation gain of just over 1,200 feet. At 4 miles you pass a right turn to Snow Valley Peak, a side trip for the very hardy. Continue ahead on the main road to Marlette Lake (the climbing is almost over). You crest the ridge and start downhill at just over 4.25 miles.

When you reach the lake at 5 miles, consider a break and a little time exploring. When you are ready to press on, turn left and ride around to the west side of the lake. The road ends by the dam, at 6.25 miles. Look for the singletrack headed downhill to the west; a sign identifies this as the beginning of the Flume Trail. Ride or walk this steep and rocky little section of trail, across Marlette Creek and around a bend, and you will be on the Flume Trail.

The Flume Trail is a narrow, 4.5-mile-long singletrack, following the ridge to the north about 1,300 feet above Lake Tahoe. If you are not a confident, experienced mountain biker or are frightened by heights, you should turn around and head back to Spooner Lake. This trail is the route of an old wooden flume that carried water and logs to Virginia City, Nevada, during the Comstock silver mining boom. Now about 120 years later, there are still a few pieces of the flume along the trail and some of the pipes that replaced the original wooden structure.

Ride the Flume Trail carefully, and slow down or stop often to enjoy the fantastic view of the Lake Tahoe Basin. You should consider bringing a camera along for this ride. There are great photo opportunities—you can get pictures of cyclists riding through the trees or alongside white granite walls with beautiful Lake Tahoe and the surrounding mountains as the backdrop!

Just about 10.75 miles from Spooner Lake State Park, the Flume Trail ends as you intersect Tunnel Creek Road. Bear left and begin the sometimes steep, sometimes sandy, and sometimes washboarded descent down to Highway 28 alongside Lake Tahoe. Advanced riders often turn right at Tunnel Creek Road and loop back to the south end of Marlette Lake, then descend North Canyon Road back to Spooner Lake.

Going left onto Tunnel Creek Road offers you three miles of downhill back to the shores of Lake Tahoe. Exercise caution on this downhill; ride in control at all times. When you reach the pavement, at 13.75 miles, turn left to head toward Sand Harbor or right to Incline Village to find your shuttle car. Where Tunnel Creek Road intersects Highway 28, you are nine highway miles north of the Spooner Lake State Park parking lot.

Options: The most popular option for the Great Flume Ride is to ride from Spooner Lake to Marlette Lake and back. This is a scenic, relatively

easy 10-mile out-and-back, suitable to hardy beginners and better. Also, as you ride from Spooner to Marlette, at 4 miles is an optional side trip to Snow Valley Peak. It is not long (about 2 miles one way), but involves over 1,000 feet of elevation gain on a rough and rocky jeep trail (for strong riders only). If you choose to take this side trip you will encounter a breathtaking, world-class view. Its breadth is so remarkable only a panorama camera would have any possibility of capturing it on film. The view of Lake Tahoe from Snow Valley Peak is as good as it gets! The north-south singletrack you encounter up high on the mountain is the Tahoe Rim Trail and is closed to mountain bikes.

As noted earlier, when riders reach Tunnel Creek Road at the end of the Flume Trail, many prefer to turn right and make a big loop east, then south, around Marlette Peak. If you choose this route, you do considerably more climbing. To make this loop ride, head up from the end of the Flume Trail to the top of the ridge. Continue straight at the Twin Lakes Road and watch for another section of the Flume Trail to your right at about 12 miles. If you miss this right turn, continue ahead and take the next main road turning right. Either route takes you past the Red House, an old flume tender's home.

At just over 14 miles your trail ends at a small diversion dam. Walk across the dam up to the main road, and turn right. About a half-mile later turn right on Forest Service Road 504 (North Canyon Road). It soon crosses a creek and then you begin a long, strenuous 2.5-mile climb with nearly 1,000 feet of elevation gain. At just over 16 miles the road forks, and you continue straight and then down to Marlette Lake. The loop ends here; turn left and head back to Spooner Lake. Upon entering the state park lot, you will have finished 23 miles of some of the best pedaling on dirt that America has to offer.

For additional rides in this area, please refer to *Mountain Biking the High Sierra, Guide 3B, Lake Tahoe North,* by R. W. Miskimins and Carol Bonser, ISBN 0-938665-27-8 (see p. 303).

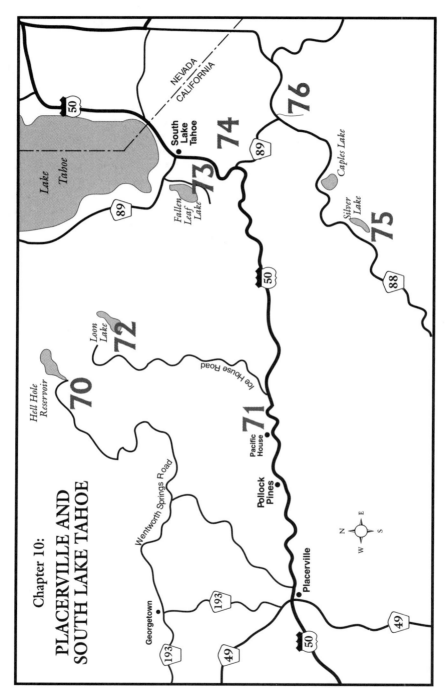

Chapter 10:

PLACERVILLE AND
SOUTH LAKE TAHOE

©1995 Fine Edge Productions

CHAPTER 10

Placerville/ South Lake Tahoe

by R. W. Miskimins and Carol Bonser

From the foothills on the western slope of the Sierra Nevada, eastward to the high country of the Lake Tahoe Basin, and southeast to the Toiyabe Forest along the Nevada border, the areas described in this chapter provide some of the most extensive, varied and beautiful mountain bike riding in the country. Located just four hours east of the San Francisco Bay Area and two hours east of Sacramento, this area offers challenging riding (elevation, plenty of climbing and rocky terrain) and gorgeous scenery.

You can begin your rides in the foothills of the Sierra in late autumn and winter on dirt logging roads that wind through oak and pine forests. As spring and summer temperatures rise, you can work your way eastward to the higher elevations, riding on jeep roads and trails that take you to the very edge of four Wilderness Areas—Granite Chief, Desolation Valley, Mokelumne and the Carson Iceberg. (Enjoy the views, but don't ride in the Wilderness Areas! Bikes are prohibited.) In June, July and August, you can still enjoy fields of flowers that you saw at lower elevations in April and May and find relief from lowland temperatures.

If you choose the right time to visit, the foothills will be full of pink dogwoods or brilliant yellow big-leaf maples. In autumn, aspen in the high country and eastern slopes of Hope Valley and Markleeville range from shades of yellow to gold and bright orange. And we haven't forgotten Lake Tahoe itself; we've included rides that let you see just how big and beautiful the lake really is.

Over the past decade, the Lake Tahoe area has become one of the most popular destinations for mountain biking in the entire western United States— and for good reason. Once you've worked your way through the rides in this chapter, you may want to try out the rides in the Reno/Carson City and Tahoe North chapters.

195

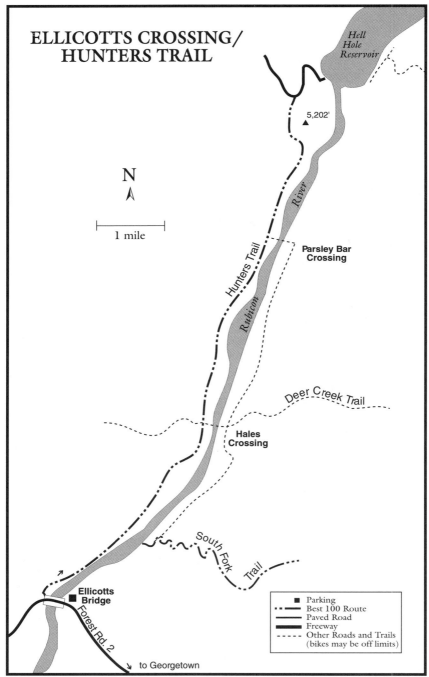

ELLICOTTS CROSSING/
HUNTERS TRAIL

Hell Hole Reservoir

5,202'

N

1 mile

River

Hunters Trail

Parsley Bar
Crossing

Rubicon

Deer Creek Trail

Hales
Crossing

South Fork Trail

Ellicotts
Bridge

Forest Rd. 2

to Georgetown

■	Parking
▪▪▪▪	Best 100 Route
——	Paved Road
▬▬	Freeway
- - -	Other Roads and Trails (bikes may be off limits)

© 1995 Fine Edge Productions

For updated trail conditions and campground information, call Eldorado National Forest (916-644-6048), Lake Tahoe Basin Management Unit (916-573-2600) or Toiyabe National Forest (702-355-5302).

70 Ellicotts Crossing / Hunters Trail

Distance: 15.5 miles
Difficulty: Strenuous, very technical
Elevation: Begin 3,300', high point 4,200' (If you ride the trail past Parsley Bar to Hell Hole, you climb to 5,200' or 5,600', depending on which trail you choose.)
Ride Type: Out-and-back on singletrack
Season: Best in April and May, whenever the road opens, or after the first rain in the fall. It is rideable all summer long, but this canyon can be *extremely* hot in the middle of the summer!
Topo Maps: Robb's Peak, Bunker Hill (7.5 min.), or Robb's Peak, Granite Chief (15 min.)
Comments: Riding in the 3,000'-4,000' elevation means watch out for poison oak and rattlesnakes along the trail! Mosquitoes can be terrible, too! Someone should know where you are riding and when you plan to return. This is a little-used trail, and if someone gets hurt, it is going to be up to the rest of the group to get help.

Overview: Do not attempt this ride if you have never done any mountain bike trail riding! The trail is narrow and the river canyon drops off steeply in many places. Everyone will walk their bike in spots on the way up the canyon, and most people will walk in spots on the way out. If you're up to the challenge, the Rubicon River canyon is spectacular, with steep granite gorge sections and beautiful deep pools. If you enjoy fishing and swimming, plan extra time to hike down to the river.

Getting There: From Sacramento, take U.S. 50 east to Placerville, turn left (north) on Highway 49. About 1 mile later, turn right on Highway 193 (follow signs to Georgetown). This highway drops down into the American River Canyon and crosses the river at Chili Bar. Continue on Highway 193 up out of the canyon to Georgetown.

Once in Georgetown, go east on Wentworth Springs Road 23 miles

to the intersection of Uncle Toms Cabin Road. Go left toward Hell Hole. The road drops quickly into the Rubicon River Canyon. Go 5 miles to the bottom, to a giant bridge. This is Ellicotts Crossing. The ride starts on the far side of the bridge. Parking is available when you first reach the bridge on the left or right side. Park here if you have a new car, one with low clearance or one that doesn't go up or down steep, rocky hills. Otherwise, go across the bridge and take the first road on the right that takes you down to the river. At 0.2 mile, look left and you can see a sign marked *Rubicon Trail, Hales Crossing 4 miles; Hell Hole Reservoir 10 miles.* (Rubicon Trail is called Hunters Trail on USGS topo maps and in "Hiking Trails of the Georgetown Area.")

Route: This ride is simple to follow. From the sign mentioned above in the *Getting There* section, head out the Rubicon Trail (Hunters Trail) toward Hales Crossing. The first mile is the toughest. You wind in and out of creek canyons and jump on and off your bike, pushing up some short steep sections. At 0.3 mile, where a trail comes in from above, go straight. At 1.5 miles a trail comes in from above. Sign: *Grey Trail; Nevada Point Road 3 miles.* Nevada Point Road at the end of Grey Trail is at 5,300 feet. This means a climb of over 2,000 feet to get out of this canyon! A trail to try *down,* not up!

At 3.8 miles, you come to an old cabin site and 0.2 mile farther you arrive at Hales Crossing, signed: *Hales Crossing and Rim Road.* If you look on the back of the tree behind the sign, you see an old Forest Service sign: *Grizzly Ranch, 8 miles [right]; Jerry's Pool, 5 miles [right].* Jerry's Pool is a small lake.

Though there is very little use in this area now, the old trail signs along this canyon show this was once a major trail for the gold miners who worked along the Rubicon River. Walk down to the river and you should be able to see where the early settlers used to cross.

After you've done your exploring, continue another 1.5 miles, and you find more old trail signs. *Big Meadows 5 miles [right]; Hell Hole 6 1/2 miles [right]; Hales Camp Trail, and Hales Camp 2 miles.* At about 6.0 miles the trail falls apart—it is rocky, washed out and, naturally, it just happens to be out in full sun. You begin to question riding any farther, but there is good riding ahead. And yes, it is worth pushing on! Pay attention to the trail, you can often ride down the rough stuff you had to push up.

At 1.5 miles past the rough section, you see a "K tag" (yellow tag on signpost) that says you are in T14N R14N, at the corner of section 20, 21 / 29, 28. This means you are at the upper end of Parsley Bar. You have traveled just over 7.5 miles so far. Parsley Bar is located to your right, along the river. Ride and walk out to see where the river has deposited an amazing pile of rocks of all sizes, from sand to very large boulders! From Parsley Bar, the trail goes up the drainage and climbs to Hell Hole Reservoir in about 2 miles, gaining 1,000 feet in elevation in one long haul. Coming down is fun, but going up is work.

After a rest and a swim, follow the trail back to Ellicotts Crossing. Going the downstream direction, you can understand why mountain bikers like this trail. So much of what you had to walk, you can now ride. In this direction, you may not need to walk at all. Total miles to and from Parsley Bar: 15.5. A good, deep swimming hole is located just downstream from the bridge—just the thing after a long, hard ride.

71 Pony Express Historical Trail

Distance: 9.2 miles
Difficulty: Moderate, somewhat technical
Elevation: 3,100' to 3,820'
Ride Type: Loop on pavement, dirt roads and trail
Season: March through June and September through November. *This area is hot in the middle of the summer!*
Topo Maps: Pollock Pines and Riverton (7.5 min.)

Overview: This short, intermediate loop has a fun 2-mile downhill a half-mile of technical singletrack and is just a suggestion of what is possible from Forest Road 35, the White Meadow Road. Several roads in this area travel through private land, most belonging to the Michigan-California Lumber Company. Some of these roads are open because they travel in and out of U.S. Forest Service land; others may be closed due to logging activities. Much of the land along the White Meadow Road is now owned by private homeowners. *Respect all private land signs by staying on the roads and traveling on through.*

Getting There: From Placerville (on U.S. 50, east of Sacramento) drive east on U.S. 50, 8 miles past Pollock Pines. Turn left on Ice House Road. Half a mile along (where the main road swings sharply to the right), go straight ahead on Forest Road 35, the White Meadow Road. Continue driving 1.2 miles to a turnout on the left side of the road in the middle of a sharp right turn. Park here.

Route: Continue out Forest Road 35 on your bike. It goes up right away with not much of a chance to warm up! At 1.9 miles, continue straight ahead on the paved road past a sign to

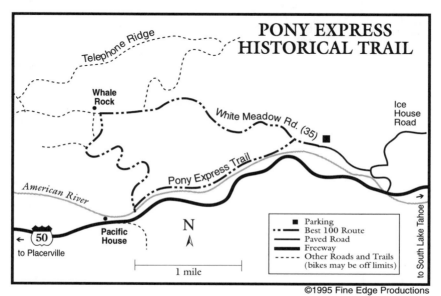

PONY EXPRESS HISTORICAL TRAIL

Telephone Ridge

Whale Rock

White Meadow Rd. (35)

Ice House Road

Pony Express Trail

American River

Pacific House

to Placerville

50

N

1 mile

■ Parking
Best 100 Route
Paved Road
Freeway
Other Roads and Trails (bikes may be off limits)

to South Lake Tahoe

©1995 Fine Edge Productions

White Meadows Camp (in the direction of Blairs Mill Site). At 3.0 miles, stay to the left on the main road (right reads "Peavine Road").

At nearly 3.5 miles, turn left (green sign reads "Peavine Ridge Rd") and prepare for a fast 2-mile downhill run! (If you missed this turn, 3.6 miles out you ride past Whale Rock, a large boulder painted to look like a whale. Look to your left and you can see another road going down into the river canyon. Go left; this spur soon ties into the main road. *Warning:* Watch out for the deep ruts at the beginning and end of the spur road!)

At 5.3 miles, when you ride through a sharp right turn, look to your left for the Pony Express Trail, which you ride to complete the loop. But continue past it if you want to get a look at the American River, go for a swim and see where the old bridge used to cross. (It was blown up several years ago.) At 5.7 miles, the road ends abruptly at a large water bar.

Leave your bikes and walk to the edge of the canyon. If you want to swim or wade, the best route down is to follow the creek drainage off to the left. As you look across the river, you can see the road that mountain bikers used to ride down before the bridge was destroyed. There is a possibility that someday a footbridge may cross the river. This would be nice, but it's probably several years away. *Warning:* The river is deep and swift at this location, usually all summer long, so do not plan your trip thinking you will be able to ford the river at this spot! When you are done enjoying the river, ride back up to the Pony Express Trail.

After riding 6.0 miles from your starting point, you turn right and head out on the remnants of the Pony Express Trail, used by Pony Express riders in the 1800s to deliver the mail. This is a challenging stretch of single-track that is worth attempting, but be careful of the washouts! Take time to

look at th e old rock wall built into the hillside to form the trail. Don't worry if you have trouble here; this is a short section you can walk if you need to. Soon the trail widens out into an old road.

At 6.8 miles, a newer, wider road crosses the road you are on. Turn right and ride down a short, steep section. Keep right again, staying on the main road. Soon you reach a take-down cattle fence. Be sure to leave it as you found it, open or closed. This is a tough fence to take down, so if you have someone with you, crawl through the fence and pass your bikes over the top. Continue, watching for cows if the gate was closed. From here the road rolls along, climbing and descending over and over as you travel along the river canyon.

When the dirt road ends at 9.0 miles, you have reached Forest Road 35. Turn left and ride the final 0.2 mile back to your car.

72 Loon Lake Loop

Distance: 16 miles
Difficulty: Strenuous, very technical
Elevation: 6,400' to 6,780'
Ride Type: Loop on pavement, dirt roads and trails
Season: June through October
Topo Maps: Loon Lake and Wentworth Springs (7.5 min.)

Overview: This ride is suggested only for those in good physical condition, with the right state of mind and solid technical skills. You need to be the kind of rider who doesn't mind pushing your bike in order to enjoy the beauty of this area. This ride also gives you an idea of what the terrain in Desolation Wilderness is like. We consider this ride a classic, but it's not for everyone.

Getting There: From Sacramento go east to Placerville. Continue east on U.S. 50, 8 miles past Pollock Pines. Turn left on Ice House Road and follow it for 23.7 miles. Take the Loon Lake turnoff. Stay on Loon Lake Road for 4.3 miles and park your vehicle at the Loon Lake Campground.

Route: Look for the wilderness trailhead located in the camp-ground—the Desolation Wilderness boundary is about 6.5 miles away. This part of the trail is only about 3.5 miles long, but is one of the "funnest" around. It follows along the lake, so for once you get to ride on a trail that isn't all up, then all down! This section is good for people just getting started in trail riding. Although there are short, steep ups, most of the trail is gentle so you can concentrate on obstacle negotiation, learning how to pick up the front of the bike and how to move the bike around. Just remember you are on a trailhead to Desolation Wilderness, so you will encounter hikers and horseback riders. If you do, *it is best to get off your bike and stand out of the way of horses.*

At 3.5 miles the trail crosses a creek and goes uphill. (Riders who are not up to the full loop should turn around here.) The trail ends and a

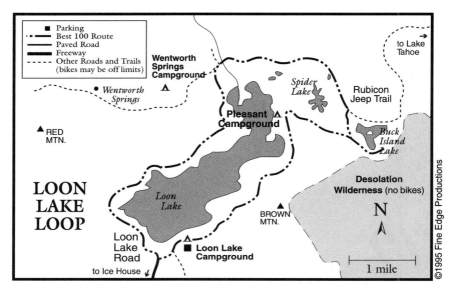

gravel road begins. Sounds simple, but this is no ordinary gravel road. Most of the roadbed has rather large rocks. At 4.0 miles the trail takes off to the left to Pleasant Campground. Not heavily used, this could be a good bike-in campground. The road surface begins to improve when the climbing is through! Follow the road as it leaves the lake.

Just over 2 miles past the turn to Pleasant Campground, after a short rideable section, the road turns back to rocks and cobbles for a technical downhill. You may prefer to walk some of this section. When the trail reenters the trees, look for a signpost without a sign (some day there might be a new sign). Remember this spot, as you will want to return here after you ride the last 0.1 mile down to the lake. You are now over 6 miles from the start of the ride, so enjoy the little lake here while you pull out your maps to see where you are and where you are supposed to go next.

To complete the loop, go back to the signpost and follow the trail

(0.6 mile to jeep road) that contours a bit then drops down to the creek. You can see the jeep road from here, just make your way over to it. After a short rideable stretch, the road becomes pretty amazing! You are now on the Rubicon Jeep Trail, a high country jeep trail that goes all the way across the Sierra, ending at the shore of Lake Tahoe. Several times through the next uphill section, ask yourself who talked you into this ride.

The trail continues to climb, sometimes rideable; sometimes it's just easier to push. After one last uphill, you can see roads and trails heading off to the left that lead to Spider Lake. Continue on the main road 1.5 miles to Little Sluice Box. This section of trail is completely composed of large rocks. Funny, jeeps can negotiate spots like this! Fortunately, with a bike you can portage around this spot. The road becomes more rideable now, with the bad sections becoming shorter and shorter.

Eventually you cross Ellis Creek. Just a little farther (0.1 mile), take the jeep trail that goes left toward Loon Lake. (The Rubicon Jeep Trail continues straight ahead here heading to Wentworth Springs.) Your spirits will rise through this next section. For most people their second wind (or third or fourth) kicks in about now, as the terrain becomes more rideable. About 0.7 mile later you reach a muddy section. One trail leads to one of the biggest natural mud holes we've ever seen! Fortunately, on a bike you can easily get around this obstacle!

Continue to the slabs, a large, open granite field. Don't get tricked into riding all the way down to the bottom. It's fun, but you need to stay fairly high and to the left up toward the trees, and you'll find the road again. 1.4 miles later go around the ridge and then you'll end up at the spillway. At just over 12.5 miles, ride up to the dam and cross it. Stay on the paved Loon Lake Road back to the campground, 3.2 miles away.

You're on your own on this ride! Go with the right frame of mind and you'll love it—it's all up to you! But we warned you, it's not easy!

73 Angora Lakes

Distance: 8 miles; 11 miles from the campground
Difficulty: Easy, nontechnical
Elevation: 770' gain/loss, 1,200' from the campground
Ride Type: Out-and-back on pavement and dirt road
Season: June through October
Topo Maps: Echo Lake (7.5 min.), or Fallen Leaf (15 min.); Fine Edge South Lake Tahoe Basin Recreation Topo Map

Overview: This is a fun ride, especially if you are staying in the Fallen Leaf or Camp Richardson areas. You can start right from your campsite. You'll travel past several lakes and you'll get some great views without too much climbing.

Getting There: From South Lake Tahoe, go north on Highway 89 along the southwest side of Lake Tahoe to the road to Fallen Leaf Lake (1 mile past Camp Richardson). Turn left and go past Fallen Leaf Campground. At a little over 1.75 miles, turn left on a paved road that goes uphill. After 0.4 mile, turn right on the dirt road. There is parking for several cars along the road just before you turn on Road 1214. If you have a larger group, or

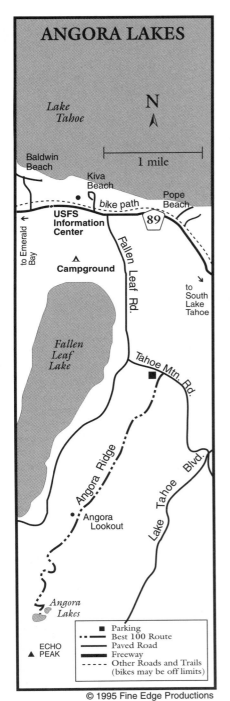

ANGORA LAKES

Lake Tahoe

N

1 mile

Baldwin Beach

Kiva Beach

bike path

Pope Beach

89

USFS Information Center

to Emerald Bay

Campground

Fallen Leaf Rd.

to South Lake Tahoe

Fallen Leaf Lake

Tahoe Mtn. Rd.

Angora Ridge

Lake Tahoe Blvd.

Angora Lookout

Angora Lakes

ECHO PEAK

■ Parking
∎·∎· Best 100 Route
── Paved Road
━━ Freeway
---- Other Roads and Trails
(bikes may be off limits)

© 1995 Fine Edge Productions

want a longer ride, park back by Fallen Leaf Campground.

Route: This is an easy ride to follow; just stay on Angora Ridge Road. (Some sections of the road are paved.) After a bit of a climb (just over 600 feet, about 2 miles out)), you come out on Angora Ridge with a spectacular view in all directions. Take a topo map with you so you can recognize the surrounding peaks – Mt. Tallac and Angora Peak—then look down on Fallen Leaf Lake and a corner of Lake Tahoe.

When you are ready, continue south toward Angora Lakes. At 3.0 miles the road arrives at a large parking lot and a gate. This is the end of the road for motor vehicles. Check the sign. Hikers, horseback riders and mountain bikes are all still allowed on the trail (an old road) to the lakes. There's plenty of room for everyone, but be sure to watch out for hikers and horseback riders!

The lower lakes are quieter, with most of the hikers heading to the upper lake. If you ride to the upper lake (4.0 miles), be prepared to park your bike. The resort owners have built a log bike rack, complete with locks and chains. Lock your bike, then go to the resort and give them your name and the number of your lock. The idea is to provide a safe place to park bikes and to keep the bikes off the beach area. The resort sells lemonade, ice cream and candy bars and rents small rowboats, so you can take a "cruise" on the lake. Swimming is good here, too.

From here, follow your tracks back to your car. *Stay in control at all times and watch out for hikers! Then watch out for vehicles once you reach the road.*

74 Mr. Toad's Wild Ride

Distance: 13.25 miles
Difficulty: Advanced
Elevation: Start at 7,320'; low point 6,340'; high point 8,820'
Ride Type: Shuttle or loop on trail and pavement
Season: June through October
Topo Maps: USGS Freel Peak, South Lake Tahoe (7.5 min.); Fine Edge South Lake Tahoe Basin Recreation Topo Map

Overview: This is definitely not a ride for novices. The climb is not very long (just over 4 miles), but it is narrow, steep, and sometimes extremely rocky and technical. The descent, at anything faster than a crawl, requires good riding skills and good judgment. Almost everyone will walk at least a few places during this ride.

Getting There: From South Lake Tahoe, go west on U.S. 50 to Meyers. Turn left on Highway 89 and travel south about 5.5 miles to the Big Meadow Trailhead for the Tahoe Rim Trail. If you are going to make a complete loop, park in Meyers and pedal the uphill section on Highway 89. There are numerous places to leave your car in Meyers—for example, the Lake Tahoe Basin Interagency Visitors Center.

Route: Mr. Toad's Wild Ride draws its colorful name from the exciting descent on the Saxon Creek Trail from Tucker Flat down to nearly lake level. It is a relentless downhill run—a drop of nearly 1,500 feet in less than 6 miles. What comes down, must first go up, however.

Start this ride at Big Meadow Trailhead by heading north on the Tahoe Rim Trail, in the direction of Armstrong Pass and Star Lake. At 0.5 mile carry your bike across the creek, then continue climbing. The trail is

narrow, uphill singletrack with lots of switchbacks and numerous rocks, in a beautiful, wooded, Sierra Nevada setting.

At just over two miles, don't turn right across the bridge/creek; instead, continue straight ahead. From here the climb gets tougher (steeper, more winding, and rockier). At about 3.5 miles you begin riding along the ridge. You can catch a few glimpses of Lake Tahoe to your left. At 4.25 miles, you reach the summit of the ride (8,820 feet).

You encounter a three-way intersection at just over 4.5 miles. There is a 4x4 post sign indicating that a left turn puts you on the Saxon Creek Trail. Turn left here and ride through Tucker Flat to begin the rapid descent alongside Saxon Creek. The descent is sometimes steep and sometimes technical, but always fun if you ride in control. There are some corners that are nicely banked for high-speed turning, and most of the trail is getting wider from increased use over the past few years. The last mile or so flattens out and follows an old fire road.

At 10.5 miles you reach Oneidas Street, a narrow, paved, single lane. Be aware that near the end of the descent there are multiple options for connecting with Oneidas and/or returning to Meyers. You need to go west (or northwest) if you

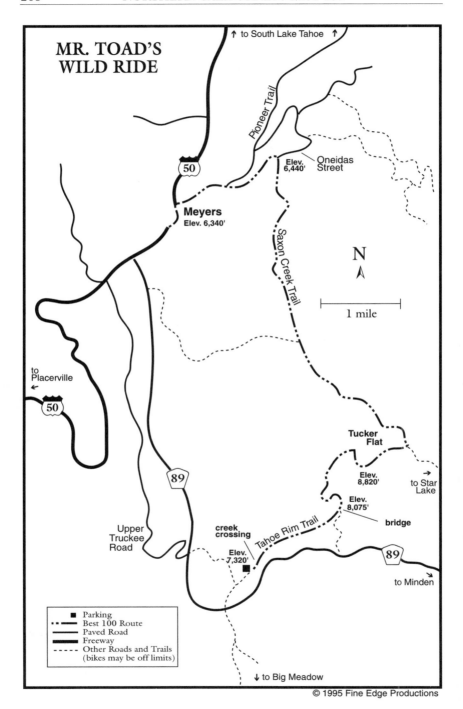

MR. TOAD'S WILD RIDE

↑ to South Lake Tahoe ↑

Pioneer Trail

50

Elev. 6,440' Oneidas Street

Meyers
Elev. 6,340'

Saxon Creek Trail

N
∧

1 mile

to Placerville
←

50

Tucker Flat

Elev. 8,820'   → to Star Lake

Elev. 8,075'

89

bridge

creek crossing   Tahoe Rim Trail

Upper Truckee Road

Elev. 7,320'

89

to Minden →

■ Parking
∙─∙─ Best 100 Route
── Paved Road
▬▬ Freeway
─ ─ Other Roads and Trails
(bikes may be off limits)

↓ to Big Meadow

© 1995 Fine Edge Productions

find yourself off the beaten path. Turn left on Oneidas, then at 11.5 miles turn left on Pioneer Trail. At 12.5 miles go left on U.S. 50. Three-fourths of a mile later, your ride ends in Meyers.

Options: As noted earlier, some cyclists ride Mr. Toad's Wild Ride as a loop, which extends the mileage from 13.25 miles to nearly 19 miles by adding the highway stretch from Meyers to Big Meadows Trailhead.

To add more miles on dirt—if you reach Oneidas Street with plenty of time and energy remaining—consider turning right. Oneidas very soon turns to a dirt road and climbs into the hills. The grade is modest and the scenery is great. It is common for mountain bikers to park their cars on Oneidas and make that road and the roads it connects with an afternoon ride. It is possible to go a few miles to the north and connect with Pioneer Trail, and then head south to create a loop.

75 Horse Canyon/ Carson-Mormon Emigrant Trail

Distance: 14.5 miles; 18.5 if you ride the pavement to complete the loop
Difficulty: Strenuous because of climbing and elevation, technical
Elevation: 7,200' to 9,000'
Ride Type: Loop or shuttle on dirt roads, trails, and pavement
Season: Mid-June through mid-October
Topo Maps: Caples Lake, Tragedy Springs, Mokelumne Peak, Bear River Reservoir (7.5 min.); Fine Edge South Lake Tahoe Basin Recreation Topo Map
Comments: No water in the first 9 miles. When you reach the Horse Canyon Trail, the creek at the top runs through July but can be dry by the end of summer. Treat all water.

Overview: This is one of the all-time great trails and jeep road rides. The entire ride is from 7,200 feet to just over 9,000 feet. Cyclists can enjoy a high-alpine experience while following one of the original pioneer trails. Called the Carson-Mormon Emigrant Trail, this route has been marked with monuments made from railroad irons. If you see them, they're worth stopping to read. This ride is only for those of you who enjoy beautiful high-alpine terrain, incredible wildflowers and don't mind walking and pushing your bike a bit to get there. You climb from 7,200 feet to over 9,000 feet in 9 miles. Much of this is rideable, except for a few short steep uphill sections.

Getting There: The best way to do this ride is to leave one vehicle at Oyster Creek Picnic Area, at the Silver Lake Campgrounds, or somewhere near Silver Lake on Highway 88. This eliminates 4 miles of mostly uphill riding on pavement. To get there from Placerville, go south on Highway 49 and east on Highway 88 to the north end of Silver Lake. The Picnic Area is on your right.

From South Lake Tahoe, head south on Highway 89 to Highway 88. Go west to the north end of Silver Lake. The Picnic Area is on your left.

After leaving one car at Oyster Creek, drive another car or ride your bikes to Tragedy Springs just southwest of Silver Lake on Highway 88.

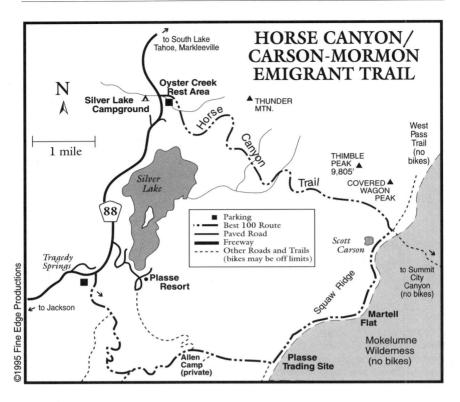

Route: From Highway 88, turn left (south) on Mud Lake Road, across the Highway from Tragedy Springs. At 2.6 miles go left at the sign that says *Allen Camp 2 miles.* (The road to the right goes to Mud Lake.) After another 1.2 miles look off to your left and you'll see a motorcycle trail that goes down to Silver Lake. At about 4.0 miles you reach Allen Camp. All that is left is an old cabin at the edge of the meadow. This is private land, so please stay on the designated roads through the area.

Continue on the newer road (the one not blocked off) which keeps you out of most of the mud. After 1.3 miles of climbing you reach Squaw Ridge. (A right down Squaw Ridge leads to Bear River Reservoir, also a good ride if you leave a car at the reservoir for a shuttle.) Along the ridge you should see railroad iron monuments giving historical information about the Mormon-Carson Emigrant Trail of 1848.

The road you are riding on is an actual wagon route used to settle the lands farther to the west. As you climb higher in elevation and start huffing and puffing for oxygen, think about how it was to get a wagon over some of the rocky stretches! All the way up the ridge you ride along the edge of the Mokelumne Wilderness Area. All roads and trails to the south (right) are closed to mechanized vehicles! *Please keep your bike on the road.*

You're at the top 3.5 miles later—and the end of the road that's open to mountain bikes. Hike over to the Wilderness Boundary and take a look down Summit City Canyon. Take a break, then follow the motorcycle signs for Horse Canyon Trail. (Turn left at the vehicle closure sign.) The first 0.75 mile is rough along the creek bed, but after that the trail is a blast with only occasional rough spots!

Take a topo map along so you can pick out Thimble Peak and Covered Wagon Peak. This is the back side of Kirkwood Ski Resort. Some 5 miles later you'll reach Highway 88. If you left a car at Oyster Creek Picnic Area, you're done (14.5 miles). If you started at Tragedy Springs, turn left on 88 towards Silver Lake and ride back to where you parked your car. This ride can also be done in reverse, starting from Oyster Creek Picnic Area, riding up the Horse Canyon Trail and down the jeep road. The motorcycle trail is more rideable in the downhill direction, but this loop is fun and spectacular in either direction!

76 Burnside Lake

Distance: 13.6 miles
Difficulty: Intermediate or better; optional expert trail section
Elevation: Begin/end 7,056', high point 8.200'
Ride Type: Out-and-back on dirt road, with some trail options and a long trail/pavement loop option
Season: June through October
Topo Maps: Carson Pass and Freel Peak (7.5 min.); Fine Edge South Lake Tahoe Basin Recreation Topo Map

Overview: This is a good ride for increasing your endurance. Best of all, it is located near Grover Hot Springs and State Park (with campground) just outside the town of Markleeville. The hot springs can be a real treat after a day of riding. To get there, go east 5 miles on Highway 88, turn right onto Highway 89 and follow the sings to Markleeville. Once in town, look for the Grover State Park sign, where you turn right and continue out to the park.

Getting There: From South Lake Tahoe, take Highway 50 west to Meyers, then Highway 89 south to the junction with Highway 88 (Pickett's Junction). Go straight across Highway 88 onto a dirt road and park out of the way of through traffic. This area seems to be a popular camping spot during fishing and hunting season. It may look

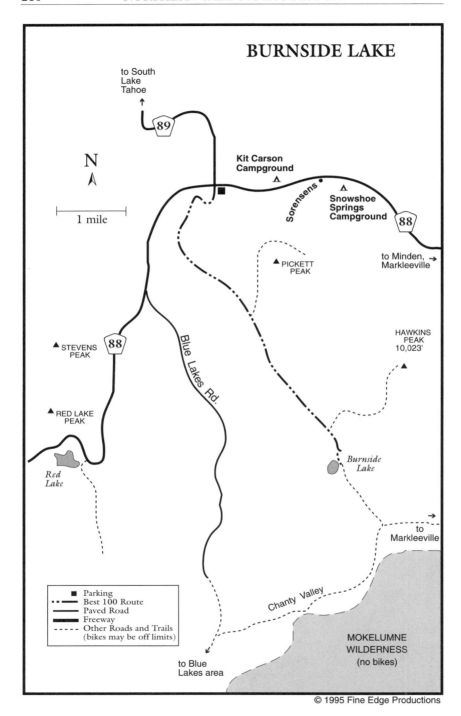

BURNSIDE LAKE

to South
Lake
Tahoe

89

N

1 mile

Kit Carson
Campground

Sorensens

Snowshoe
Springs
Campground

88

to Minden,
Markleeville

PICKETT
PEAK

HAWKINS
PEAK
10,023'

STEVENS
PEAK

88

Blue Lakes Rd.

RED LAKE
PEAK

Red
Lake

Burnside
Lake

to
Markleeville

Chanty Valley

■ Parking
Best 100 Route
Paved Road
Freeway
Other Roads and Trails
(bikes may be off limits)

MOKELUMNE
WILDERNESS
(no bikes)

to Blue
Lakes area

© 1995 Fine Edge Productions

crowded, but hardly anyone goes out this road except during deer hunting season in the fall.

Route: The directions are easy. Follow the dirt road 6.2 miles to Burnside Lake. You can see roads taking off to the left that you may want to explore for extra mileage. Most of them climb quickly. At 3.2 miles the road to the left contours around Pickett Peak. Another left at 5.7 miles is for the "peak bagger" in the crowd. It goes to Hawkins Peak (10,023'), with about 1,800 feet of climbing. Don't attempt it on a hot day, since there is no shade on the peak.

At 6.2 miles you reach Burnside Lake. If you continue on, the road turns into a trail that offers good introductory trail riding for about 0.6 mile. At that point you reach the edge of a canyon, and Markleeville is below you. The view is worth the effort, even for those who would rather walk the trail section. When you are done sight-seeing, ride back the way you came in.

Expert downhill riders may want to continue on the trail into the canyon beyond the overlook. It is about a 3-mile descent, and most riders have to walk down some of the switchbacks. Please control your speed and watch out for hikers. Unless you have a shuttle waiting at the bottom, ride the pavement from Markleeville back to your vehicle at Pickett Junction. This makes for quite a long haul with a sustained uphill on Highway 88, so if you want to do this ride, consult your maps and make preparations accordingly.

For additional rides in this area, please refer to *Mountain Biking the High Sierra, Guide 3A, Lake Tahoe South,* by R. W. Miskimins and Carol Bonser, ISBN 0-938665-40-5 (see p. 303).

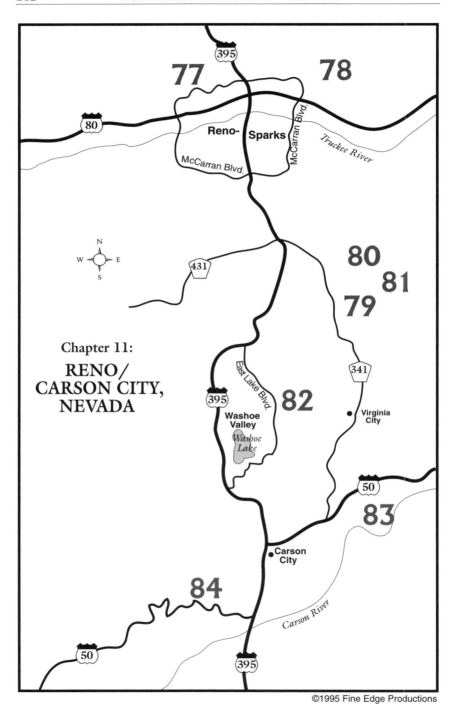

Chapter 11:
**RENO/
CARSON CITY,
NEVADA**

CHAPTER 11

Reno/Carson City, Nevada

by R.W. Miskimins

The climate, the hills and the "wild west" outdoor attitude of Nevadans make mountain biking extremely popular in the northern part of the state. Most of the population lives in the Truckee Meadows, or Washoe and Eagle valleys, each pretty much surrounded by mountain ranges. There is always the option of riding in one of the valleys or picking a nearby hill and trying to climb it. The popular mountain bike rides for the Reno-Carson City area, including the ones offered in this guidebook, provide a lot of variety in terrain—from tall pine forests to juniper and scrub-pine-covered highlands, sagebrush-covered hills, and barren dry lake beds.

Generally, heading west from the valleys leads to pine forests and heading east takes you to more arid country. The elevations of the rides described in this chapter range from 4,400 to over 8,000 feet. Included as features of interest are sites of several now extinct mining towns and cattle ranches,

3,000-year-old Native American petroglyphs, lakes (both wet and dry), creeks, springs, a couple of rivers, and plenty of fantastic views of both mountains and valleys. One thing for sure about the state of Nevada—there is a re-markable amount of unpopulated, open ter-ritory, making it a great place to ride a moun-tain bike!

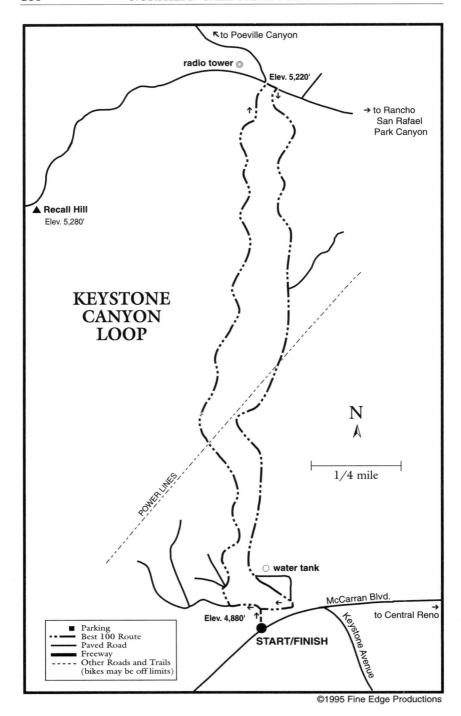

KEYSTONE
CANYON
LOOP

to Poeville Canyon

radio tower ◎

Elev. 5,220'

→ to Rancho
San Rafael
Park Canyon

▲ Recall Hill
Elev. 5,280'

N
^

1/4 mile

POWER LINES

○ water tank

McCarran Blvd.

to Central Reno →

Keystone Avenue

Elev. 4,880'

START/FINISH

■ Parking
∙—∙ ∙— ∙ Best 100 Route
Paved Road
Freeway
Other Roads and Trails
(bikes may be off limits)

©1995 Fine Edge Productions

77 Keystone Canyon Loop

Distance: 3.75 miles
Difficulty: Moderate, somewhat technical
Elevation: Begin/end 4,880'; 5,280' high point
Ride Type: Out-and-back on dirt roads and singletrack, loop option
Season: Year-round
Topo Map: Reno (7.5 min.)

Overview: This ride, located in the southeastern foothills of Peavine Peak, is most commonly called Keystone Canyon, but dubbed by some as "Upper Canyon" (those using the latter name usually call Rancho San Rafael Park Canyon "Lower Canyon"). The name Keystone Canyon comes from the fact that the trailhead is located just east of the intersection of Keystone and McCarran. This is a delightful ride up an interesting little canyon, some of it on singletrack. The entire route, up and back, is only 3.75 miles long and has a total elevation gain of 400 feet if you take the high road loop back to McCarran (340 feet if you just turn around and come back down the canyon). With caution in a couple of rocky sections, this ride is suited to riders of all levels.

Getting There: From downtown Reno, take Virginia Street (business 395) north to McCarran and turn left. Go west on McCarran to a point just past Keystone. Look for the parking area on the north side of McCarran, almost directly under a giant, light brown water storage tank.

Route: From the parking area along McCarran, ride through the gate and follow the main road swinging to the left. After a few hundred feet you encounter a fork—bear right. Then turn right to go under power lines (through here, if you look to the right

you can see the canyon you are headed for). Stay on the main road to drop into Keystone Canyon. Head up the canyon on the two-track jeep trail. At just over 0.5 mile you simultaneously ride through the wash and under high power lines. At 0.75 mile go straight ahead into the rocky wash (don't turn left to steep uphill).

At just under 1 mile you go through the wash and switch to singletrack. This section of the ride, 0.75 of a mile in length, is what has made Keystone Canyon popular—watch for high-speed bike traffic coming the other way! Check out the interesting rock formations and varieties of flora. At a little over 1.75 miles, back on two-track jeep trail, you reach an area of radio towers. Just before you actually reach the first tower is a four-way intersection—here there are some choices to make.

For advanced or expert riders who like a challenge, try a side trip to the left. A left turn in front of the first tower starts a 1-mile climb to the top of Recall Hill (an elevation gain of nearly 650 feet and some of it unrideable). This side trip is not recommended for beginners, but provides the hardy with a fantastic view of the Truckee Meadows when they reach the top.

For the adventurous, you can go west from the top, then downhill to the south and come out on McCarran about 1.5 miles west of

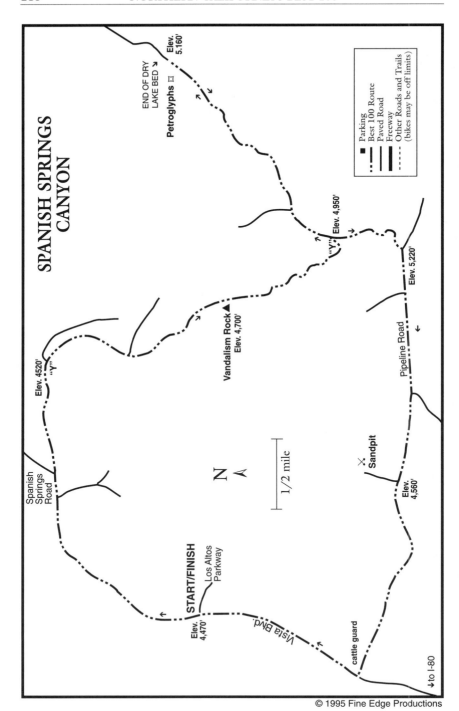

SPANISH SPRINGS CANYON

Elev. 5,160'

END OF DRY LAKE BED ↗

Petroglyphs ⊞

"Y" Elev. 4,950'

Elev. 5,220'

Vandalism Rock ▲ Elev. 4,700'

"Y" Elev. 4520'

Pipeline Road

Spanish Springs Road

Sandpit ✕

Elev. 4,560'

N

1/2 mile

START/FINISH

Los Altos Parkway

Elev. 4,470'

Vista Blvd

cattle guard

↘ to I-80

Parking ■
Best 100 Route
Paved Road
Freeway
Other Roads and Trails (bikes may be off limits)

© 1995 Fine Edge Productions

Keystone (not shown on map). Another choice at the four-way intersection is to go straight ahead and by maintaining a northwesterly direction intersect with Poeville Canyon (in this maze of jeep trails it's a little difficult to do it the first time you try). Once at Poeville Canyon you can climb up to the main Peavine Peak road or drop down to North Virginia Street (at Seneca in Horizon Hills).

Those not interested in side trips must make a choice at the four-way intersection just before the radio towers. Either make a U-turn and go back down the canyon (a great downhill experience, especially around banked corners) or turn right for an alternate route back to your starting point. The two routes back are the same distance (total ride of 3.75 miles), but the right turn adds a little

climbing. To do the "loop," turn right at the four-way intersection, ride through the wash and up the little hill. Immediately past the fence line turn right again and head uphill south, following the fence line. Your road swings away from the fence for a short distance (don't take roads to the left) and then back uphill to rejoin it. On your left through here is a large flat—directly to the east of it is Rancho San Rafael Park Canyon, another nice place to ride. At 2.75 miles from your starting point you ride through a gate and shortly thereafter pass a small power station. Go past the power station and then bear right at the fork (stay along power lines) at 3 miles. Follow the main road south, then down to the parking area along McCarran to conclude your ride.

78 Spanish Springs Canyon

Distance: 16 miles
Difficulty: Strenuous, technical
Elevation: Begin/end 4,470'; 5,220' high point
Ride Type: Loop on dirt and paved roads
Season: Spring, summer, fall
Topo Map: Vista (7.5 min.)

Overview: Around the turn of the century, local landowners dubbed an area of natural springs in the Pah Rah Range "Spanish," because they were frequented by Mexican squatters. Today, Spanish Springs Canyon and the dry lake beds above it give cyclists a feeling of the Nevada "outback" even though you are actually very close to town. For much of the ride you cannot see any signs of the nearby urban population (other than the inevitable litter along the road).

This ride is suited to advanced mountain bikers and above. It is not

extraordinarily long but involves some steep and rocky ascents and descents. There are a couple of hills where only very strong riders can avoid getting off their bikes and walking.

Getting There: From downtown Reno, go north on Virginia Street (business 395) to McCarran Boulevard and turn right. Follow McCarran to northeast Sparks (where McCarran swings south), and then turn onto Baring Boulevard. Go east, past Reed High School, until Baring ends at a T. There you turn left onto Vista

Boulevard. Follow Vista until the pavement ends (just past Los Altos Parkway). There is room to park on the right.

Route: From Los Altos Parkway head north on Vista. After about 1.5 miles you swing to the right and head due east. At 2.25 miles the main road turns left to the north, but you go straight ahead on a wide dirt road. Ride on this road until you reach a Y at 3.5 miles— proceed on the smaller road, the right fork. Follow this road south, to the mouth of Spanish Springs Canyon, ignoring little roads to the right and left. At 5.5 miles from where you started you'll see Vandalism Rock, a large boulder on your right with white paint reading "Bud Loop." Continue ahead for a gentle climb on up the canyon.

Near the end of this box canyon there is an intersection, a Y (at almost 6.5 miles). You must turn left here and ride up the steep hill to the top (it is possible to shorten your total ride to 12 miles by turning right here, but you miss the very interesting dry lake area). After the climb, follow the main road down along the edge of the large dry lake bed. The lake bed has rounded black lava rocks strewn all over with soft sand and silt. It calls to mind a lunarscape.

At 8.5 miles the lake bed ends. At this point look uphill to your left; the very large rock outcropping on the hillside has some interesting Native American petroglyph art. These carvings include several bighorn sheep

and rattlesnakes, and are estimated to be about 3,000 years old. Please do not disturb them! And if you see anyone vandalizing them (it is illegal, as well as immoral, to disturb them and the penalties are substantial), please report it to the Washoe County Sheriff. Pause here for a rest break and hike up the hill to see fascinating prehistoric rock art.

After your break, turn around and return the 2 miles back to the intersection at the top of Spanish Springs Canyon (10.5 miles). Go left at this intersection and soon you climb another steep hill. Up on top, as you go past a road coming from the left, a view of the Truckee Meadows appears (11.25 miles). Head downhill, following the main road to the west— you have merged with Pipeline Road. There is a right turn to a large sand pit at 13 miles (you continue straight ahead). This intersection marks the base of a very steep hill. Proceed ahead (west), following the power lines to Vista Boulevard (14 miles). Turn right onto Vista and ride the shoulder for two miles to return to where you started.

79 Virginia Mountains to the Valley

Distance: 13.5 miles
Difficulty: Moderate, somewhat technical
Elevation: Begin 5,790'; 5,960' high point
Ride Type: Can be done as an out-and-back, loop or shuttle
Season: Spring, summer, fall
Topo Map: Steamboat (7.5 min.)

Overview: The Virginia Mountains offer an interesting and very scenic high desert ride. The mountain range and Virginia City were named after "Old Virginia" Fennimore, a prospector who lived and worked around the Comstock in the 1850s. You ride in sagebrush covered hills dotted with cedars and pines—interesting and beautiful high desert terrain. There are herds of wild horses roaming the highlands, as well as numerous other animals and birds.

This ride, from the fire station to Highway 341, is best suited to intermediate or better cyclists. The climbs, except for one short steep portion near the top, are relatively easy. The difficulty is in the descent—it is long and sometimes steep and rocky. There are repeated possibilities for novice riders to lose control and crash. If you choose to cycle Virginia Mountains to the Valley (to Highway 341) as an out-and-back (27 miles), then it becomes an expert ride (double the distance and considerably steeper climbing)—when going back to the fire station you climb from 4,420 feet (at the power station) to 5,960 in just a few miles!

Getting There: Heading south from Reno on U.S. 395, drive 10 miles to the Mt. Rose junction and turn left onto Highway 341 toward Virginia City. Climb Geiger Grade (341) up to the Virginia Highlands turnoff (about 7 miles). Turn left onto Cartwright Road. Follow Cartwright a little over 3 miles to its junction with Lousetown Road (watch for the fire station). There is plenty of parking near this intersection. Unless you want to ride a long and arduous loop (described later) or to backtrack the ride outlined herein (also difficult), you need to have a car waiting for you at the power station near Mira Loma (8.5-mile ride) or at the intersection of Mira Loma and Highway 341 (just over 13.5 miles).

Route: The ride begins at the intersection of Cartwright Road and Lousetown Road (next to the fire station). Head north on Lousetown Road and you'll pass Panamint (just over 0.25 mile), Wildrose (just over 0.75 mile) and Bull Frog (1 mile). Two miles from Cartwright Road and after crossing the creek bed twice, a network of roads appears ahead (including one to a house in the canyon to the west). This is the site of "Lousetown," a small burg populated by thieves and scoundrels during Virginia City's heyday (mid-1800s). Apparently, this settlement was originally called Louisetown, but due to the nature of the folks who populated it, the name was changed. Very little indication of the dozens of buildings and the racetrack that used to be there can be found today.

Avoid roads to the left and the

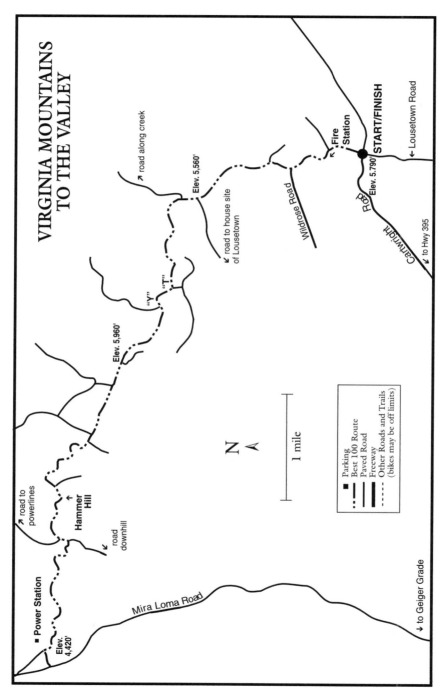

VIRGINIA MOUNTAINS TO THE VALLEY

road along creek

Elev. 5,560'

road to house site of Lousetown

"Y"

"T"

Elev. 5,960'

Fire Station

START/FINISH

Wildrose Road

Cartwright Road

Elev. 5,790'

Lousetown Road

to Hwy 395

road to powerlines

Hammer Hill

road downhill

Power Station

Elev. 4,420'

Mira Loma Road

to Geiger Grade

N

1 mile

■ Parking

·—·— Best 100 Route

Paved Road

Freeway

······ Other Roads and Trails (bikes may be off limits)

© 1995 Fine Edge Productions

low road to the right which continues along Lousetown Creek. Just to the left of that creekside road you can see another road headed gently up the hillside—this begins the 2-mile, mostly gradual climb to the flats up high in the Virginia Mountain Range. At 3.5 miles you'll encounter a T; turn right and continue to a Y (3.75 miles) where you turn left. The crest is just over 4 miles from the fire station and offers your first view of downtown Reno. This begins several miles of panoramic views of the Truckee Meadows with a high mountain (Carson Range) backdrop. Continue on the main road, ignoring left and right turns. At about 6 miles the descent steepens, and about 0.50 mile later you'll encounter Hammer Hill—this is a short little "up one side and down the other" hill. After you carefully go down the backside of the hill, for a challenge turn around at the lone tree and try to ride back up!

Continue, ignoring side roads (mostly headed up to power lines). At about 7.25 miles there is a four-way intersection—do not take the road to the left headed downhill or the one to

the right uphill to the power poles. You want the road that goes straight very briefly then curls around the hillside to the right. Stay on the main road, descending to the power station (8.5 miles) back in the valley. To get to Highway 341, turn left in front of the power station, go 0.25 mile to Mira Loma, turn left and follow it for 4.75 miles to Geiger Grade and a total ride of 13.75 miles.

Advanced riders should consider a full loop starting with the 6-mile Toll Road Climb (consult your topo map). Access the Toll Road off of Geiger Grade, about 0.5 mile east of U.S. 395. When Toll Road ends, just ride across Highway 341 onto Cartwright Road and follow it to Lousetown Road (as described above under "Getting There"). The advanced rider's loop is as follows: (a) Toll Road Climb (6 miles); (b) Cartwright Road to the fire station (3 miles); (c) fire station to Mira Loma (8.75 miles); and (d) Mira Loma to Highway 341 and Toll Road (4.75 miles). This entire loop involves plenty of climbing and descending and a total of 22.75 miles.

80 Lagomarsino Petroglyphs

Distance: 15 miles
Difficulty: Strenuous, technical
Elevation: Begin/end 5,790'; 6,040' high point
Ride Type: Out-and-back on dirt road
Season: Spring, summer, fall
Topo Map: Steamboat and Chalk Hills (7.5 min.)

Overview: Deep in the Virginia Mountain Range, which borders the Truckee Meadows (Reno-Sparks area) to the east, is located one of the West's finest petroglyph sites. Petroglyphs ("rock writing") are figures, lines and symbols carved by

Native Americans on the face of boulders. The designation "Lagomarsino" comes from the name of a rancher who in years past grazed cattle in the area. This site has hundreds of well-preserved petroglyphs dating between 2,000 and 5,000 years. The canyon containing the rock art is believed to have been a game ambush site and the carvings are thought to represent magic to help the Indians in their hunt.

This ride is best suited to advanced mountain bikers. Although the entire run (out and back) is only 15 miles, very little of it is flat. With several ascents and descents, many of them very rocky– the highest elevation is 6,040 feet and the lowest is 5040—there are repeated possibilities for novice riders to lose control and crash. Taken cautiously, with some walking on steep hills, strong intermediates may also enjoy this ride.

Getting There: Heading south from Reno on U.S. 395, drive 10 miles to the Mt. Rose Junction and turn left onto Highway 341 toward Virginia City. Climb Geiger Grade (341) up to the Virginia Highlands turnoff (about 7 miles) and turn left onto Cartwright Road. Follow Cartwright a little over 3 miles to its junction with Lousetown Road (fire station). There is plenty of parking near this intersection.

Route: The ride begins at the fire station at the intersection of Cartwright Road and Lousetown Road. Go east on Cartwright, past Bull Frog to a road labeled Aurora (a little under 1 mile). Turn left onto Aurora and go to Panamint (1.25 miles from the fire station). Turn right and climb Panamint hill, then

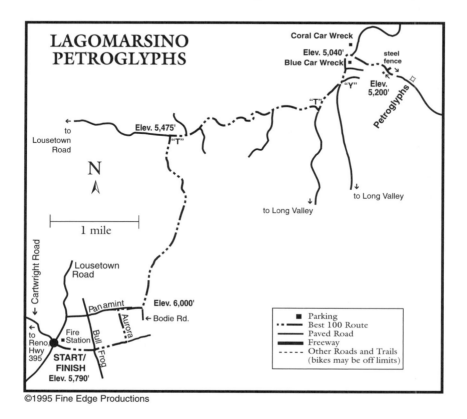

LAGOMARSINO
PETROGLYPHS

©1995 Fine Edge Productions

swing left at Bodie (just over 1.5 miles). Follow this road until you encounter a T (at about 4 miles), and then turn right. Make sure you can find this turn again for your return trip. Stay on the main road, headed east, until you reach another T at 6 miles from the fire station. Turn left at this T, then 0.25 mile later go left at the Y. Ride north down toward the creek (you'll intersect and follow power lines)—look for a blue wrecked car (at about 6.5 miles). This wreck marks an old home site (consider a little exploring here to find some building remains, a beautiful tree-lined cottonwood canyon, and some remarkable hand-stacked rock fences).

Continue north past the blue wreck until you reach the coral-colored car wreck (about 0.25 mile apart). The road swings right, past the coral wreck into a Y—take the road furthest to the right (immediately cross the creek bed and swing left, then right to start a slow steady climb up the canyon). On your left, at about 7.25 miles, you can see a small grouping of petroglyphs. Shortly thereafter you'll pass through a short steel fence and at just under 7.5 miles you reach a large turnaround area. Take the road to the left (a short, steep down and up) and you can ride right alongside the main concentration of petroglyphs (7.5 miles).

The carvings are almost non-stop from the road level all the way to the rim rock. Get off your bike, hike around and enjoy. You can see big-horn sheep, human figures, snakes, birds, circles, grids, rakes, spirals, lizards, groups of dots, and lots of lines both straight and wavy. For some, interpretations come easily; but for many of these carvings, you will have to stretch your imagination to figure out their mystical purpose. The area is a "designated archaeological site," making vandalism here illegal as well as immoral. Please do not in any way alter or deface this remarkable prehistoric art museum—let's save it, in good condition, for the generations that follow us. If you witness any vandalism, please report it to the Storey County Sheriff's Office.

81 Long Valley Loop

Distance: 19.75 miles
Difficulty: Strenuous, technical
Elevation: Begin/end 6,460'; 5,120' low point
Ride Type: Dirt road out-and-back with a loop
Season: Spring, summer, fall
Topo Maps: Virginia City and Flowery Peak (7.5 min.)

Overview: For an enjoyable tour through the high desert, this is a great ride. There are pines and junipers, fascinating rock formations, bubbling springs and green meadows and interesting little canyons. Virtually any time of the year you can see herds of wild horses—hundreds of mustangs live in this area.

This loop is best suited to cyclists with advanced technical skills and endurance. Riders with less

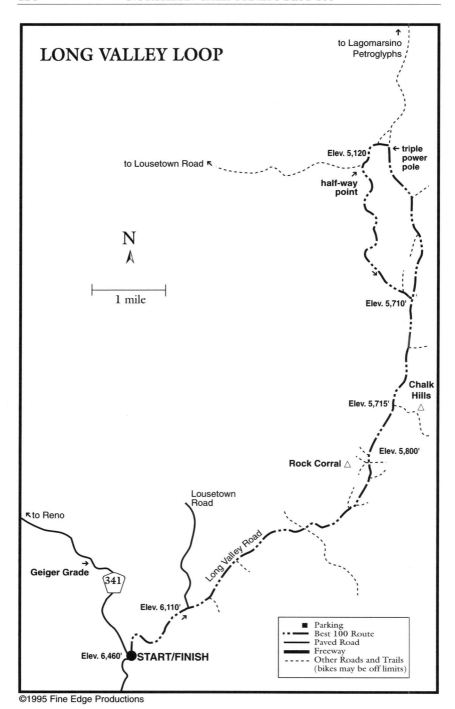

LONG VALLEY LOOP

to Lagomarsino Petroglyphs

to Lousetown Road

Elev. 5,120'

← triple power pole

half-way point

N

1 mile

Elev. 5,710'

Chalk Hills

Elev. 5,715'

Elev. 5,800'

Rock Corral △

Lousetown Road

to Reno

Long Valley Road

Geiger Grade

341

Elev. 6,110'

Elev. 6,460' ● START/FINISH

■ Parking
▬·▬· Best 100 Route
▬▬ Paved Road
▬▬ Freeway
---- Other Roads and Trails
(bikes may be off limits)

©1995 Fine Edge Productions

experience frequently run the first few miles of it; the ride out to the rock corral and back is relatively flat and only 9.5 miles total distance. There are several sections beyond the rock corral that are steep uphill or downhill and/or very rocky. To avoid a lot of walking, you should have good technical riding ability and enough endurance to keep rolling for 20 miles. The highest elevation is at the start next to Geiger Grade (6,460') and the lowest you will encounter is just prior to the halfway point, over 1,300 feet less (5,120').

Getting There: Heading south from Reno on U.S. 395, drive 10 miles to the Mt. Rose junction and turn left onto Highway 341 toward Virginia City. Go up Geiger Grade (341) and watch for the turn about 2 miles past the summit (Geiger Summit is identified by a highway sign). The turn is labeled "Lousetown Road"—make a left turn and park your vehicle in the parking area just off the highway.

Route: Begin your ride by heading north on Lousetown Road. When you encounter a fork at 1.25 miles, bear right onto Long Valley Road. Stay on this road as it heads northeast. You pass under power lines at just over 3.75 miles.

At about 4 miles, begin a brief descent to the fork in the road around 4.5 miles. Go left at this Y and 0.25 mile later you pass an "oasis"—look for the remains of a handbuilt rock corral and numerous trees just below it. Either now or on your return trip, consider some exploring. In the little canyon right behind the corral are natural year-around springs, tall trees, green grass, a little creek and a tiny pond.

From the rock corral take the road going northeast (alongside the power poles). Follow the power lines and at almost 5.5 miles you'll pass the remains of an old wooden corral on your left; then at 5.75 miles you encounter "Chalk Hills" on your right (very light colored low hills). There is a fork just before you pass these hills— the two roads rejoin (at 6 miles) so take either option here. At just under 6.25 miles, the road forks again. Take the road to the left. The loop portion of this ride begins at 7.25 miles—as you're climbing bear right. Very soon thereafter you crest the hill and then descend for several minutes. This downhill ends at 7.75 miles (you go through a wash and immediately head uphill). You'll crest the next hill at 8.25 miles and encounter panoramic views to the north. The next 1.5 miles is all downhill, sometimes steep and sometimes rocky.

At 9.75 miles from the start of this ride, next to a power structure with three poles, swing left under the power lines (continuing straight ahead takes you to the Lagomarsino Petroglyphs). Do not turn right a few hundred feet later, but swing left and up a gentle hill. You pass a right turn (it goes west to Lousetown Road) at 10 miles—don't turn here, but note that this spot marks the halfway point on this ride.

Continue south and soon you start a long 2-mile uphill. Climb to the top, then descend briefly to reach the fork where the "loop" started. Go right to retrace your route all the way back to Geiger Grade. At about 14 miles you pass the Chalk Hills again, and around 15 miles is the rock corral. When you reach 18.5 miles, Long Valley Road rejoins Lousetown Road, and at just over 19.75 miles you are back to where you started next to Geiger Grade.

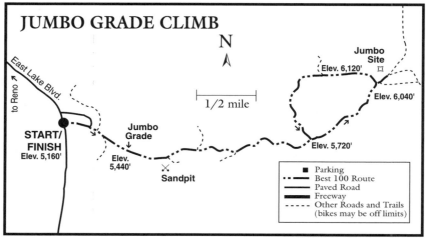

©1995 Fine Edge Productions

82 Jumbo Grade Climb

Distance: 6.5 miles
Difficulty: Moderate, somewhat technical
Elevation: Begin/end 5,160'; 6,120' high point
Ride Type: Dirt road out-and-back with a loop
Season: Summer, fall
Topo Maps: Washoe City and Virginia City (7.5 min.)

Overview: The Jumbo Grade Climb takes you into the Virginia Range to a loop through an area with numerous old mines. The flat along the creek below the mines was the location of an early twentieth-century camp named Jumbo. There was a post office there from April 1908 to November 1910. The nearby mines include Boss Jumbo, Mahoney, Campbell, Empire and Pandora.

The ride is for strong intermediate or better cyclists. It is only 6.5 miles long, but involves nearly 1,000 feet of elevation gain in the first 3.5 miles and some steep downhilling on your return trip.

Getting There: To reach the starting point for this ride, go south on U.S. 395 from Reno to East Lake Boulevard (a left turn off of 395, about 15 miles south of downtown Reno). Take East Lake south, about 4 miles, to Jumbo Grade (identified by a street sign). There is plenty of space across East Lake to park vehicles.

Route: To begin this ride take the paved road east. At just under 0.5 mile bear left, across the cattle guard, onto a dirt road—stay on the main road, riding along the wash. You reach another fork at 1 mile. Bear left to stay along the wash (don't turn right through an iron gate, into a sand pit). Throughout this area there are many side roads (made by motorcycles and 4-wheel drive vehicles) to play on if you choose, but your main route continues on up the canyon, along the wash. Springs and trees and shrubs make this part of the ride very scenic. At 2 miles you cross the wash. Year round, even in a drought, there is some spring water flowing here. Just ahead is a fork. Go right and through the wash again (continue on the main road, staying along the tree-lined wash/creek).

At just over 2.5 miles, just past large concrete pylons on your right, you reach another fork. The left is a very steep, short hill (it goes up and out of the wash and is badly rutted). You can bear right, avoiding the little hill, and ride in the wash, if there is not much water in it. After about 100 yards the road is up above the wash again; continue up the canyon. At 3 miles your trail makes a sharp right, downhill through the wash and back up. Here you enter a small, relatively flat area—ahead and to your left is the site of the mining camp called Jumbo. The Jumbo site is a great area to explore. If you go right (east) and up the hill (about 0.33 mile) you reach a spring (grassy area and pond); if you continue east it is possible to connect with Ophir Grade leading into Virginia City. If you go straight, you encounter numerous trails and roads that ultimately can lead east toward Virginia City or west to Washoe Valley.

Immediately past the down and up through the wash at 3 miles is a left turn (goes northwest). To continue your loop, turn onto that road and ride through the wash. Stay on the main road as it winds

up the hill, then bear right at just over 3.25 miles (go left if you want to explore some of the work of the Pandora Mine). After bearing right at 3.25 miles bear left at another fork at 3.5 miles and ride past a dangerous, fenced mine shaft (it is on your right). Just after you bear left, look ahead and you can see a road winding up the hill in front of you—that is your route to the south. You can see Slide Mountain and Mt. Rose on your right to the west.

At the top of the hill stay on the main road, swinging left, then right and down the hill to the south (as you descend you can see Jumbo Grade down below). This is a serious, steep descent. You encounter a fork at just under 4 miles where you can go left, toward the concrete pylons to get back down to the bottom of the canyon. At 4 miles, turn right onto Jumbo Grade and head toward East Lake. At 5.75 miles you pass the iron gate and sand pit again. At just over 6.25 miles you ride over the cattle guard and back onto pavement. The ride ends when you rejoin East Lake Boulevard. If you did not explore or take any side trips, your ride was 6.5 miles long.

83 Carson River Loop

Distance: 10.5 miles
Difficulty: Moderate, somewhat technical
Elevation: Begin/end 4,610'; 4,800' high point
Ride Type: Dirt road out-and-back with a loop
Season: Year-round
Topo Map: New Empire (7.5 min.)

Overview: If you appreciate desert rivers, you will appreciate this ride. It provides interesting scenery from start to finish, and there is always a possibility of catching a glimpse of a wide assortment of wild creatures (including rattlesnakes).

The Carson River Loop is a ride of medium length (10.5 miles) and only moderate difficulty. It is well-suited to intermediate level cyclists or better.

Getting There: This ride is located a few miles east of Carson City, just off of U.S. 50. To get to the starting point from U.S. 395 (Carson Street), go east on U.S. 50 (William Street). Go past Airport Road and 4.25 miles from 395 turn right (south) on Deer Run Road. You encounter a bridge about 0.75 mile after the turn. Park along the river, just before and to the left of the bridge.

Route: This ride begins by heading east from the bridge on a wide gravel road. At 1 mile you can see a primitive bridge going across the river. If you cross it and follow the road up Brunswick Canyon, you'll encounter a maze of jeep trails—cyclists can explore for hours up there. Also across the bridge, there are roads going right alongside the river in both directions for more exploration opportunities. For the Carson River Loop, do not cross the bridge, but continue

straight ahead (the road gets smaller and rougher).

At 1.75 miles the road swings away from the river. To accomplish this, go straight at the four-way intersection (you won't ride past a tunnel-looking structure ahead on the left, but turn away from the river before it). At 2 miles from your starting point you pass a large, abandoned concrete structure (on your left). Go straight through here. A few hundred yards later you are back along the river again. Continue on the main road.

The road soon begins to climb steadily up the canyon wall, staying parallel with the Carson River. At just over 3.75 miles the road swings left, through a narrow draw. As you exit the draw you can see a road on your right. Don't turn now, but note that it is the road that completes the loop part of this ride. Continue, staying up high above the river.

At a little over 4.5 miles you ride under low power lines (right next to a power pole). Watch for a sharp right turn (headed downhill, following the power lines). Drop down and go through the creek and back up to a four-way intersection. Turn right here and head down the canyon, along (and sometimes through) the wash. You exit the canyon at just over 5.5 miles and work your way down to ride along the river's edge. Once you reach the river, you can turn left and ride east if you want to extend the ride and explore along the river. However, for the Carson River Loop, you continue heading south.

Pause here for a rest break if you like, but then double back up the little canyon a few hundred feet to pick up a road heading west (up and over the hill, then down to the river's edge). Ride upstream (southwesterly), following along the river.

At 6.25 miles you turn right and start up the hill. If you miss this turn, the road along the river dead ends. There is a fork at 6.5 miles— go right and continue climbing back to the main road (left goes down to the river). Look to your left at just under

6.75 miles to see the rock foundation remains of an old, turn of the century ranch house. At just over 6.75 miles, go right at the fork and keep climbing. (To the left is another road down to the river's edge.) You finish the loop portion of this ride, rejoining the main road at 7 miles. Then turn left and go back through the narrow draw.

From this point you retrace your route all the way back to where the ride started. At 8.5 miles you pass the large concrete structure again. At 9.5 miles you ride by the bridge to Brunswick Canyon. One mile later you reach your starting point, for a total ride of 10.5 miles.

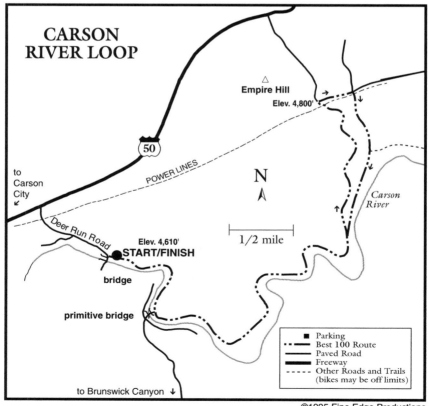

CARSON
RIVER LOOP

Empire Hill
Elev. 4,800'

50

to
Carson
City

POWER LINES

N

Deer Run Road

Elev. 4,610'
START/FINISH

Carson
River

1/2 mile

bridge

primitive bridge

■ Parking
Best 100 Route
Paved Road
Freeway
Other Roads and Trails
(bikes may be off limits)

to Brunswick Canyon ↓

84 Kings Canyon Climb

Distance: 19 miles
Difficulty: Strenuous, somewhat technical
Elevation: Begin/end 5,380'; 7,270' high point
Ride Type: Out-and-back on jeep road
Season: Summer, fall
Topo Maps: Carson City and Genoa (7.5 min.)

Overview: This is a delightful ride. It begins in the foothills and ends in a mountain forest. The entire route is on a non-maintained jeep road, so there is not a lot of traffic to contend with.

This ride is suited to advanced riders or better. Technically it is not particularly difficult, but it is long (9.5 miles each way, for a total ride of 19 miles) and the ride up to the road's end at Spooner Summit (Highway 50) involves an altitude gain of about 1,900 feet.

Many cyclists do not ride Kings Canyon as an out-and-back—they have someone drop them off on top

and they ride 9.5 miles back to the pavement, virtually all flat or downhill after the first 0.5 mile.

Getting There: To get to the trailhead, you first need to get on King Street in Carson City. It runs west, directly from the Nevada State Capitol (domed building). However, it no longer comes through to U.S. 395 (Carson Street)—it starts one block west. To get onto King Street turn west one block before or one block after the Capitol Building (Musser Street or Second Street), go a few blocks, then turn one block to King Street. Follow King west until

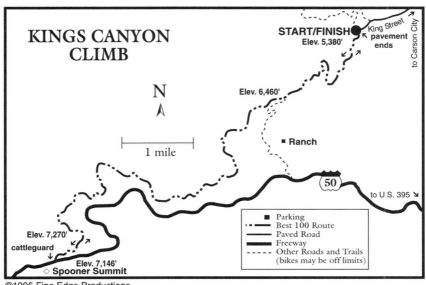

KINGS CANYON CLIMB

START/FINISH
Elev. 5,380'

King Street
pavement ends

to Carson City

N

1 mile

Elev. 6,460'

■ Ranch

50

to U.S. 395

Elev. 7,270'
cattleguard

Elev. 7,146'
◇ Spooner Summit

■ Parking
Best 100 Route
Paved Road
Freeway
Other Roads and Trails
(bikes may be off limits)

©1995 Fine Edge Productions

the pavement ends (3 miles from downtown). Park off the blacktop.

Route: At the trailhead, the end of the pavement, there are roads going right and left. The road to the right is gated and climbs very steeply up through private land to a mine. Take the road going left (south). Stay on this main road, climbing steadily and sometimes steeply. You achieve two-thirds of your elevation gain in the first 3 miles (over 400 feet per mile).

At just under 2.5 miles you encounter a fork—the left goes down-hill to a giant meadow and a ranch, the right is your route (continues climbing). Shortly after the fork, there is a breathtaking view to the south! At just under 3 miles you enter National Forest land. After 4 miles, the climb-ing eases and there is about 3 miles of fairly flat riding, followed by some more steep sections. At just under 9 miles, you reach your maximum el-evation (7,270') and start a brief downhill to the highway. When you cross the cattle guard just prior to the pavement you have ridden 9.5 miles.

For an out-and-back ride, turn around and retrace the route that brought you to Spooner Summit. If you would like a different road back to your starting point and don't mind pavement and the possibility of lots of traffic, you can descend back to U.S. 395 on U.S. 50 (9 miles). When you reach 395, ride north to pick up King Street (3 miles), then west to where you began (another 3 miles). This loop increases the total ride from 19 to 24.5 miles.

For additional rides in this area, please refer to *Guide 13, Mountain Biking the Reno-Carson City Area,* by R. W. Miskimins, ISBN 0-938665-22-7 (see p. 303).

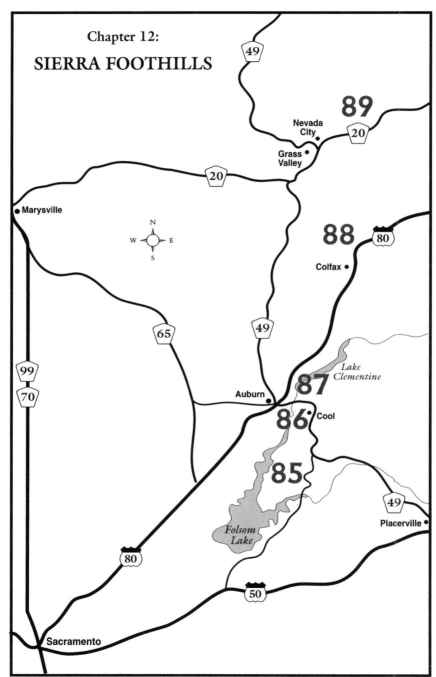

Chapter 12:

SIERRA FOOTHILLS

CHAPTER 12

Sierra Foothills

by Robin Stuart

Imagine a world of primeval beauty, where the trees reach all the way to the sky, the terrain varies between mellow fire roads and rugged singletrack, and the trail user conflicts consist of "after you." A perfect world? You bet. And the good news is that it really exists. About 20 miles north of Sacramento on Interstate 80, nestled below the jaw-dropping beauty of the northern Sierra Nevada mountain range is Placer County, an area commonly known as the Sierra Foothills.

This region is as rich with California history as the hills once were with gold. In fact, many of the hundreds of miles of trails that exist today were mining routes, blazed by those that heeded the call of the Mother Lode in 1849. Hanging out up here, you encounter far more old than new; the original buildings still stand, some lovingly restored and some which never fell into disrepair in the first place. Trains still roar through towns, and open mine shafts yawn from hillsides, deserted for over 100 years.

Through it all, fed by snow and rain runoff from the higher elevations, runs the American River. Its three forks, North, South and Middle, converge just south of Auburn and feed into Folsom Lake in Sacramento. Thanks to the heavy winter storms of the last few seasons that sloughed off layers of earth untouched for over a century, gold flakes, and even a few nuggets, have been found along the banks of the American, sparking a new wave of gold fever. Although gold mining has never gone completely out of style here, it hasn't enjoyed this much popularity since the early 1900s.

The foothill communities of Placer County, as well as its neighbors to the north, just recently realized that they sit on another type of gold mine. County planners and business associations, several members of which are mountain bikers themselves, have embraced the fat-tire movement, throwing open trails and aggressively marketing their services to us. Walk into any given visitor information center or Chamber of Commerce and identify yourself as a mountain biker, and you'll be welcomed like long-lost family and handed bundles of information proclaiming the foothills "Mountain Bike Country." People in local grocery stores and restaurants love us, too. They are apparently well aware of our post-ride appetites!

Looking for big-city, flashy-jersey attitude at the trailhead? Sorry, none of that here. There is a lot of smiling, chatting and waving to and from passers-by, however. Hikers will likely startle you with the boisterousness of their cheery greetings, and horseback riders (they don't call them "equestrians" up here) will warn you of any dangers up ahead before wishing you a pleasant ride.

The following trails are a sample plate of what you can find in this neck of the woods. They're the rides that locals take their out-of-town friends on. Once you try them, you'll see why. So, warm up your waving hand, smile like you mean it and practice saying "hi" really loud.

85 Salmon Falls Trail

Distance: 16 miles
Difficulty: Moderately strenuous, mildly technical
Elevation: 500' gain/loss
Ride Type: Out-and-back on singletrack
Season: Spring through fall
Topo Maps: Pilot Hill, Clarksville (route not shown on maps)
Comments: Water is available at the turnaround point. Be on the lookout for rattle-snakes, particularly in the summer months.

Overview: Although its official name is the Darrington Trail, everyone knows and loves this ride as the Salmon Falls Trail, named for the waterfall that feeds into the American River just beyond the trailhead. If rolling singletrack through breathtaking scenery sounds like a great way to spend a few hours, this ride is for you.

Not challenging enough, you say? Well, let's toss in a little acropho-bia, then. The trail spends a fair amount of time clinging to a wall along the South Fork canyon, giving you a heart-stopping vertical view of the river rushing 50 feet or so below. The only thing between you and it are a lot of rocks and the oddly placed tree. It's not really that technical—as long as you don't look down.

Getting There: From Sacramento,

take Interstate 80 east to the Highway 49 exit, following the signs for 49 through Auburn. At the American River confluence, bear right over the bridge to stay on 49 and follow it 4 miles past Cool. Turn right onto Rattlesnake Bar Road, followed by a quick left onto Salmon Falls Road. Follow Salmon Falls Road 6 miles to the trailhead and parking lots. There are two paid parking areas, one on each side of the road, and a large dirt turnout across of the bridge. Parking in a paid area is $2.

Route: The trailhead is located at the left end of the first parking lot on the right side of the road. As you round the first corner and the left side of the

trail falls away, you get a spectacular view of the American River's South Fork winding below and ahead of you. The feeling is a little unsettling at first, but you get used to it. The singletrack is actually on the wide side. It's not a fire road by any means, but there is room to pass—as long as somebody stops.

The trail is generally buff, with minor sandy exceptions, and it couldn't be easier to follow; there are no turns. It starts with a very short, loose climb then rises and falls along the contour of the canyon wall. The trail follows this pattern for most of its 8 miles, interspersed with cuts into oak woodlands at the plateau level.

As you close in on Folsom Lake,

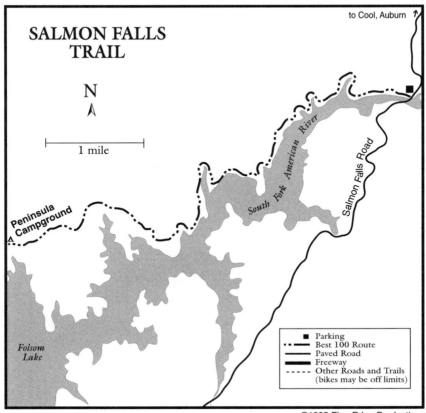

SALMON FALLS
TRAIL

N

to Cool, Auburn

South Fork American River

Salmon Falls Road

Peninsula Campground

Folsom Lake

1 mile

■ Parking
▪▪▬ Best 100 Route
▬▬ Paved Road
▬▬ Freeway
---- Other Roads and Trails
     (bikes may be off limits)

©1995 Fine Edge Productions

the trail heads inland away from the river and leads to a fast fire road descent into the Peninsula Camp-ground. This is the turnaround point and water is available for refills. Head back the way you came to experience the vertigo from the right side.

86 Olmstead Loop

Distance: 9 miles
Difficulty: Moderately strenuous, technical sections
Elevation: 900' gain/loss
Ride Type: Loop on fire roads, single and doubletrack
Season: Spring through fall
Topo Map: Auburn (most of the route is not shown)
Comments: No drinking water is available. Be on the lookout for rattlesnakes, particularly in the summer.

Overview: Cool isn't just a state of being, it's also a small town in the Sierra Foothills. And, yes, it is a cool town. Cool proper consists of a small town center where you can take your pet to the Cool Animal Hospital or have some Cool Pizza. Or you can ride a cool trail—the Olmstead Loop.

The trail is named in memory of a local mountain bike advocate, Dan Olmstead, who succeeded in gaining access to what was previously a horse trail. The Olmstead legacy lives on in Dan's wife and son who own the Auburn Bike & Hike in nearby Auburn. For the last three years, the Olmsteads have held an annual February mudfest of a race on this loop. The race and the trail are so popular they have had to limit the number of entrants at the behest of the Bureau of Land Management,

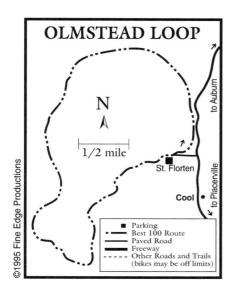

OLMSTEAD LOOP

N

1/2 mile

to Auburn

St. Florten

Cool

to Placerville

■ Parking
• — Best 100 Route
—— Paved Road
■■■ Freeway
---- Other Roads and Trails
      (bikes may be off limits)

©1995 Fine Edge Productions

sign, turn right onto Saint Florten, in front of the fire station. The dirt parking lot and trailhead are behind the fire station.

Route: The trail is well-marked and easy to follow. From the trailhead, follow the doubletrack as it heads back out toward the highway then curves around to the left, turning into a fire road as you reach the trees. The fire road rolls along the ridge line for about a mile or so. As you reach the last rise, you can almost hear the click-click-click that tells you the E-ticket ride is about to begin.

Where the trail veers to the left again, it narrows as it pitches steeply, sending you on a rocky slalom-like downhill. The trail snakes its way through a forest of black oak with lots of fast berms, rock jumps and deep sand. At about the time you start to realize that you've been going downhill for a long time, the trail levels and you see how you have to pay for it. Looming in front of you is an exasperatingly steep and sandy climb. Although it's only a half mile long, this granny-grinder feels like so much more.

At the top of the climb, the trail rolls along the ridge again, a little faster and steeper than before. At about the 4-mile point, the trail again pitches downhill, along a steep and rocky singletrack that leads through a creek. On the other side, you begin the steep grind back up. Around the first bend, the trail hugs the side of the mountain while to your right, the canyon falls away just past the trees, giving you a nice view of the American River valley below you.

The trail quickly leads away from the mountain's edge and through a meadow to the first of several cattle gates. From this point, the rest of the

who asked that they keep it down to 250. The first year, almost 500 racers showed up.

So what's all the fuss about? Well, it's a really fun loop, for one thing. It's got a little bit of everything: a little fire road, a little singletrack, a little doubletrack (and one triple), some rocks, a little steep climbing, a little steep descending, a couple of water crossings. All of these come in one tidy 9-mile package.

Although there aren't any services available at the trailhead, except for the outhouse at the rear of the staging area, the town center is on the other side of the fire station (see directions). Among the possibilities are two restaurants, a deli and a liquor store.

Getting There: From Sacramento, take Interstate 80 to the Highway 49 exit and follow the signs for 49 through Auburn. At the American River confluence, bear right across the bridge and follow the highway south into Cool. Just past the town climb gets decidedly easier. Within a half mile, the trail levels, becoming fire road again, as you make your way past a stand of towering pine at about 4.7 miles. The trail leads along a short rolling section through an orchard, then gives way to doubletrack along grassland hillsides.

The rest of the loop rolls along the exposed hillsides on single- and doubletrack, and for one brief stretch it splits into tripletrack. You come to the last steep climb at about 8 miles. Thankfully, this one is short. At the top, it's all downhill, a little steeply near the bottom, back to the staging area and parking lot.

87 Lake Clementine Loop

Distance: 10.5 miles
Difficulty: Moderately strenuous, mildly technical with a couple of very technical sections
Elevation: 1,500' gain/loss
Ride Type: Loop on fire roads and singletrack
Season: Spring through fall
Topo Map: Auburn (part of the route not shown)
Comments: No drinking water is available along this ride so bring plenty. Be on the lookout for rattlesnakes, particularly in the summer. Summers get very hot and the proximity to water throughout the ride means lots of sun; even if you don't burn easily, slather on the sun block.

Overview: The hugely popular Lake Clementine Loop is a must for anyone new to the area. The trail follows two different branches of the magnificent American River, the North and Middle Forks. As you make your way along the canyon floors, you see the river at its calmest points. Past Lake Clementine to the north, its rapids are a favorite among rafters from all over.

The trail leads down from a high ridge in the town of Auburn to the North Fork canyon, climbs back up and drops down into the Middle Fork Canyon. The ride takes place on mostly smooth, narrow fire roads and singletrack, with a couple of rocky and rutted sections thrown in for good measure. If you ride early enough, the only sound you hear is the river gurgling and rushing by.

Getting There: From Sacramento, take Interstate 80 east to Auburn and

exit at Russell Road. At the stop sign, go straight (the cross traffic doesn't have to stop). The trailhead is half a mile down the road, in a large dirt turnout on the left. Park in the turnout.

Route: Starting from the Stagecoach trailhead, follow the fire road as it makes its 1.5-mile rolling descent to the Old Foresthill Bridge. Overall, the trail is smooth and not terribly steep, which is good since you have to climb this at the end of the ride. At the bottom, the trail ends at the Old Foresthill Bridge (you can see the new bridge up behind you). Turn left across the bridge, which is Old Foresthill Road, and cross the river. On the other side of the bridge, turn left onto Old Clementine Road, a narrow fire road which rises above the North Fork.

At about 2 miles, you come to a fork in the trail. Veer left, following the trail that hugs the river. Just past the fork, the trail becomes a single-track. The singletrack is smooth and scenic, widening to a fire road about a mile later. At this point, the trail climbs up a little steeply to the North Fork Dam and Lake Clementine (called North Fork Lake on the Auburn topo map), which is actually a section of the American River.

At the top of the climb, you come to a gate at a paved road. Turn right and continue climbing on the road for about 0.5 mile. At about 4.8 miles, you see a bunch of boulders and a gate on your right. Turn right here. Just inside the gate, you have your choice of three trails. Head up the trail to the right, which takes you up and down a little rolling section that turns into a downhill straightaway.

At approximately 5.3 miles, you see a singletrack on the left. Turn

onto it and continue descending. The trail ends at a culvert which leads under Foresthill Road. Head on through and begin the next downhill section. This one gets a little steep and a little rocky, ending at Old Foresthill Road (not to be confused with Foresthill Road).

Cross the road and pick up the signed bike trail as it continues to head downhill. At just under 6 miles, turn right to stay on the bike trail. Immediately, the fire road narrows to a singletrack that follows the north bank of the Middle Fork of the river. It's mostly downhill, leveling out before ending with a little rise. Keep your speed in check—this stretch is popular with hikers.

The trail ends at the Old Foresthill Bridge. Cross the road and the bridge, and turn right onto Stagecoach. Climb up Stagecoach back to the parking lot on Russell Road.

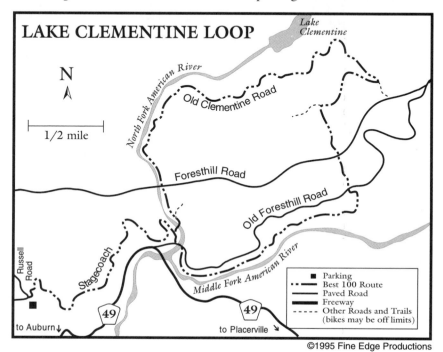

©1995 Fine Edge Productions

88 Stevens Trail

Distance: 9 miles
Difficulty: Strenuous, very technical
Elevation: 1,200' gain/loss
Ride Type: Out-and-back on singletrack
Season: Spring through fall
Topo Map: Colfax (beginning of trail not shown)
Comments: No water is available. Be on the lookout for rattlesnakes, particularly in the summer.

Overview: This trail is fairly short but it's very well trod. Its popularity stems from its technical nature. It's severely rutted, very rocky and the lower half follows a ledge of granite boulders that leads down to the North Fork of the never-far-from-reach American River. One person said of this section of trail, "It's scary to *hike* it."

Stevens is a hit with history buffs, too. It was originally built by Truman Allen Stevens in 1859 as a

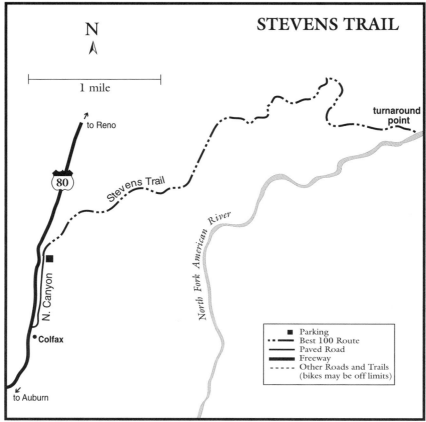

toll road for miners going back and forth between the river and the town of Colfax. In the mid-1880s, a public road was built nearby, putting Stevens out of business. Since that time, very little has been done in the way of developing the trail, testament to the quality of its original construction.

Getting There: From Sacramento, go east on Interstate 80 to the Canyon Way exit in Colfax and head north. Follow North Canyon to its end at a dirt parking area and trailhead.

Route: From the well-signed trailhead, simply go down the singletrack. The descent is gradual, carved out like giant steps. It goes down a little, then levels, then repeats, all the way down. It starts off fairly smooth and clear but the bushes, including poison oak, soon close in as the trail narrows. Within 100 yards, the excitement begins as a deep but narrow

rut runs down the middle of the trail, leaving very little pedal clearance. Once you pass the rut, the trail smoothes out as it heads down into the trees.

The trail winds along, heading steadily down through a forest before coming out in the open about a mile later. Then the rocks begin. The rest of the trail alternates between really rocky and nearly unrideable with brief relatively smooth respites along a few of the level sections. If the terrain gets too much for your abilities, turn around. Keep in mind that you have to go back up whatever you make it down.

As you near the river, look for a couple of cave-like holes in the canyon wall. These are old mining tunnels, now sealed off.

At the bottom of the trail, take a break, watch the river and then head back up the way you came.

89 Pioneer Trail

Distance: 20 miles
Difficulty: Moderate, mildly technical
Elevation: 600' gain/loss
Ride Type: Out-and-back on single- and doubletrack
Season: Spring through fall
Maps: Tahoe National Forest (much of the route not shown). (Free map is also available at the Harmony Ridge Market.)
Comments: Water is available at various points.

Overview: The Pioneer Trail is actually two trails, Lower and Upper, that flank Highway 20 just inside the boundary of the Tahoe National Forest. The trails were originally developed as horse trails, and a couple of years ago mountain bikers asked permission to use them. The local equestrian group that maintains the trails

said, "Sure, why not?" Makes you wish it was always this easy.

The trail consists of singletrack that at times widens to doubletrack, that gradually climbs and descends through a dense forest of pine and oak. It looks pretty and it smells good, too.

The trails are very easy to fol-

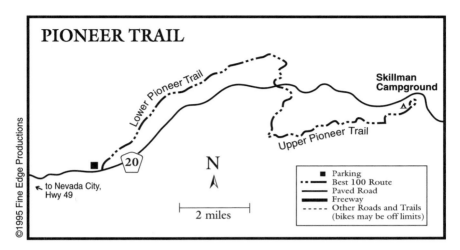

low; every few trees are marked with a white diamond-shaped sign. When riding this route, show your appreciation to the horse folks by treating them courteously.

Getting There: From Interstate 80, take the Highway 49 turnoff and follow it north through Nevada City. Bear east at the 49/20 junction and take Highway 20 about 5 miles past Nevada City. When you see the Five Mile House restaurant on the right, turn left into the parking lot for the Harmony Ridge Market (park near the rear of the lot). The trailhead is on the right side of the market, between two big boulders.

Route: From the trailhead, follow the Lower Pioneer singletrack as it parallels the highway. Within the first mile, it veers a little to the left so you won't have to look at the highway the whole time. From that point, the trail meanders through the trees and through several crossroads. Just keep heading straight.

The trail climbs so gradually it almost feels level. This section is also pretty smooth with a few smatterings of small rocks, ruts and tree roots. At about 5 miles, you reach the White Cloud Campground. Some people cut the ride short by turning around here. But we're not going to do that. At the campground, turn right and head out and across the highway. The Upper Pioneer Trail begins on the other side.

From the Upper Pioneer trailhead, the trail continues up to the left. This portion of Pioneer is again a virtual straight line, paralleling the highway. However, the trail gets a little more interesting. The singletrack is more consistently narrow and the rocks are a little bigger. Still not too imposing, though.

At 10 miles, you reach the Skillman Campground. Turn around here and head back. Going this direction is a lot of fun because, although it's not steep, you do pick up speed. Keep an eye out for horses and have a good time.

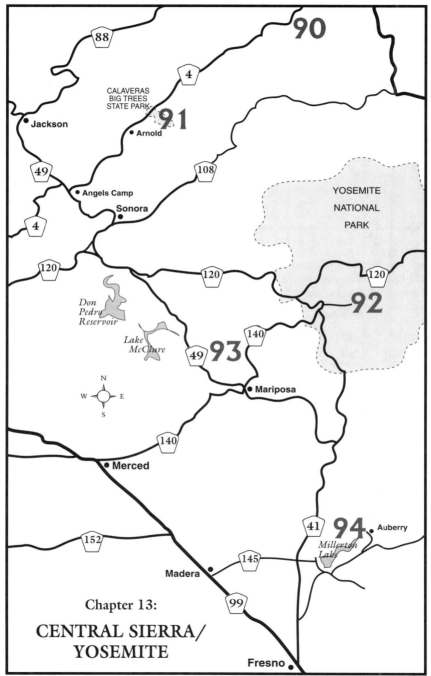

88

90

4

CALAVERAS
BIG TREES
STATE PARK

91

• Jackson

• Arnold

49

108

• Angels Camp

YOSEMITE

NATIONAL

PARK

Sonora
•

4

120

120

120

92

Don
Pedro
Reservoir

140

Lake
McClure

49 93

N
W ✦ E
S

• Mariposa

140

• Merced

41 94 • Auberry

152

Millerton
Lake

145

Madera •

Chapter 13:

99

CENTRAL SIERRA/
YOSEMITE

Fresno •

Central Sierra/ Yosemite

by Delaine Fragnoli

Thanks largely to the images of Ansel Adams, the granite beauty of Yosemite National Park is familiar to those who have never even been to the area. More than any other natural landmarks, Half Dome, El Capitan, Sentinel Rock and other Yosemite rock formations have been firmly etched into the American consciousness.

No travel book on California would be complete without a section on Yosemite. While the riding opportunities within the park are limited to paved roads, bike paths and one trail on the valley's floor, bicycling in Yosemite is still something special. Besides the incredible scenery you can see from your saddle, a bike makes the ideal way to get around the valley and to avoid the park's traffic.

To the northwest, Stanislaus National Forest borders the park and offers more off-road opportunities. (The ride included in this chapter is just one example.) With the exception of three wilderness areas (Mokelumne, Carson-Iceberg and Emigrant), most of the forest's roads and trails are open to bikes. This is high-alpine country, bisected by four major rivers: the Mokelumne in the north, the Stanislaus and the Toulumne in the center, and the Merced in the south.

Nearby is Calaveras Big Trees State Park. Although the park is popular, you can escape the crowds by heading to the less-visited south end. Here you can explore seldom-used fire roads while taking in the grandeur of some of the western Sierra's biggest tress.

On the south side of the Merced River, the Sierra National Forest tucks up against Yosemite's southwest boundary. There is virtually unlimited riding in the Sierra Forest. Few trails are closed to bikes, and only your conditioning and the altitude will restrain you.

Besides the two river trails included in this chapter which cross forest land, the Sierra National Forest contains several popular OHV routes. Contact the Forest Service (209-487-5155) for excellent route sheets and information if you feel like tackling one of these challenging rides.

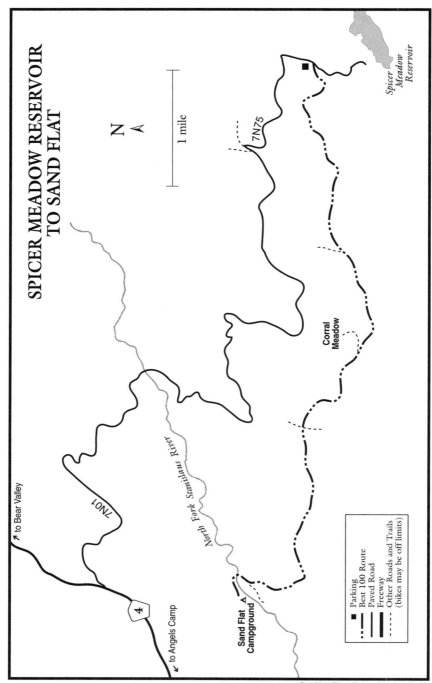

SPICER MEADOW RESERVOIR
TO SAND FLAT

N

1 mile

Spicer Meadow Reservoir

7N75

Corral Meadow

North Fork Stanislaus River

7N01

to Bear Valley

4

to Angels Camp

Sand Flat Campground

■ Parking
Best 100 Route
Paved Road
Freeway
Other Roads and Trails
(bikes may be off limits)

© 1995 Fine Edge Productions

Last but not least, the Bureau of Land Management's Folsom Resource Area manages acres of public land west of Stanislaus and Sierra National Forests. The Merced River Trail and the San Joaquin River Trail, both included in this chapter, cross BLM land. BLM's Squaw Leap Management Area and Millerton Lake State Recreation Area make good weekend getaway destinations or excellent jumping-off spots for exploring the Sierra National Forest.

90 Spicer Meadow Reservoir to Sand Flat

Distance: 10 miles
Difficulty: Moderate, technical
Elevation: 1,300' gain/loss, high point 6,880'
Ride Type: Out-and-back on singletrack
Season: Late spring through fall; check snow levels
Topo Maps: Spicer Meadow Reservoir, Tamarack. (The route is also clearly shown on the USFS Sierra National Forest map.)
Comments: Be careful, especially if you decide to camp in the area, because this is bear country. Camping is available at Spicer Reservoir Group Campground, Sand Flat and Stanislaus River Campgrounds.

Overview: In the northeast section of the Stanislaus National Forest, Spicer Reservoir sits up against the western boundary of the Carson-Iceberg Wilderness Area. This is high-alpine scenery at its best.

Your route, almost all singletrack, travels from the forested reservoir area into Corral Meadow—especially beautiful in spring—before dropping steeply down to Sand Flat and the North Fork of the Stanislaus River, the forest's namesake. Rugged terrain and several streams add some technical spice to the ride.

Getting There: From Stockton, take Highway 99 to Highway 4 and head east. From Angels Camp, continue northeast another 43 miles on Highway 4. Just past Big Meadow Campground, go right on Forest Road 7N01. Take it to Forest Road 7N75 and turn right. Follow 7N75 to the Spicer Meadow Reservoir trailhead. (west side of the road—your right). Park off of the road.

Route: From the trailhead you head west and begin to climb. You climb just over 200 feet before the trail begins to level out. From here it's rolling with a generally downward trend.

Soon you cross two intermittent streams (wet in spring, but dry by the end of summer). After these and just before a third stream, the trail joins a jeep road coming in on your right. The trail soon narrows as you continue due west and enter Corral Meadow. A trail crosses the meadow if you want to explore; the main route continues west.

You have four more stream crossings to maneuver. Just after the fourth one, the trail intersects a jeep road. Cross the road and continue on the trail on the other side. Less than a mile and one more stream crossing later, you begin to lose elevation in earnest, dropping 600 feet to Sand Flat and the Stanislaus River.

Cross the footbridge over the river for views upstream and down.

It's worth continuing to Sand Flat Campground, where you can refill your water bottles. When you're ready, return the way you came. The first climb back out of the river bottom is tough, but after that things ease up.

If you want, you can do this ride in reverse, from Sand Flat to Spicer Reservoir, or you can ride it one way and arrange for a shuttle. But be forewarned—the road into Sand Flat campground is a 4WD road.

91 Calaveras Big Trees State Park/ South Grove Loop

Distance: 9 miles
Difficulty: Moderate, not technical
Elevation: 1,200' gain/loss
Ride Type: Loop on fire roads and pavement
Season: Spring through fall
Topo Map: Dorrington. (Brochure and trail map available from the park office for $1.)
Comments: There are several campgrounds in the park. Reservations should be made well in advance through MISTIX, especially if you are planning to visit in the summer months. Call (800) 444-PARK in California, and (619) 452-1950 outside of California.

Overview: Calaveras County seems to be famous for two things: as the setting for Mark Twain's short story "The Notorious Jumping Frog of Calaveras County" and as the home of two of the most impressive groves of giant sequoia trees in the state.

Commonly confused with redwoods, their coastal cousins, *Sequoiadendron giganteum* are stouter but shorter and thrive in a drier climate. Sacred to the local Indians, the Calaveras sequoias were brought to the attention of whites in the 1850s when a lost hunter stumbled into the area by mistake.

All hell broke loose after that, and several entrepreneurs cut down some of the most impressive specimens to cart around the country and exhibit for money.

Thankfully, two magnificent groves, the North Grove and the South Grove, have been preserved, largely through the work of the Save- the-Redwoods League and the

Calaveras Grove Association. Today the park houses not only the two groves but also 6,000 acres of pine forest in the Stanislaus River and Beaver Creek watersheds.

Although all hiking trails are closed to bikes, you can enjoy the park on paved roads and dirt access roads. Most visitors are content to hike the trail through the North Grove and few make it to the South Grove; even fewer explore the fire roads. So relatively wild and remote is the South Grove that it has been given special status as a "natural preserve." Please behave accordingly when you visit.

Getting There: From Stockton, take Highway 99 to Highway 4 and head east. Follow Highway 4 past the junction with Highway 49 at Angels Camp. The park is 4 miles past the town of Arnold. Take the park's main thoroughfare, the Walter Smith Memorial Parkway, for 9 miles to the parking area for the South Grove

Trail. You can also park at the Beaver Creek Picnic Area. There is a park entry fee of $5 per vehicle.

Route: Leave the parking area and continue northeast on the park's main paved road. You pass two gates before the pavement ends. Continue around a third gate and onto a dirt road. When the road forks soon thereafter, veer right.

The road drops into Beaver Creek, which you cross. On the other side, the road sweeps southward and begins to climb. You cross the Bailey Grove hiking trail and then cross another fire road. Almost immediately, the road you're on ends in a T. Go left and continue climbing.

The next 3 miles are a gradual climb to the northeast end of the South Grove. The road begins to curve southward and ends in a T at a small saddle. There's a gate to your left, but you want to go right.

You're at the top of a ridge here

and your route starts to roll, then to head downhill for real. After about 1.5 miles of downhill you pass a spur road to the left. Just past that, your road forks, with each route going around a small hill and rejoining on the other side. Take your pick.

About 3.5 miles into the downhill, you cross a fire road, then recross the same fire road just as you reach Big Trees Creek. Here you are down in the belly of a mature sequoia grove.

Either fire road will work out, but the left fork is a bit easier. After you cross the creek, you almost immediately intersect the South Grove Trail (off-limits to bikes). Up and over a small ridge and you're back to where your loop began. Backtrack the way you came: down to and over Beaver Creek and out to pavement.

While you're here, take the time to hike the South Grove Trail. Be sure to take the spur out to the Agassiz Tree and the Palace Hotel Tree, the two largest trees in the park.

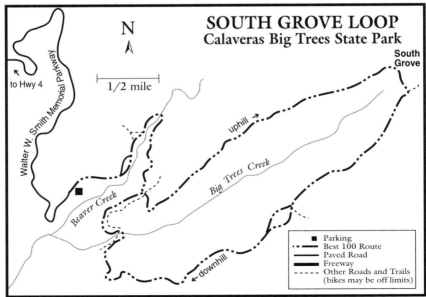

SOUTH GROVE LOOP
Calaveras Big Trees State Park

N

1/2 mile

to Hwy 4

Walter W. Smith Memorial Parkway

South Grove

uphill

Big Trees Creek

Beaver Creek

downhill

■ Parking
·-·-· Best 100 Route
▬▬▬ Paved Road
▬▬▬ Freeway
----- Other Roads and Trails
(bikes may be off limits)

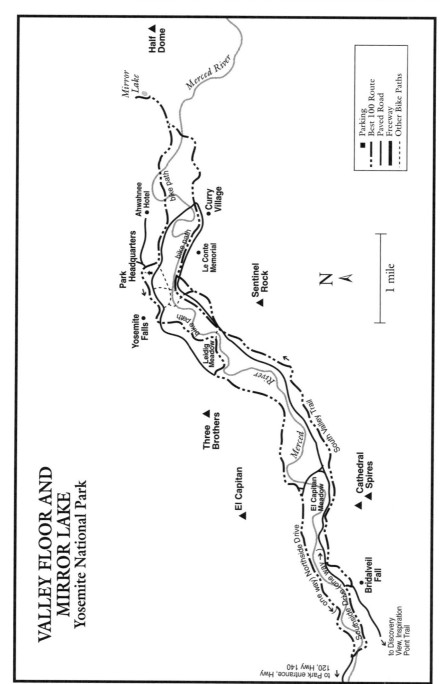

VALLEY FLOOR AND
MIRROR LAKE
Yosemite National Park

Half Dome

Mirror Lake

Merced River

Ahwahnee Hotel

bike path

Curry Village

Park Headquarters

bike path

Le Conte Memorial

Sentinel Rock

Yosemite Falls

bike path

Leidig Meadow

River

N

1 mile

Three Brothers

Merced

South Valley Trail

El Capitan

El Capitan Meadow

Cathedral Spires

(one way) Northside Drive

one way)

Southside Drive

Bridalveil Fall

to Discovery View, Inspiration Point Trail

to Park entrance, Hwy 120, Hwy 140

Parking
Best 100 Route
Paved Road
Freeway
Other Bike Paths

92 Yosemite National Park/ Valley Floor and Mirror Lake

Distance: Varies, depends on options taken; entire loop is about 17 miles
Difficulty: Easy, not technical
Elevation: Minimal elevation gain/loss
Ride Type: Loop on pavement and dirt
Season: Spring through fall
Topo Maps: Wilderness Press produces a topo map of Yosemite Valley. Trails Illustrated makes one for Yosemite National Park.
Comments: For camping and general information on Yosemite, contact the Public Information Office at P.O. Box 577, Yosemite National Park, CA 95389, (209) 372-0200. The Yosemite Association, P.O. Box 230, El Portal, CA 95318, is another good source of information.

Overview: In *Desert Solitaire* (1968), Edward Abbey described Yosemite National Park as "a dusty milling confusion of motor vehicles and ponderous camping machinery" and went on to suggest that the park "...could be returned to relative beauty and order by the simple expedient of requiring all visitors, at the park entrance, to lock up their automobiles and continue their tour on the seats of good workable bicycles supplied free of charge by the United States Government. Let our people travel light and free on their bicycles...their backpacks, their tents, their food will be trucked in for them, free of charge, to the campground of their choice by the Park Service. Why not?"

Unfortunately, the Park Service has not heeded Abbey's advice and Yosemite Valley continues to be choked with motor traffic. Although shuttles have helped and plans are afoot to further minimize traffic, congestion can still be a problem. All the more reason then for you to take to two wheels. A bicycle is by far the easiest, most efficient, and healthiest way to tour Yosemite.

You are limited to paved roads and bike paths, with a section of dirt, so the riding is not really *mountain* biking. Still, it is some of the most

incredible scenery in the world, and any kind of bike is a great way to visit the park's awesome sights.

Getting There: From the west, the most direct route is via Highway 140 from Merced. For those coming from the north, access is by Highway 120. Those coming from the east side of the Sierra have no choice but to take Interstate 395 to the junction with 120 near Lee Vining. From there, it's over Tioga Pass (check snow conditions as late as June or even July in a heavy snow year) and into the valley.

Route: You can start this ride virtually anywhere on the valley floor. Basically two one-way roads, Northside Drive and Southside Drive, circle the valley. A paved bike path parallels each road for much of the way, giving you freedom from vehicle traffic most of the time.

However, the bike path sees a lot of foot traffic and, increasingly, rollerbladers. Families with kids running every which way, joggers, tourists gaping at the scenery, parents pushing baby strollers—all combine to crowd the path. Be careful, watch for people stepping out in front of you suddenly, and keep your speed down. I've found that a bell helps immeasurably.

For lack of a better place, I'll start at the Park Headquarters in Yosemite Village. From here, the clearly marked bike path heads west, paralleling Northside Drive. Your first scenic stop, Lower Yosemite Falls, comes up quickly, about 0.5 mile. Park your bike—there are bike racks—and walk up the asphalt to the base of the falls.

The bike path continues to head west, still paralleling Northside Drive. You cross the road and head south past Yosemite Lodge and down toward the Merced River. You contour along Leidig Meadow before circling back out to Northside Drive. You may want to stop at the meadow and look behind you for views of North Dome and Half Dome.

Past the meadow you have to get out on the road to continue your tour. (The North Valley Trail which leads from the meadow is closed to bikes.) There's no bike path for the next several miles, but there is a good shoulder.

If you're uncomfortable riding with vehicle traffic or have young children with you, I recommend that you do an out-and-back on the north or south side of the valley, or fashion a much shorter loop using the footbridge at Leidig Meadow or Sentinel Bridge.

As you merge onto the road, the towering rock formation above you is known as the Three Brothers because of its three distinctive ridgelines. You pass several picnic areas as you make your way around the Brothers and on to the base of world famous El Capitan.

Just past the Devils Elbow Picnic Area, if you're tired already or want to do a short loop, take Northside over the El Capitan Bridge to Southside Drive and start heading back. For a longer loop which takes you to Bridalveil Fall, continue west on Northside.

You pass the slight but graceful Ribbon Fall on your way to the intersection with Southside Drive. Be careful of traffic here as you cross over the Merced on Pohono Bridge and loop onto Southside Drive. All the traffic coming into the park has to take Southside Drive.

The terrain is a little hillier on the south side. So far your route has been gradually downhill and on the way back you have to gain back the elevation lost.

You will want to stop at Bridalveil Fall. Visiting Bridalveil is the primary reason for doing the longer loop in the first place. From the road which leads to Bridalveil you can pick up the South Valley Trail, a 6-mile dirt trail, sections of which are open to bikes (obey the signs). Cross a creek and head up an old road bed to the base of Cathedral Rocks.

The trail soon rejoins the road near a picnic area before continuing east. (This is a good spot to watch rock climbers on El Capitan across the valley—bring binoculars.) You cross Sentinel Creek and get a good look at Sentinel Fall, which runs in the spring. Just past here you can drop down to the pavement and pick up the paved bike path on the other side of the road.

Soon you pass Le Conte Memorial, a tribute to Berkeley's first geology professor, who was also a Sierra Club hero and supporter of Yosemite. Then you continue on to Curry Village.

Expect more traffic as you approach Curry Village. Near the village you can take the path left over Stoneman Bridge to see the architectural splendor of the Ahwahnee Hotel and complete your loop, or, if you want to take a trip out to Mirror Lake, you can continue east past Stoneman Meadow.

Pass through Lower Pines and Upper Pines campgrounds and cross the Merced on Clark Bridge. Continue around the stables. At the fork go left and head northward toward Mirror Lake. At the next fork go right.

This is the only real hill in the whole loop as you head up to Mirror Lake. There is a horse path and a foot path, but you must stay on the pavement. (The pavement is closed to motor vehicles.) The climb doesn't last for long and soon deposits you at the lake. The lake may be a disappointment to you since it is quickly turning into a meadow and, thus, does not "mirror" much of anything anymore. Still, it's pretty, offers views of Half Dome looming above you, and makes a nice rest stop. Note that bikes are not allowed on the trail that loops around the meadow/lake.

Backtrack down the hill and watch your speed. At the fork go straight. Pass Indian Caves and circle around the group campground. Cross Sugarpine Bridge and head on to the Ahwahnee Hotel. Just past the hotel are park headquarters. The entire loop is roughly 17 miles.

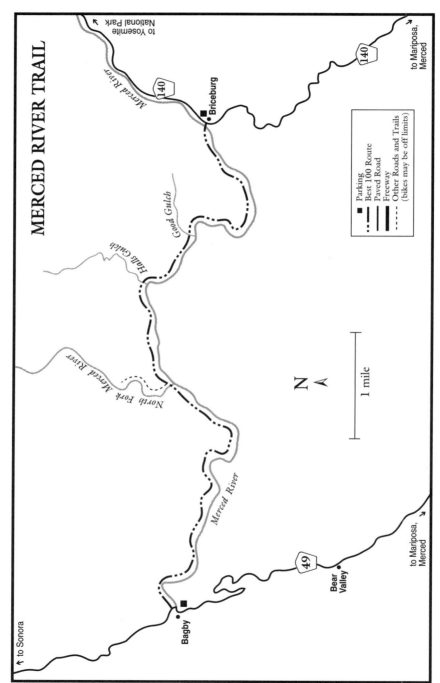

MERCED RIVER TRAIL

to Yosemite
National Park

Merced River

140

Briceburg

to Mariposa,
Merced

140

Good Gulch

Halls Gulch

North Fork Merced River

Parking
Best 100 Route
Paved Road
Freeway
Other Roads and Trails
(bikes may be off limits)

N

1 mile

Merced River

to Mariposa,
Merced

49

Bear
Valley

Bagby

to Sonora

© 1995 Fine Edge Productions

93 Merced River Trail

Distance: 14 miles one way, 28 miles out and back
Difficulty: Easy, technical in spots
Elevation: 420' loss one way
Ride Type: One way with shuttle option or out-and-back on singletrack
Season: Year-round; can get brutally hot in summer
Map: A trail guide (actually it's a boating trail guide) of the Merced River is available at the Briceburg Visitor Center.
Comments: Seasonal fluctuations in the reservoir may make the trail unpassable below the North Fork of the Merced River. Seasonal runoff may at times make the North Fork dangerous to cross. Call for trail conditions, (916) 985-4474. Nearest campgrounds are Indian Flat and Jerseydale in the adjacent Sierra National Forest.

Overview: This route follows the old Yosemite railroad grade from the Briceburg Visitor Center to the Highway 49 bridge at Bagby. Briceburg is a popular put-in and take-out spot for boaters rafting the Merced River, and Bagby is the final take-out point. The trail parallels the river as it heads downstream to Lake Mc Clure (Exchequer Reservoir). As is true of most railroad grades, this one is pretty level the whole way, about a 1 percent grade.

Along the way you pass vestiges of a water-diversion dam from the turn of the century. In addition to rafters, you may see modern-day prospectors working dredges. Also keep your eyes peeled for lizards—the area is home to the rare limestone salamander.

The railroad was originally built to cart out timber cut by the Yosemite Lumber Company. The river's slopes used to be covered with sugar pine but, thanks to the logging folks, today's route is largely unshaded, which makes this an uncomfortably hot ride during the height of summer. Besides timber, the railroad also carried tourists from Merced to El Portal. This was the most popular method for getting to Yosemite until the 1940s.

Before that the river was popular with miners, who arrived in the 1850s. The area is dotted with old mines, the most productive of which was Hite's Cove mine. It produced more than $3 million of the precious metal before ceasing operations.

The river actually got its name from a Mexican soldier. In 1806, Lieutenant Gabriel Moraga, exhausted after a 40-mile march, came upon the river. In his gratitude he called it El Rio Nuestra Senora de la Merced (The River of Our Lady of Mercy). It has since mercifully been shortened to Merced!

Today much of the river belongs to the National Wild and Scenic River system. Mountain bikers are free to join hikers and equestrians on the generally easy trail. Areas where slides and washouts have occurred make the trail difficult in spots. The 1-mile section of trail between the Mountain King Mine and the North Fork of the Merced River confluence is the most challenging.

Getting There: From Merced (on Highway 99), head east on Highway 140 to Highway 49 and go north. Past Bear Valley you cross the Merced

River at the Bagby bridge. If you choose the shuttle option, leave your shuttle vehicle here. To get to the ride start, backtrack to Highway 140 and go left (northeast). Follow Highway 140 through Midpines and down to Briceburg. Park at the Briceburg Visitor Center (open seasonally).

Route: The trail starts on the north side of the Merced River. Just over a mile later you pass Vanderkarr Crossing, a good swimming spot late in the summer. There are also toilets here should you need them.

At about 2.5 miles you come to McCabe Flat Camp, an undeveloped campground. Here the river curves northward, a spot known to rafters as Corner Pocket. Just under 4 miles, you cross Good Gulch.

You pass Willow Placer and Railroad Flat undeveloped campgrounds at 5 miles. Both are popular with the boating crowd. Just past these you cross Halls Gulch. At about 5.5 miles you come to the remains of an old diversion dam.

In the next mile, the river really begins to churn as a major set of rapids serves warning of the upcoming North Fork Falls. Between 7 and 8 miles, the trail begins to degenerate. Here high water levels frequently wash out the trail. The winter and spring of 1995 were very wet, so there's no telling what shape the trail may be in this spring and summer.

At just under 8 miles, you come to where the North Fork runs into the main Merced River. In the spring, especially in heavy snow years, this may be impassable. Use your common sense: if it's too dangerous to cross, turn around and go back the way you came. It still makes for a nice ride! The main river is so rough at this point that rafters must make a mandatory portage.

At one time, railroad bridges provided a safe route over all the side streams, several of which are swift-moving and can be difficult to cross, but they have fallen. Plans are underway to improve this situation.

If you can get past the North Fork you have 6 more undulating miles of river to follow. Miles 11 to 13 cross private land, so be sure to stay on the trail and behave yourself. Once you get to Bagby you may want to hang out for a while. There is an undeveloped campground as well as picnic facilities. You can also go swimming there once the water level is low enough, usually by late July.

94 Squaw Leap National Recreation Trail

Distance: 8 miles, optional 8-mile out-and-back section
Difficulty: Strenuous, technical
Elevation: Roughly 2,400' gain/loss
Ride Type: Loop on singletrack
Season: Year-round; best in spring and fall, can get hot in summer
Topo Map: Millerton Lake East (trail not shown on map)
Comments: I rode this loop in the spring when it was very muddy and the trail was in very bad shape. By the time you ride it, the loop may be considerably easier and less technical. There is a toilet but no water at Squaw Leap campground.

Overview: From the Squaw Leap campground on the San Joaquin River it's possible to do two rides. One, Squaw Leap Trail, is a loop on the north side of the river; the other, the San Joaquin River Trail is still under

SQUAW LEAP
NATIONAL
RECREATION TRAIL

Squaw Leap Trail

River Trail

River Trail

to Millerton Lake

Ridge Trail

N

1/2 mile

Kerckhoff
Powerhouse

Smalley Road

to Powerhouse
Road, Auberry

San Joaquin River

■ Parking
-■-·- Best 100 Route
——— Paved Road
▬▬▬ Freeway
- - - - Other Roads and Trails
         (bikes may be off limits)

©1995 Fine Edge Productions

construction. It follows the river along its south side and will eventually run all the way from Friant Dam on the west to Devils Postpile on the east side of the Sierras, a distance of about 73 miles! Check with land management officials to see which segments are ready to ride when you visit.

Administered by the Bureau of Land Management, the Squaw Leap area is a great place for a weekend getaway. You're just upstream from the Millerton Lake State Recreation Area, which offers good fishing. In fact, you can ride a 4-mile piece of singletrack from the Squaw Leap Trail to the Recreation Area. Future plans include extending this singletrack so that it hooks up with a state hiking trail. The campground also has a Native American on site who offers interpretive programs.

This rolling landscape is chaparral country, where you see mountain mahogany, manzanita and mountain lilac *(Ceanothus)*. Near the river you find oaks and digger pines. Expect lots of spring wildflowers. As for wildlife, you're likely to see mule deer, quail, band-tailed pigeons, Audubon cottontail rabbits, grey squirrels, and mourning doves.

The highlight of the area, however, is the view into San Joaquin River gorge with its granite walls and tumbling rapids. Interesting rock formations sit atop the ridges on both sides of the river. In fact, the area is named for the rock formation to the southwest of Squaw Leap Campground.

Getting There: From Fresno take Highway 168 (Shaw Avenue) east to Prather. Follow the signs to Auberry. In Auberry, take Power House Road west (left). Be on the lookout for this intersection; it's easy to miss. Follow Power House Road to Smalley Road and go left. Follow Smalley as it drops steeply down to the San Joaquin River. There are good views of the river gorge as you make your way down. Pass the turnoff to the powerhouse and to the group campground. The Squaw Leap campground is just past the group camp on your right.

Route: The trailhead is clearly marked with a large sign. You head straight toward the river on singletrack. At 0.1 mile you come to a gate. Be sure to close it behind you as there are many cattle in the area. The trail rolls along, descending gradually. At about 0.5 mile you come around a bend and have your first good view down to the river. In the spring this hillside is covered with wildflowers and is spectacular.

Near the 0.8-mile mark you come to a second gate. Once again, be sure to close it. From here the trail drops more steeply and gets more technical. Two switchbacks lead you to a bridge, 0.9 mile, which crosses the river. It's worth stopping here to look up and down the gorge. This first mile of singletrack may be the best of the whole ride!

On the other side, you have to portage your bike up a rocky section. Good technical riders are able to ride down this, but even the best have to carry their bikes up.

At 1.1 miles you reach a trail sign. Straight ahead is the River Trail (not to be confused with the San Joaquin River Trail) and to the right is the Ridge Trail. You can go either way to do the loop. I went toward the River Trail because at the time trail conditions were better for climbing this portion and then descending the Ridge Trail.

At 1.5 miles a foot trail goes off

to your right, but you stay left. The terrain here is rolling, with short, steep climbs which contribute to an overall elevation gain. There are also several small stream crossings to maneuver—invariably with steep climbs on the other side!

You come to another trail junction at 1.9 miles. The left fork is the River Trail which leads west for about 4 miles to Millerton Lake. If you want, you can ride this section of trail out and back. From this trail you have good views of Squaw Leap across the river. If you just want to do the Squaw Leap loop, then go right at the intersection.

You continue to climb in short, steep bursts as the trail makes its way up a ridge. At 2.6 miles you pass a trail sign and take the right fork. Soon the trail begins to curve to the east. From here it's more of the same—rolling terrain interspersed with steep climbs until about the halfway point. Then you get to lose all the elevation you've gained.

The descent is fun, if rocky and rutted. Keep your eyes on the trail even though you are tempted by views down to the river and across the gorge. The downhill and the views are why Fresno cyclists flock to the area on weekends.

Did you clean that rock section leading back to the bridge? Now you have to pay for all that fun you just had as you climb back up to the campground. Actually it's not that steep, but there are some rocky sections that will probably have you off your bike. It levels off the closer you get to the campground.

Note: If you want to try the partially completed San Joaquin River Trail, there is a trailhead at the southeast corner of the Squaw Valley campground. You can ride eastward from there, or you can catch the trail westward across Smalley Road from the campground. (Look for a trail post next to a telephone pole and a gate.)

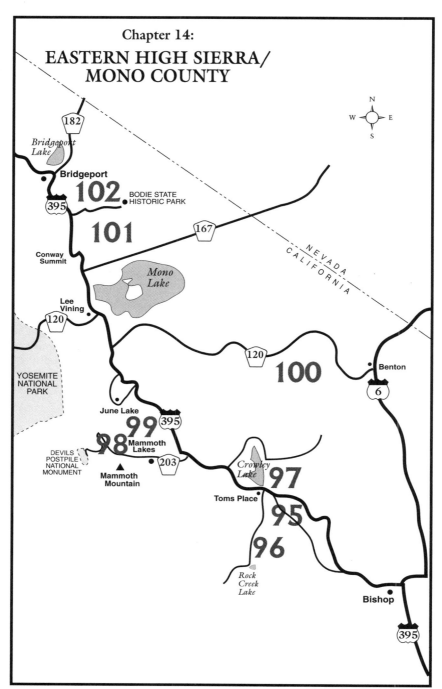

Chapter 14:
EASTERN HIGH SIERRA/ MONO COUNTY

Eastern High Sierra/ Mono County

by Don Douglass and Réanne Hemingway-Douglass

The Eastern High Sierra, home to some of the most scenic mountain and basin terrain in America, offers unlimited outdoor challenges in all seasons. Popular recreation includes camping, hiking, fishing, alpine and cross-country skiing, boating, hunting, horseback riding and packing. Mountain bike riding, four-wheel-driving, and snowmobiling are allowed in designated areas.

Approximately 98 percent of the land in Mono County is held in trust for the public. Among these lands are Inyo National Forest, Mono Basin National Scenic Area, Devils Postpile National Monument, Bureau of Land Management holdings, and the John Muir and Ansel Adams Wilderness areas.

The Inyo National Forest itself is one of the most highly visited areas of the country's national forest system. Its 1.9 million acres are managed primarily for recreation and wilderness preservation, with contracts held also for timber harvest, grazing, mining, and research. The Mono Basin National Scenic Area covers unique Mono Lake and its adjacent tufa-lined shores and pinyon forests— a total of 116,000 acres of Great Basin topography. Devils Postpile National Monument is administered by the National Park Service, while most of the large alluvial plains, valleys and meadows to the east of the Sierra Nevada are managed by the Bureau of Land Management.

95 Lower Rock Creek Trail

Distance: 3.3 miles or 8 miles (double the mileage if you ride it as a loop)
Difficulty: First half easy to moderate; second half moderate to advanced with some technical sections
Elevation: 7,000' to 5,000' (500' to 2,000' loss/gain)
Ride Type: One way with shuttle or loop—singletrack and pavement
Season: April to November; especially nice in early fall
Topo Maps: Toms Place, Rovana (7.5 min.)

Overview: For a real mountain biking treat, the Lower Rock Creek Trail is hard to beat. This route follows an old fishermen's trail along the edge of Rock Creek as it flows south, creating its own gorge of natural scenic beauty. The upper section of the trail can be navigated with easy to moderate skill and simple care. Due to rocks and logs obstructing the lower section of the trail at certain points, the route becomes something of a trials competition requiring moderate to advanced skill. You can do part or all of the trail, depending upon your skill and love of adventure. Fortunately a paved road crosses the trail at the appropriate bailout point. The narrow trail is used by hikers and fishermen, so please yield to all others by stopping and dismounting if necessary. (It's a good idea to avoid the heaviest part of the fishing season to minimize traffic.)

Note: The BLM and USFS have been conducting a study regarding the designation of Rock Creek as a Wild and Scenic River. The agencies feel that current recreational use will be compatible with their findings, and they invite public input. Please contact the BLM in Bishop for information or to volunteer for trail work on the Rock Creek Trail.

Getting There: From the junction of Highways 203 and 395, drive south 15.0 miles to a turnoff marked *Swall Meadow, Lower Rock Creek.* (When you pass the turnoff for Tom's Place, it's only a quarter-mile to your turnoff.) About 75 yards south of Highway 395 on the west side of Lower Rock Creek Road, there is parking for four or five cars next to a sign marked: *Inyo National Forest Day Use Area, Lower Rock Creek.* Park here. To do the entire 8-mile downhill ride as a shuttle, drive a second car to Paradise Lodge, 8 miles down Lower Rock Creek Road, and park off the road beyond the lodge wherever you can find a place. Do not park behind the lodge or block their driveways.

Route: The trail takes off from the east side of the road between two small boulders. Head east down to Rock Creek, which flows in from a culvert under Highway 395. The trail narrows around the culvert, and it's best to walk your bike here. At 0.2 mile you pass a catch basin, then it's sandy for the next 100 yards until you come to the side of the creek. At 1.5 miles the trail narrows to handlebar-width among aspens.

The next section along the creek is frequently wet and muddy, and you may have to walk your bike. At 1.7 miles the trail is fast, but keep a lookout for rocks and logs. At 2.1 miles you cross a dry wash—carry your bike at this point. Make a hard right at 2.2 miles and drop down to the paved road. Then cross the bridge to the west side of the creek and pick up the trail, continuing down the west side of the creek.

At 2.9 miles you ride across Witcher Creek Bridge. Within 75

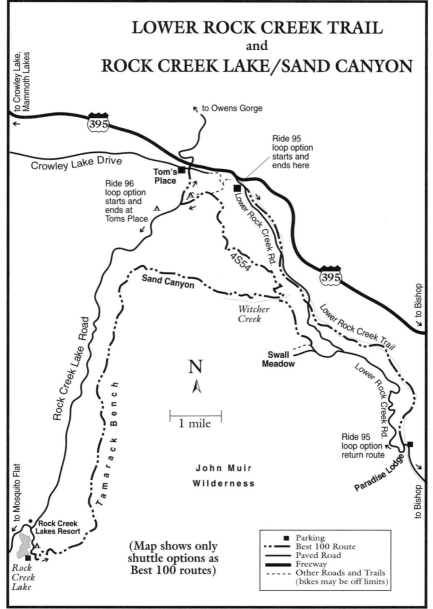

LOWER ROCK CREEK TRAIL
and
ROCK CREEK LAKE/SAND CANYON

to Crowley Lake, Mammoth Lakes

to Owens Gorge

395

Ride 95 loop option starts and ends here

Crowley Lake Drive

Tom's Place

Ride 96 loop option starts and ends at Toms Place

Lower Rock Creek Rd.

4S54

Sand Canyon

Witcher Creek

395

to Bishop

Lower Rock Creek Trail

Rock Creek Lake Road

Swall Meadow

Lower Rock Creek Rd.

N

1 mile

John Muir Wilderness

Ride 95 loop option return route

Paradise Lodge

to Bishop

Tamarack Bench

to Mosquito Flat

Rock Creek Lakes Resort

Rock Creek Lake

(Map shows only shuttle options as Best 100 routes)

■	Parking
·─·─·	Best 100 Route
───	Paved Road
▬▬▬	Freeway
- - -	Other Roads and Trails (bikes may be off limits)

yards there's another stream crossing without a bridge that you can usually cross without dismounting. At 3.2 miles you're on a high-speed trail in the shade, but watch out for rocky outcroppings above the stream; it's very narrow at this point. At 3.3 miles you come back to the paved road at a parking area for about six cars.

The trail crosses the pavement at this point and continues down Rock Creek. You can bail out here and ride the 3.3 miles back up the pavement to your car. Or if you're an experienced, hearty cyclist and wish to continue down the trail, cross the road and within 150 feet to the south, pick up the trail down to the creek. (*Caution:* From here down, there are no bailout points, and only experienced cyclists should continue.) We don't recommend this lower section during times of earthquake swarms.

At 3.5 miles you pass an old rusty car, circa 1930. At about 3.8 miles the canyon starts to narrow, so watch out for brush. At the very bottom of Sherwin Hill where you see several old rusted car bodies (4.0 miles), turn left and cross a log bridge. *Caution:* Watch the cracks between the logs! The canyon continues to narrow, and the trail becomes rocky for 100 yards. From here down, the canyon is deep with sheer cliffs.

At 4.2 miles a fallen tree, almost six feet in diameter, has been sawed through to free the trail for passage. For fun, count the rings of the tree to determine its age. At 4.4 miles the trail is blocked by a boulder half the size of a Volkswagen. During a 1985 earthquake, the pink rocks lying around this area split off from the east wall of the cliff above and tumbled clear across the creek, taking numerous trees in their path. The large pink rock blocking the trail at

4.6 miles fell in a 1986 earthquake. If you look up the canyon wall to the east, you can see where the rock broke away. At 4.8 miles ride to the left of a 5-foot-wide boulder obstructing the trail. Note that the original trail lies underneath that rock!

At 4.9 miles you pass a downed 6-foot-diameter "grandfather" tree. Look east up the canyon and notice the cabin-sized boulders that have tumbled down. There's a nice picnicking area along this particular stretch of the creek. You can also spot columnar rock formations here similar to those of Devils Postpile.

At 5.1 miles, where the stream flows more gently, there are several elbows where you can find primitive campsites. As you leave this area, the trail curves up a scree and talus slope, and the next 100 yards are miserably rocky. At 5.3 miles you return to the creek. At 5.8 miles heavy rocks cover much of the trail. The trail peters out on the east side and you have to cross to the west side of the creek.

Over the next nine-tenths of a mile, a series of bridges take you back and forth across the creek. At 6.9 miles beware of a 4-foot-diameter rock in the center of a high-speed section of trail. You cross to the west side again at 7.0 miles on a wide bridge, and continue on a high-speed trail, and within 0.2 mile you pick up a jeep trail. At 7.5 miles cross the stream to the east, or to avoid a cold-water crossing, use the footbridge 30 feet downstream. At 8.0 miles, you reach Paradise Lodge and the paved road. The lodge is on private property, so please respect any signs posted. Pick up your shuttle vehicle here. If you're riding to your starting point instead, turn right on Lower Rock Creek Road and return uphill on the pavement.

96 Rock Creek Lake/Sand Canyon

Distance: Approx. 22 miles (loop) or 14 miles as a shuttle
Difficulty: Strenuous due to the elevation and climb; technical
Elevation: 7,000' to 10,000'; 3,000' gain and loss
Ride Type: Loop on pavement, dirt roads and trail; or shuttle, leaving one car at Tom's Place and one at Rock Creek Lake Campground
Season: June through October
Topo Maps: Mt. Morgan and Tom's Place (7.5 min.)

Overview: This is a strenuous trip that covers a lot of ground over varied terrain with fantastic scenery. You can do this ride either as a loop or as a mostly downhill ride using a shuttle. If you're prepared for the brutal combination of elevation gain, "thin air," long distance, and some challenging bicycle handling, the entire loop trip may be for you. This route may get early snow, so carry extra clothing to be prepared for abrupt weather changes.

Be sure to carry adequate water. Springs that feed into Witcher Creek on the downhill run can be used, but all water must be treated. Note that since Rock Creek Canyon faces north-south, as you go up the canyon you are technically heading south. This route crosses the migration path for the Sherwin deer herd, and in both spring and fall, numerous deer travel along these slopes. Please be careful not to frighten them.

Getting There: From the junction of Highways 203 and 395 (near Mammoth Lakes), drive south 14.8 miles to Tom's Place. Turn west (right). If you plan to do the full pavement-dirt loop, park your car to the left on the pavement spur parallel to 395.

If you're planning to do the shuttle option, park one car on the pavement spur parallel to Highway 395 at Tom's Place and the second

car in the day-use parking lot at Rock Creek Lake.

Route: For the full loop starting at Tom's Place, hop on your bike and head up the canyon on the paved road for 8 miles to Rock Creek Campground. Just after you pass Rock Creek Lakes Resort, turn left and head to the parking lot at the east end of the road at Rock Creek Lake. This parking area is the starting point for the shuttle ride.

From here, pick up the dirt road that heads past the summer cabins on the slopes a little farther south. Watch for and take the trail that leads sharply northeast (left), contouring across an open rock face. Across the face, the trail turns more easterly and climbs up a small, shallow canyon. As you reach the relatively flat Tamarack Bench at the 10,000-foot contour, you pick up a jeep road that starts a long 3,000-foot descent back out of the canyon. This beautiful, high area is seldom visited. (Do not be tempted to enter the John Muir Wilderness Area—bikes are prohibited.)

Six miles north of Rock Creek Lake, the road reaches the northern extreme of Wheeler Ridge, veers sharply east, and drops steeply down Sand Canyon. Walk your bike down the 1-mile stretch if necessary. The road can be badly rutted by runoff and 4WD vehicles, so use caution.

After climbing out of Sand Canyon, you pass through a stand of old-growth Jeffrey pine, and once again drop down a gnarly path that challenges the hardiest cyclists. At about the 6,700-foot elevation mark when you come out into the open

along Witcher Creek , take the power line road 4S54 left (north). This dirt road winds its way north for 5 miles, eventually rejoining Rock Creek Road just below Holiday Group Campground. Head left through the campground to Rock Creek Road. A right turn take you back to Tom's Place.

97 Great Wall of Owens River Gorge

Distance: 3.5 miles
Difficulty: Easy, nontechnical, but with steep dropoffs
Elevation: Begin/end 7,000'; 350' loss
Ride Type: Loop on trail and pavement
Season: May through October
Topo Maps: Tom's Place (7.5 min.); Fine Edge Eastern High Sierra Recreation Topo Map

Overview: For those of you who like a mystery, this ride should arouse your curiosity. Who made the rock wall along this trail with such careful craftsmanship? What was its purpose? When was it built? This simple loop drops to the bottom of Owens River Gorge just below Long Valley Dam (Crowley Lake), then circles back up the pavement. The trail section is an easygoing downhill ride, except for occasional small pine trees and brush that obstruct the trail. The pavement section, just above the dam, is steep at first, but after that it rises fairly gently.

Getting There: From the junction of Highways 203 and 395, head south 14.8 miles to Tom's Place. Turn east, and follow Owens Gorge Road (4S02) approximately 1.5 miles. Where the paved road turns left toward Crowley Lake, take the straight dirt road that heads out to the rim of the gorge, where you park your car.

Route: From the rim, look left and take the trail that contours gently in a northwesterly direction down the can-

yon wall to the bottom of the gorge. Although the trail is not well-maintained, it is quite rideable. Watch for debris and ride cautiously.

As you proceed, part way down the trail you come to the "great wall," where fine rock work has kept this old trail from washing out. The work appears to have been done entirely by hand without modern tools or drilling equipment. It is precision craftsmanship that has withstood the test of time and numerous earthquakes. Perhaps someday the story of this work will be uncovered.

From a vantage point above the wall, you can often spot red-tailed hawks, golden eagles, gulls, and cranes, as well as deer, rabbits, and coyotes. When you reach the canyon floor, proceed up-river to the Long Valley Dam (at the south end of Crowley Lake). Turn left onto paved Owens Gorge Road, which takes you back to your starting point.

To add more mileage to your ride, check out the maze of dirt (and sand) roads in the vicinity.

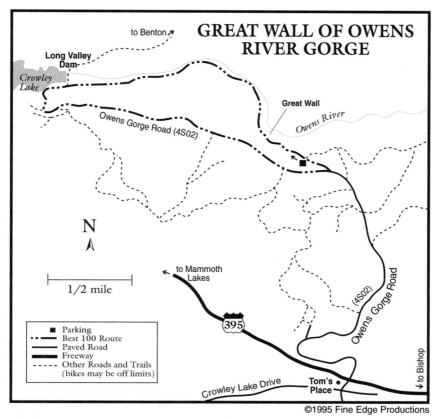

GREAT WALL OF OWENS RIVER GORGE

to Benton

Long Valley Dam

Crowley Lake

Great Wall

Owens Gorge Road (4S02)

Owens River

N

1/2 mile

to Mammoth Lakes

Owens Gorge Road (4S02)

395

to Bishop

- ■ Parking
- ·-·- Best 100 Route
- —— Paved Road
- ▬▬ Freeway
- ----- Other Roads and Trails (bikes may be off limits)

Crowley Lake Drive

Tom's Place

©1995 Fine Edge Productions

98 Minaret Summit to Deadmans Pass

Distance: 5 miles
Difficulty: Strenuous, nontechnical
Elevation: 9,200' to 10,250'; 1,050' gain and loss
Ride Type: Out-and-back on dirt road
Season: Summer only
Topo Map: Mammoth Mountain and Old Mammoth (7.5 min.); Fine Edge Eastern Sierra Recreation Topo Map

Overview: The headwaters of the middle fork of the San Joaquin River from Agnew Meadows to Red's Meadow, including Devils Postpile National Monument, form one of the most accessible and heavily used areas of the High Sierra. Here you can enjoy outstanding granite formations, waterfalls, wildflowers, hot springs, and high alpine scenery. One of the best mountain views in the entire country is from the Sierra Crest about 3 miles north of Minaret Summit at Deadmans Pass. This ride begins at Minaret Summit and takes you along the ridge, with breathtaking views of

the Minarets, the Ansel Adams Wilderness to the west, the granite peaks of Yosemite National Park toward the north, Mono Basin to the northeast, and the Glass and White mountains to the east and southeast. This is a strenuous trip due to the high elevation, but it's well worth it, even if you end up walking a good part of the way uphill. Since the weather can be blustery, dress accordingly.

Getting There: From the junction of Highways 395 and 203, drive west on 203 for 8.2 miles, passing through the town of Mammoth Lakes and continuing up past the main lodge of Mammoth Mountain Ski Area to Minaret Summit (9,265') and the Forest Service kiosk. Turn north (right) at the summit of Highway 203 and drive a short way to Minaret Summit Vista, where you park.

Route: The jeep trail to Deadmans Pass takes off to the northeast, just after you leave Highway 203. The rocky trail opens up into a grassy area at 0.6 mile. You cross a broad saddle through a stand of short fir trees, staying fairly close to the ridge that heads north along the Sierra Crest. At 2.1 miles you have a steep climb to the top of the ridge. The next mountain to the north is Two Teats Mountain, which forms the north end of Deadmans Pass. You are now above tree line at approximately the same elevation as the 11,053-foot summit of Mammoth Mountain, and the 360-degree view from here is truly magnificent. Due west you can see the Ritter Range with the needles of the Minarets. To the north across Donahue Pass, the granite peaks of upper Yosemite National Park are in full view. Mono Lake Basin and the Inyo and Mono craters lie below to

the northeast. To the east the White-Inyo Mountains are visible, and to the south you can see Mammoth Mountain and the entire spine of the Sierra Crest.

The jeep trail ends at 2.5 miles slightly above Deadmans Pass. At this point you must turn around. This is the turnaround point. There is talk of lengthening this trail, but as of summer 1995 bikes were prohibited beyond this point. If you want to take a hike, there's a short trail that drops 200 feet to Deadmans Pass and the upper bowl of Owens River. From there it climbs up the west side of Two Teats where there's another great panoramic view.

To return to Minaret Summit, simply turn around and retrace your route south to the parking lot.

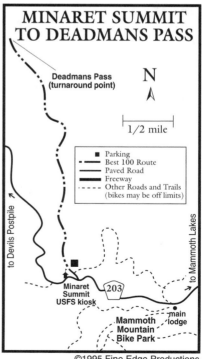

MINARET SUMMIT TO DEADMANS PASS

©1995 Fine Edge Productions

99 Inyo Craters Loop

Distance: 10.5 miles
Difficulty: Moderate, somewhat technical
Elevation: 500' gain and loss
Ride Type: Loop on dirt roads and pavement
Season: June through October
Topo Map: Mammoth Mountain and Old Mammoth (7.5 min.); Fine Edge Eastern Sierra
Recreation Topo Map

Overview: This fine mountain bike tour of moderate difficulty, but almost ideal length, starts in the Dry Creek drainage from Mammoth Mountain, heads north contouring west of Inyo Craters, and proceeds down Deadman Creek before crossing south back to the starting point.

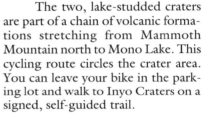

The two, lake-studded craters are part of a chain of volcanic formations stretching from Mammoth Mountain north to Mono Lake. This cycling route circles the crater area. You can leave your bike in the parking lot and walk to Inyo Craters on a signed, self-guided trail.

A sign at the site explains the area's geology: "These craters are one of the youngest features, probably less than 1500 years old, on a belt of old volcanoes, extending from Mono Lake to Mammoth Mountain. They were formed by violent explosions of volcanic gas which hurled more than five million tons of rock and debris into the surrounding terrain. The uppermost 30 to 40 feet of the northwest wall of the south crater is composed of this debris. The debris shows distinct horizontal beds and rests on a layer of white pumice a few feet thick. This is the same layer of pumice which elsewhere in this region blankets the surface. This relationship shows the craters are younger than the pumice. The pumice rests on a thick layer of reddish

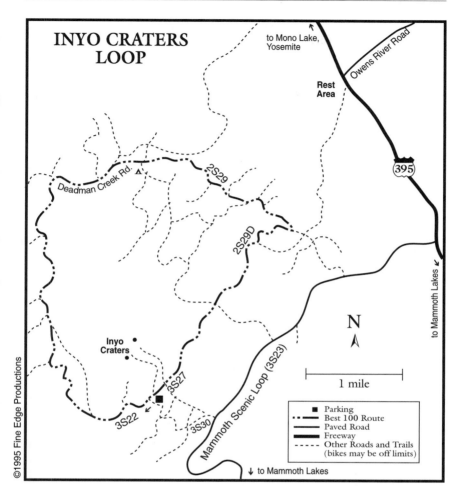

INYO CRATERS LOOP

to Mono Lake, Yosemite

Owens River Road

Rest Area

395

Deadman Creek Rd.

2S29

2S29D

to Mammoth Lakes

Inyo Craters

Mammoth Scenic Loop (3S23)

3S27

3S22

3S30

N

1 mile

■ Parking
▪▪▪ Best 100 Route
— Paved Road
▬ Freeway
- - - Other Roads and Trails
      (bikes may be off limits)

↓ to Mammoth Lakes

©1995 Fine Edge Productions

ash which overlies dark gray massive lava and andesite."

The sign has been in place for many years; geologists now set the craters' age at about 600 years. Both craters have small lakes several hundred feet down from the rim, an unusual feature, since most craters in this region are dry.

Getting There: From the junction of Highways 395 and 203 head west through Mammoth Lakes. Continue on 203 for 0.9 mile from the traffic signal at Lake Mary Road and Highway 203, and turn right on the Mammoth Scenic Loop Road. Drive 2.7 miles to the signed Inyo Craters turnoff, turning left onto 3S30 and continuing another mile to the parking lot at the craters' trailhead, where there is ample parking.

Route: Start the ride by heading back on 3S27 to the major intersection, where you reset your odometer to 0.0 mile and head west on 3S22. At 0.6 mile you reach Crater Flat, a large meadow with a view of Mammoth Mountain to the southwest. The preferred route is through the lodgepole pines to the left side of the meadow. The road divides at 1.1 miles. Stay right, along the edge of the meadow. There are not many trees in this area, so the views of Deadmans Pass and the Sierra Crest are excellent.

At 2.1 miles you rejoin the other fork, head steeply downhill, and continue through the trees. At the intersection at 2.6 miles, keep right. At 3.0 miles go slowly—the roadbed gets bumpy and gravelly. Notice the lava flow to your right and the Sierra Crest to your left. Cross a creek at 3.4 miles and keep left. There is a meadow downstream to the north side of the stream. Cross Deadman Creek (which can be deep and hazardous) at mile 4.0 and turn right onto Deadman Creek Road.

Head downstream on the road, passing a dome to your left. The road widens at 4.5 miles and is well graded. Continue straight ahead. At 5.0 miles you reach a major intersection. (The road north leads to Upper Deadman Campground with 18 campsites and picnic tables.) Continue east, crossing a stream (Lower Deadman Campground is to your right—south). Stay on the 30-foot-wide road until mile 5.8, where you turn right onto dirt road 2S29, and head southeast. You can take it all the way to Mammoth Scenic Loop (paved) and follow signs back to the crater parking area, or you can turn right on 2S29D about a mile before the paved road. This becomes 3S22 and takes you to your starting point, all on dirt roads.

Mammoth Mountain Bike Park

As soon as the snow melts, Mammoth Mountain Ski Area (MMSA) turns into one of the best mountain biking parks in the West. The first ski area in the U.S. to lift bicyclists and their bikes to the peak by gondola, Mammoth Mountain burst upon the mountain biking scene in 1985 with its famous Kamikaze Downhill. That year, approximately 150 entrants rode up the gondola and screamed four miles down the side of 11,053-foot Mammoth Mountain. Nowadays, that number has increased more than fivefold, and the full-fledged park offers trails for cyclists of all abilities. You can cruise the flats, challenge your uphill muscles, or try your skills on an obstacle course. New trails are being added yearly, and in addition, the Park offers clinics, guided tours and mountain bike vacation packages. Weather permitting, the Park opens July 1 and operates daily through September 24, then weekends through October 8. Hours are 9:00 a.m. to 6:00 p.m. For information, contact Mammoth Adventure Connection at 619-934-0606 or 800-228-4947. Maps of the Park trails are available at Mammoth Mountain Bike Center.

100 Sagehen Loop

Distance: 20 miles
Difficulty: Moderately strenuous; remote; high elevation
Elevation: Begin/end 8,100'; high point 9,000'; about 1,600' gain
Ride Type: Loop on dirt roads, trails and pavement
Season: June to October
Topo Maps: Cowtrack Mountain and Dexter Canyon (7.5 min.); Fine Edge Eastern Sierra Recreation Topo Map

Overview: Sagehen Loop, which travels through little-known country east of Mono Craters, is an outstanding trip if you want to enjoy the fall colors. In this remote area, you need to be self-sufficient at all times. Carry adequate supplies and water. Any spring water you use must be treated.

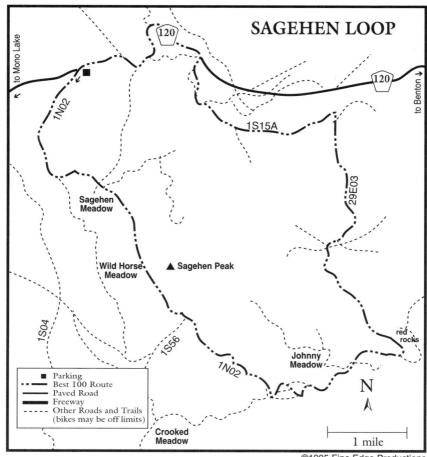

©1995 Fine Edge Productions

Getting There: On Highway 395 from the junction of Highways 203 near Mammoth Lakes, drive north 24.8 miles to Highway 120. Turn east for approximately 14 miles to signed Sagehen Summit. Park here.

Route: Begin your ride by heading south on Road 1N02, gradually ascending to Sagehen Meadow in just over 2 miles. The route continues to climb until you reach an aspen grove on the west side of Sagehen Peak (mile 4.4). From there you descend in a southeasterly direction through Wild Horse Meadow. The road curves eastward and levels out between miles 6.3 and 8.0. About 0.6 mile beyond the Johnny Meadow turnoff at a red rock outcropping (mile 9.2), turn left

(north) and follow the doubletrack.

About 1.6 miles from the red rocks, veer right. (The first doubletrack you pass on this section goes west for 0.75 mile to a year-round stream, an area often used by sheepherders—good primitive camping.)

Continue north, following 29E03 to an old mine site. Within a mile you cross a major stream with another good primitive campsite, then turn west on 1S15A, going steeply uphill to a corral at Baxter Spring, approximately mile 16.3. Head north three-quarters of a mile on 1S15 to paved Highway 120 at mile 17.5. Turn west (left) here and ride 2.5 miles on the paved road to return to your starting point.

101 Bodie via Cottonwood Canyon

Distance: Option 1: 17.7 miles; Option 2: 30.7 miles; Option 3: 44.1 miles
Difficulty: Strenuous, nontechnical
Elevation: 6,400' to 9,000'
Ride Type: Shuttle or loop on dirt roads and pavement
Season: June through October, depending on snow level
Topo Maps: Bodie SE, SW, NW (7.5 min.)
Comments: Nearest services are at Bridgeport or Lee Vining. Carry plenty of water and refill at Bodie State Historic Park. Do not drink from springs in the canyons, which may be contaminated by mining operations. (Cyanide and arsenic are present in the soil.) Because temperatures can vary from below freezing to 80° F at any time of the biking season, and winds are sometimes exceedingly strong, dehydration and hypothermia can become serious concerns. Be prepared with extra clothing, water, and food. Other than water and restrooms, Bodie has no facilities. If you plan to camp, you must carry all the supplies you need. You may camp on Bureau of Land Management land if you stay over 3 miles from the Park. Fire permits are required.

Overview: The hills to the east of Conway Summit and north of Mono Lake are rich in mining history, and the dirt roads in the area provide excellent mountain biking. The highlight of this area is Bodie State Historic Park, the largest unrestored ghost town in the American West. Bodie still contains over 100 build-

ings, and the State Park System is trying to keep it in a state of "arrested decay"—as pure a ghost town as possible. When gold was discovered here in 1859, it triggered the Eastern Sierra's greatest mining stampede. During its heyday—1874 to 1882—Bodie personified the rowdy spirit of the West. Stage holdups, street fights, and robberies occurred almost daily. Just visit the town cemetery, where the gravestones tell quite a story!

The area can be explored in one day with shuttles, or as a multi-day tour, combining the routes into a long loop, with overnight camping near Bodie advised. (Remember that you must camp 3 miles from the Park boundaries.)

Getting There: To leave one car and to begin the ride, drive north from Lee Vining for 5.6 miles to Cemetery Road. Turn east and drive a short distance to Mono Lake County Park, where parking, water, and restrooms are available.

To get to Bodie to park a second car for the Option 1 shuttle, head north from Lee Vining on Highway 395 for 18 miles. Turn east on Highway 270 and drive 13 miles to the Park. There is an entrance fee.

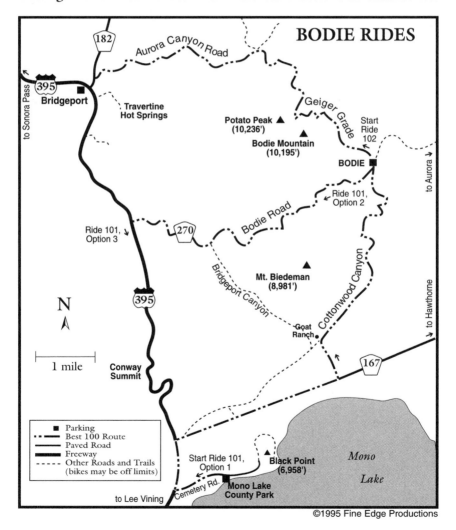

BODIE RIDES

Aurora Canyon Road

Geiger Grade

Bridgeport

Travertine Hot Springs

Potato Peak ▲ (10,236')

Bodie Mountain (10,195') ▲

Start Ride 102

to Sonora Pass

BODIE ■

to Aurora

Ride 101, Option 2

Ride 101, Option 3

Bodie Road

Bridgeport Canyon

Mt. Biedeman (8,981') ▲

Cottonwood Canyon

to Hawthorne

N
∧

1 mile

Conway Summit

Goat Ranch

167

■ Parking
Best 100 Route
Paved Road
Freeway
Other Roads and Trails (bikes may be off limits)

Start Ride 101, Option 1

Black Point (6,958') ▲

Mono Lake County Park

Cemetery Rd.

to Lee Vining

Mono Lake

©1995 Fine Edge Productions

Park your shuttle vehicle here.

To park a shuttle for Option 2, head north from Lee Vining on Highway 395 for 18 miles to Highway 270. Turn east and park well off to the side of Highway 270, just east of the junction.

Option 3, the loop, requires no shuttle vehicle. While you can start the ride just about anywhere, our directions begin from Mono Lake County Park.

Route (Option 1): Hop on your bike at Mono Lake County Park and head back to Highway 395. At the junction, set your odometer to 0.0 mile and head north for 2.5 miles to Highway 167, where you turn east. You pass signs reading *Hawthorne* and *Next Services 55 mile*.

As you descend through Mono Valley, you pass an area of juniper, pinyon and sage, and looking to the south, you can see Negit Island where California gulls nest each year. At 6.6 miles a dirt road to the south (right) leads to a road that contours above the Mono Lake shore at the 6,450-foot level. (This dirt road also connects to another one that heads back west to the cemetery near Mono Lake County Park.) At 7.0 miles, turn left (north) at the sign reading: *Ghost town of Bodie to left 10 miles.* Elevation is 6,488 feet.

Reset your odometer to 0.0 upon leaving Highway 167, and head northeast on the wide, well-graded road until you come to a Y at 1.6 miles. The main road goes right to Cottonwood Canyon and up to Bodie. (The road visible to the northwest, left, heads up Bridgeport Canyon. It's a 4WD road that could provide a loop trip if you wish; inquire about conditions of this road at the State Park. Although the county

grades the road, in years of heavy runoff or rain, it may become impassable at times.)

After turning right toward Cottonwood Canyon, you encounter another sign at 2 miles: *Bodie State Historical Park 11 miles. Very rough road, 1 hour travel time (by car). No services. Park open 9 AM to 7 PM. Use fees collected. Through traffic no charge. Bodie State Park is accessible by over-snow equipment. Wheeled vehicles not advised November through April.*

Continue up Cottonwood Canyon, passing Goat Ranch on the left (elevation 6,942 feet), and continue to the northeast. At 2.9 miles, a short trail leads north, up and into juniper trees from where you can get a good view of Mono Lake, the Sierra, the White Mountains, and Boundary Peak, which marks the California-Nevada border, as well as of Glass Mountain due south.

You cross a cattle guard at 3.8 miles and pass a dirt road on the right that drops back down to Highway 167. Continue straight ahead. At mile 4.5 you cross a stream bed. The road along this stretch is rocky but well-graded. At 6.4 miles you leave the area of scrubby trees and enter a brushy area at the 7,500-foot elevation.

A mile later, as you climb steeply, you pass lava formations on the left. A short road on the right at 8.3 miles leads to a mining prospect. In this treeless area there are nice displays of paint brush, California poppies and wild roses in the summer and early fall. Near the summit at 9.4 miles, there are numerous yellow diggings and mining prospects. You pass under the power lines as you skirt the north side of Sugarloaf, and from here, there are great views back down Cottonwood Canyon. You reach the summit at 9.7 miles, and as the road turns north to Bodie, there is a beautiful view of the valley ahead.

At 10.3 miles you enter California State Park property. At the junction of Bodie Road (Highway 270) at 10.7 miles, you cross a cattle guard and come to the entrance station where fees are collected and information is available. In another three-tenths of a mile, you reach the parking lot where you can pick up your second car. You can refill your water bottles with treated water at the Park entrance below the parking lot or next to the museum in "downtown" Bodie.

Note: Only foot traffic is allowed in Bodie proper, so if you plan to pay a visit, lock your bike in or near the parking lot, or walk it to the Ranger Station and ask permission to walk it through town. The private property outside the Park to the east is closed to public entry due to numerous mining hazards. Mountain bikes, like other vehicles, are restricted to existing trails and roads. (No riding across meadows!)

Option 2: Follow the directions for Option 1 to Bodie. After you've visited the Park, ride west (left) from the entrance station and head down Bodie Road. After 3 miles of rough dirt, it's 10 miles of pavement to the junction of Highway 395. Take time along your downhill run to stop and enjoy the meadows at Murphy Spring and Mormon Meadow. (The latter is the takeoff point for Bridgeport Canyon mentioned above.)

Option 3: Follow the directions for the Option 1 up Cottonwood Canyon to Bodie, and then for Option 2 out to Highway 395. Unless you're iron-man material, you should plan to camp overnight somewhere along Bodie Road. At the junction of Bodie Road and Highway 395, turn left (south) and ride Highway 395 back to Mono Lake. This section of ride, although it follows the main highway, is both challenging and spectacular. It starts right off with a sustained uphill push to Conway Summit (8,138'), gaining nearly 2,000 feet of elevation in a little over 5 miles.

Just past the summit your reward is the memorable Mono Lake overlook. Here you can feast your eyes on the panorama of Mono Lake and the volcanoes to its immediate south, as well as a sizeable section of the eastern Sierra Nevada. When you are ready, zip down the grade and continue south to Cemetery Road after 13 miles of freeway riding. Turn left (east) to return to your car at Mono Lake County Park.

If you have any energy left at this point, you might want to con-tinue east on Cemetery Road to Black Point. It's about 5 miles to the parking lot at Black Point, where you must leave your bike. The hike around the crater takes you past some fascinating volcanic fissures.

102 Bodie to Bridgeport via Geiger Grade/Aurora Canyon

Distance: 16.7 miles
Difficulty: Strenuous, nontechnical
Elevation: 6,400' to 9,000'
Ride Type: Shuttle on dirt roads and pavement
Season: June through October
Topo Maps: Bodie SE, Bodie SW, Bodie NW (7.5 min.)

Overview: This ride gives you a chance to explore Bodie while you are fresh, and then take off into remote, but easily accessible terrain. You'll pass through some lightly forested areas and ride along open rolling hills. This area attracted numerous prospectors during the last decades of the nineteenth century, and the very Nevada-like terrain on this ride certainly allows your imagination to conjure up their lonely and rugged life style.

Getting There: Leave a shuttle vehicle car in Bridgeport. Then from Bridgeport, drive south for 7 miles on Highway 395. Turn east on Highway 270 (Bodie Road) and drive 13 miles to the State Park (the last 3 miles are rough dirt road). Park in the parking lot (entrance fee for vehicles).

Route: After you've had a chance to explore Bodie, begin your ride on the north side of the parking lot. (The dirt road that heads east from the parking lot is signed: *Aurora 18 straight ahead; Hawthorne 41 straight ahead*. Do not confuse the historical site of Aurora ghost town with Aurora Canyon, which is in the opposite direction.)

Set your odometer to 0.0. Take the Geiger Grade Road (also known as the Old Pipeline Grade), which heads north climbing toward Bodie Mountain—10,195'. (No sign identifies the Geiger Grade Road, which is perpendicular to the Aurora Road.) Immediately after you cross a cattle guard, you pass a sign: *Rough road. Travel at your own risk.* Bodie Mountain is to your left as you contour down through an open saddle. Watch your downhill speed—the road is rocky and grassy in some spots.

At 2.3 miles you pass the Sage Grouse and Antelope Habitat Improvement Project. The road to the west leads to Bodie Mountain where there are outstanding views in all directions. Around 3.0 miles the road turns westerly toward Potato Peak (10,236'). Half a mile later the road gets rocky. If you're planning to camp, there's a primitive campsite to the right in a nice, quiet area. A road to the west climbs the saddle next to Potato Peak.

At 4.3 miles you reach the head of the canyon and contour to the north. You can find primitive campsites and short trails in this vicinity. By 6.0 miles you're on the ridge, and if you look left and down, you can see the pipeline grade for Old Bodie's water supply. The road to the right leads to Rough Creek. At this point, there's nothing manmade in sight, and the views of the Nevada peaks to the east and the Sweetwater Mountains to the north are outstanding!

Dropping down, you come to a broad, shallow valley with an almost glaciated surface where you can see glacial erratic rocks lying about. There's a nice meadow here with a nearly year-round spring that once provided additional water for Bodie's development. (It's a good primitive campsite.) A road left climbs the upper canyon to the headwall on the north side of Potato Peak.

At 6.7 miles, you come upon a weathered aspen grove and springs. Within less than a half-mile, you pass a well-graded road that heads east to the Paramount Mine. Continuing northwesterly you soon catch a view of Bridgeport Reservoir and the Sierra. Cross a cattle guard at 7.5 miles, then at 8.7 miles you hit a saddle and the junction with Aurora Canyon Road. A sign painted on rock reads: *Masonic left 7 mi. Bridgeport left. Bodie back 7 mi.* If you were to take the road to Masonic, you would actually cross Aurora Canyon Road and head north toward Masonic Mountain (9,217').

At the junction of Geiger Grade and Aurora Canyon Roads, turn west and downhill toward Bridgeport. There's a cattle crossing at 9.1 miles, then the road drops steeply downhill. Beware of rough and muddy conditions caused by runoff or small springs. At 9.7 miles a primitive campsite with a fire ring is located in the aspen grove to your left. Cross a stream at 11.1 miles. Sign: *Narrow cattle guard.*

Around the 14-mile mark the terraces you can see to your left were caused by mining activity. Cross a cattle guard at 14.6 miles. A half-mile later (15.1 miles), the canyon opens out into a fan, and Bridgeport is visible ahead.

At 15.3 miles the road to the left is signed: *D & B Enterprises. Private Mill Site. Mercury Health Hazard.* Stop for a moment to enjoy the view across the valley to the north—you can see the canyon through which the east fork of the Walker River flows, as well as the Sweetwater Mountains. At 15.8 miles you pass Bridgeport Ballpark and Sagebrush Road. Continuing downhill, guide to the left to intercept Highway 395 at 16.7 miles on the south side of Bridgeport. Head north (right) on Highway 395 to finish your ride and pick up your shuttle vehicle.

For additional rides in this area, please refer to *Mountain Biking the High Sierra, Guide 2, Mammoth Lakes and Mono County,* by Don and Réanne Douglass, ISBN 0-938665-15-4 (see p. 303).

APPENDIXES

APPENDIX A

THE CARE AND FEEDING OF A MOUNTAIN BIKE
By R. W. Miskimins

ROUTINE CHECKUPS FOR YOUR BICYCLE

The key to years of fun and fitness from your mountain bike is giving it checkups on a regular basis. You need to know how to clean it, lubricate a few places, make simple adjustments, and recognize when something needs expert attention. For the average rider, most bike shops recommend tuneups once a year and complete overhauls every two to three years. All of the maintenance in between your trips to the bike shop you can do yourself. Given below is a nine-step checkup procedure—a list to run through after every extensive ride—before you head back out into the hills again.

1. CLEANUP

Unless the frame is really filthy, use a soft rag and a non-corrosive wax/polish such as Pledge to wipe off the grime and bring the old shine back. If you need to use water or soap and water prior to the polish, don't high-pressure spray directly at any of the bearing areas (pedals, hubs, bottom bracket or head set). You should clean all your components, too (including the chain and the rear cogs), but use a different rag and a lubricant such as Tri-Flow or Finish Line for wiping them down. Do not use polish or lubricants to clean your rims— an oily film will reduce your braking ability. Instead, wipe off the rims with a clean dry rag. If you need to remove rubber deposits from the sidewalls of the rims use acetone as a solvent.

2. INSPECTION

After you get the grit and grime off, check out the frame very carefully, looking for bulges or cracks. If there are chips or scratches that expose bare metal (especially when the metal is steel), use automotive or bicycle touch-up paint to cover them up. Your inspection should also include the components. Look for broken, bent or otherwise visibly damaged parts. Pay special attention to the wheels. When you spin them, watch the rim where it passes the brake pads. Look for wobbles and hops, and if there is a lot of movement, the wheel needs to be trued at home (or take it to a bike shop) before using it. Look for loose or broken spokes. And finally, carefully check your tires for sidewall damage, heavy tread wear, cuts and bulges, glass and nails, thorns, or whatever.

3. BRAKES

Grab the brakes and make sure they don't feel mushy and that the pads are contacting the rim firmly (be certain the brake pads do not rub against the tires!). If the brakes don't feel firm, there are barrel adjusters at one or both ends of the wire cables that control the brakes— turn them counterclockwise to take up some of the slack. If you are unsure as to the dependability of your brakes, for safety's sake let a bike shop check them.

4. BEARING AREAS

Most cyclists depend upon professional mechanics to fix any problems in the pedals, hubs, bottom bracket or head set, but they should be able to recognize when something is wrong. Spin the wheels, spin the crankarms (and the pedals) and move the handlebars from side to side. If you feel notches or grittiness, or if you hear snapping, grating or clicking noises, you have a problem. Check to make sure each of the four areas is properly tightened. To check for looseness, try to wiggle a crankarm side to side or try to move a wheel side to side. Check your headset adjustment by holding the front brake, rocking the bike forward and backward, and listening for clunking sounds.

5. SHIFTING

Presuming your bike has gears, check to make sure you can use all of them. The most common problem is the stretching of the inner wire that operates the rear derailleur. If your bike is not shifting properly, try turning the barrel adjuster, located where the cable comes out of the derailleur. Turn it just a little; usually a counterclockwise direction is what you need. Unless you know what you are doing, avoid turning the little adjustment screws on the derailleurs.

6. NUTS AND BOLTS

Make sure the nuts and bolts which hold everything together are tight. The handlebars and stem should not move around under pressure, and neither should your saddle. And make certain that the axle nuts or quick-releases that hold your wheels are fully secure—when a wheel falls off, the result is almost always crashtime. If you have quick-release hubs, they operate as follows: Mostly tighten them by holding the nut and winding the lever, but finish the job by swinging the lever over like a clamp (it's spring-loaded). Do not wind them up super tight as you would with a wingnut—for safe operation they must be clamped, and clamped very securely, with considerable spring tension! If you are at all uncertain regarding the use of quick-releases, go by a bike shop and ask for a demonstration.

7. ACCESSORIES

Make sure all your accessories, from water bottles to bags to pumps to lights, are operational and secure. Systematically check them all out and if you carry flat-fixing or other on-the-road repair materials or tools, make sure you've got what you need and you know how to use what you carry. Statistics show that over 90% of all bicycle breakdowns are the result of flat tires, so it is recommended that you carry a pump, a spare tube, a patch kit, and a couple of tire levers with you whenever you ride.

8. LUBRICATION

The key to long-term mechanical happiness for you and your bike is proper and frequent lubrication. The most important area of lubrication is the chain—spray it with a Teflon-based or other synthetic oil (WD-40, household oil, and motor oil are not recommended), then wipe off all the excess. You can use the same lubricant for very sparsely coating the moving parts of your brakes and derailleurs.

9. INFLATION

You now are ready for the last step. Improper inflation can lead to blowouts or pinch flats. Read the side of your tires to see what the recommended pressure is and fill them up. If there is a range of pressures given, use the high figure for street cycling, the low figure or near it for off-road riding.

After going through these nine steps of getting your bike ready you've earned another good long ride!

Everybody knows how to ride a bike—at least almost everybody can ride around the neighborhood. But with the advent of the mountain bike, riding a two-wheel pedal-powered machine has gotten more complicated. Watch a pro-level mountain bike race and the need for "technical skills" will become obvious. Can you handle steep hills, big rocks, creeks, muddy bogs, loose sand, big tree roots, deep gravel, or radical washboards? These are the kinds of factors that differentiate mountain biking from road riding and that demand skills and balance above and beyond those required to ride around the neighborhood. The key to acquiring these abilities is practice— start easy and work diligently until you achieve high-level control of your bike (see Appendix C).

APPENDIX B

ROADSIDE REPAIR
By R. W. Miskimins

Cyclists who take a little time to prepare for equipment failure before riding will get the most enjoyment out of their bicycle. Although there are dozens of things that can go wrong on a ride, especially if you crash, most of them happen so rarely that it doesn't make a lot of sense to worry about them. The chance that you will need to replace a bent axle or replace a wheel with a dozen broken spokes or tighten the lock ring on your cassette (rear sprockets) or replace a defective shift lever is always there, but thankfully these are not the common trailside problems. For these kinds of difficulties, most cyclists ride, carry or coast the bike back to their car, any way they can, and head for a bike shop.

It has been written that more than 95% of all trailside or roadside repairs involve either fixing flats or simply tightening something that has rattled loose. With this in mind, consider the following as insurance against long walks home.

PRE-RIDE PROTECTION
Bicycles arrive from the factory with regular tubes and no added protection to cut down on the possibility of flats. There are three different approaches to minimizing the possibility of air loss while riding your bicycle. The most popular over the years has been "thorn-resistant" tubes (they used to be called "thorn proof"). They do help, but are not very effective against much of what might create problems for you. Two more effective products are tire liners (plastic strips that go inside the tire, between the tire and the tube) and sealants (goo that goes inside the tube and seals the holes that thorns, staples, and so on make). Some cyclists employ two and sometimes three of these measures to minimize flat tires. Bear in mind that each of them adds a significant amount of weight to your bike, so it is best to select one and hope for the best. Short of using solid, airless tubes (which is not recommended), nothing is foolproof. Always be prepared to fix flats.

BICYCLE BAGS
Whatever you choose to carry in the form of tools and spare parts will require a comfortable means to haul them. Although you could carry what you need in a fanny pack or backpack or even in your pockets, the most popular kinds of bike bags are those that fit under the rear of your saddle (underseat bags). They do not interfere with mounting or dismounting or handling and they carry a remarkable amount of gear. The best ones have some form of plastic clips, rather than just straps, to attach them to the bike. The extremely small ones are best suited to racing since they carry very little. The extremely big ones are best suited to slow, nonaggressive riding; they tend to bounce around on rough terrain and, when full, add too much weight. Other forms of bags include the frame pack, which doubles as a shoulder strap when carrying your bike; handlebar bags, which are suitable when off-road handling is not an issue; and bags that attach to racks (either on top or hanging down alongside the wheel), which are most often used for long-distance touring.

REPAIR KIT
Once you have chosen a bag for your bike, consider the following as essentials to put in it: a spare tube (whenever possible, put patches on punctured tubes at home rather than in the outback), a patch kit to cover you if you get more than one flat on an outing, tire levers (plastic tools for getting the tire off and back on the wheel), and a set of Allen wrenches—especially 4mm, 5mm and 6mm—to tighten up loose stem, saddle, handlebar, shifters, and so on. Be certain, before you go riding, that you know how to take your wheels on and off and how to replace a bad tube. A lot of people carry the right repair materials but don't know how to use them.

These suggestions will take care of a remarkable number of trail/road repairs. At many shops this is all that is recommended for the typical cyclist to carry. There are a few other tools, however, that some cyclists—especially mountain bikers who ride far from civilization—like to carry. Again, if you bring these tools along, be sure they will work for your specific bike and that you know how to use them.

Consider the following possibilities: crescent wrench (needed if both your wheels are not quick release), chain tool to repair damage to the chain by taking out a link or two, spoke wrench for straightening slightly bent wheels, crank wrench for tightening loose crankarms, small screwdriver for derailleur adjustments, cone wrench for tightening loose hubs, or socket wrenches (8mm, 9mm, or 10mm) to use for brake adjustments and the like. In addition, some long-distance cyclists carry spare parts such as cables, brake pads, and a rag to wipe their hands.

BICYCLE PUMPS
Since flat tires are the primary problem for cyclists, a pump becomes important.

It doesn't do any good to replace a punctured tube with a new one if you cannot inflate it. There are basically three kinds of bicycle pumps.

Floor pumps are generally too awkward to carry on a ride; but since they pump high volumes of air and fill tires rapidly, they are perfect for home and shop use.

For many years, most cyclists have carried frame-fit pumps on their bikes for emergency use. With the proper size they can be squeeze-fit on to a bicycle frame with no additional hardware needed. If you use a frame-fit pump on a mountain bike and you like to ride rough terrain, however, consider a secondary velcro tie or something similar to ensure that the pump doesn't fly off the bike as you negotiate bumps. Also, consider placing the frame-fit pump behind your seat tube rather than in the usual position below the top tube, so it is not in the way if you need to carry your bike.

Mini-pumps, the third type, have become most popular for mountain bikers over the past few years. They are very small and can fit into out-of-the-way places on your bike, such as alongside a water bottle cage. This requires special hardware, but it is a very tidy application. The down side to these pumps is that they move very small volumes of air at a time. Many of them now are "double shot," meaning they move air when both pushed and pulled. Since pumps are for emergencies, inflating a tube beats hours of walking, no matter what size your pump.

Finally, be aware that there are two different kinds of valve stems on bicycles now. The "regular" ones, like those on cars, are called Schrader valves. The skinny metal ones are Presta valves or French valves, and they require that you first unscrew the little gadget on the top before applying a pump. All the standard pumps now can be altered to work for either type of valve. Also available at a very nominal cost are adaptors that allow you to use Presta valves at a regular gas station pump connection.

Below is a checklist for the most basic, inexpensive roadside repairs:

[ ] tire liners	[ ] patch kit	[ ] mini pump
[ ] underseat bag	[ ] tire levers	[ ] Allen wrenches
[ ] spare tube	[ ] Presta adaptor	
	(if needed for your bike)	

APPENDIX C

BASIC SKILLS FOR MOUNTAIN BIKING
By R. W. Miskimins

1. BICYCLE

All mountain bikes are not created equal. Some are better suited to staying on pavement. They have too much weight, too long a wheelbase, ineffective braking systems, sloppy shifting, too smooth of tread on the tires, poorly welded frames, and so on. As a general rule, the mountain bicycles marketed by the discount store chains, department stores, and sporting goods stores are only suited to on-road, non-abusive use. Bicycles from bike stores, excepting their least expensive models, are generally suited to heavy duty, skilled off-road use. They should be relatively light (under 30 pounds), and have a fairly short wheelbase and chainstay (for agility), moderately steep head angle (again for agility), strong and dependable braking and shifting systems, well-made frames, and knobby/aggressive tires.

For details on choosing the right bike for you, consult the experts at your local bike shop. They can help you not only with selecting a bicycle, but also with various accessory decisions, in such areas as suspension forks, bar ends, and gear ratio changes. And of extreme importance, whatever bike you decide on, get the right size for you. If a bike is too big for your height and weight, no matter how hard you try, you will never be able to properly handle it. If you are in doubt or in between sizes, for serious off-road riding opt for the smaller bike.

2. FUNDAMENTAL PRINCIPLES

There are some very general rules for off-road riding that apply all the time. The first, "ride in control," is fundamental to everything else. Balance is the key to keeping a bike upright—when you get out of control you will lose your ability to balance the bike (that is, you'll crash). Control is directly related to speed and excessive speed for the conditions you are facing is the precursor to loss of control. When in doubt, slow down!

The second principle for off-road riding is "read the trail ahead." In order to have time to react to changes in the trail surface and to obstacles, you should be looking ahead 10 to 15 feet. Especially as your speed increases, you want to avoid being surprised by hazardous trail features (rocks, logs, roots, ruts, and so on)—if you see them well ahead, you can pick a line to miss them, slow down to negotiate them, or even stop to walk over or around them.

The third principle is to "stay easy on the grips." One of the most common reactions by novices in tough terrain is to severely tense up, most noticeably in a "death grip" on the handlebars. This level of tightness not only leads to hand, arm and shoulder discomfort but interferes with fluid, supple handling of the bike. Grip loosely and bend at the elbows a bit—don't fight the bicycle, work with it!

The last general principle to be presented here is "plan your shifting." If you are looking ahead on the trail, there should be no shifting surprises. Anticipate hills, especially steep ascents, and shift before your drivetrain comes under a strong load. Mountain bikes have a lot of gears and their proper use will make any excursion more enjoyable.

3. CLIMBING

Mountain bikes were originally single-speed, balloon-tired cruisers taken by truck or car to the top of a hill and then used for exciting and rapid descent. After a few years, they were given gears to eliminate the shuttle. Today's off-road bikes have 18 to 24 speeds, with a few extremely low gears so they can climb very steep hills. One of the keys to long or difficult climbs is "attitude"—it's a mental thing, in that you need to be able to accept an extended, aerobic challenge with the thoughts "I can do it" and "this is fun."

Your bike is made with hill-climbing in mind. Find a gear and a pace that is tolerable (not anaerobic) and try to maintain it. Pick a line ahead, stay relaxed, and anticipate shifting, as noted earlier. In addition, be alert to problems in weight distribution that occur when climbing. It is best to stay seated, keeping your weight solidly over the traction (rear) wheel if possible. However, if the slope is so steep that the front wheel lifts off of the ground, you will have to lean forward and slide toward the front of the saddle. Constant attention to weight distribution will give you optimum traction and balance for a climb. And make sure your saddle height is positioned so when your foot is at the bottom of a pedal stroke, your knee is very slightly bent— a saddle too low or too high will significantly reduce both power and control on a steep and difficult climb.

4. DESCENDING

This is where most serious accidents occur, primarily because a downhill lends itself to high speed. It is unquestionably the most exciting part of mountain bike riding—expert riders reach speeds up to 60 mph! For descents, the "stay in control" and "read the trail ahead" principles can be injury-saving. Know your ability and don't exceed it. And be certain your brakes are in good working order—don't believe the slogan "brakes are for sissies." On steep and difficult downhills everyone has to use them. Regarding braking, always apply the rear brake before the front (to avoid an "endo"—that is, flying over the handlebars), and if possible, brake in spurts rather than "dragging" them. On easy hills, practice using your brakes to get comfortable with them.

As was the case for steep uphills, steep descents require attention to weight distribution. Many riders lower their saddle an inch or two prior to descending (to get a lower center of gravity). All cyclists quickly learn to lift their weight slightly off the saddle and shift it back a few inches to keep traction and to avoid the feeling of being on the verge of catapulting over the handlebars. Practice this weight transfer on smooth but steep downhills so you can do it comfortably later on obstacle-laden terrain. Finally, it is possible to go too slow on a difficult downhill, so slow you can't "blast" over obstacles. Instead, because of lack of momentum, hazards can bring you to an abrupt stop or twist your front wheel, and both of these results can cause loss of control.

5. TURNING

A particularly treacherous time for mountain bikers is high speed or obstacle-laden turns. The first principle is: don't enter a curve too fast. Turns often contain loose dirt and debris created by all the mountain bikes that preceded you. Slow down before you get to it; you can always accelerate during the turn if you choose. Lean around the turn as smoothly as possible, always keeping an eye out for obstacles. It is common for the rear wheel to skid in turns. To take the fright out of that phenomenon, go find a gentle turn with soft dirt and practice skidding to learn how you and your bike will respond.

6. OBSTACLES

If you get into the real spirit of off-road cycling, you will not ride just on smooth, groomed trails. You will encounter rocks, roots, limbs, logs, trenches, ruts, washboards, loose sand (or dirt or gravel), and water in a variety of forms from snow and ice to mud bogs to free-flowing springs and creeks. Obviously, the easiest means for handling an obstacle is to go around it; however, you can't always do that. For raised obstacles, those you need to get up and over, riders need to learn to "pop the front wheel." To practice this, find a low curb or set out a 4x4 piece of lumber. Approach it, and just before the front wheel impacts it, rapidly push down then pull up the front wheel. The wheel lift is enhanced if you simultaneously lower and raise your torso and apply a hard pedal stroke. After your front wheel clears the obstacle, shift your weight up and forward a little so the rear wheel can bounce over it lightly.

If you encounter "washboards," the key to relatively painless negotiating is to maintain a moderate speed and get into a shock absorbing posture—slightly up and off the saddle, knees slightly bent, elbows slightly bent, loose grip on the handlebars, and relaxed. Soft spots in the trail can make your bike difficult to control and create an instant slowdown. If you have to deal with loose, deep sand, dirt or gravel, the key is to go slower but "power through." Shift your weight back a little (for better traction), then keep your bike straight and keep pedaling. Maintaining momentum and a straight line is also important in mud holes, and be certain to do any shifting prior to soft spots or muddy bogs (otherwise you will lose momentum). Sharp turns can present a particular problem in these conditions— you will be much more prone to losing the rear wheel to a slide out, so be extra cautious in sandy or muddy curves.

Going through water can be a lot of fun, or it can be a rude awakening if you end up upsidedown on a cold February afternoon. Before any attempt to cross a waterway, stop and examine it first. Make sure it isn't so deep that it will abruptly stop you, then find the route that has the least obstacles (look for deep holes, big rocks, and deep sand). Approach the crossing at a fairly low speed and plan on pedaling through it (rather than coasting) for maximum traction and control. Be aware of the potential for harmful effects that riding through water can have on your bearings (if they are not sealed) and exposed moving parts— plan on lubricating your chain, derailleurs, inner wires, and so on, when you return home. Finally, regarding snow and ice, just stay away from ice as much as possible. Snow riding can be fun but if it's deep, it can be very laborious. Maintaining momentum and avoiding buried obstacles are the two major tasks for snow riders. Also, the difficulty of steep ascents and descents are significantly magnified by a few inches of snow—most mountain bikers riding on snow prefer flat or nearly flat terrain.

APPENDIX D
AGENCIES AND VISITOR CENTERS

Annadel State Park
6201 Channel Drive
Santa Rosa, CA 95409
707-5393911

Bodie State Park
P.O. Box 515
Bridgeport, CA 93517
619-647-6445

Bureau of Land Management
California State Office
2800 College Way
Sacramento, CA 95825
916-979-2805

Bureau of Land Management
Arcata Resource Area
1125 16th Street, Room 219
Arcata, CA 95521
707-825-2300

Calaveras Big Trees State Park
P.O. Box 120
Arnold, CA 95223
209-795-2334

California Department of Forestry
Steve Sagers or Bob McDonnell
P.O. Box 839
Cobb, CA 95426
707-928-4378

Carson Ranger District
1536 South Carson Street
Carson City, NV 89701
702-882-2766

East Bay Regional Park District
11500 Skyline Blvd.
Oakland, CA 94619
510-531-9300

El Dorado National Forest
Forest Supervisor
100 Forni Road
Placerville, CA 95667
916-622-5061

El Dorado National Forest
  Interpretive Association
3070 Camino Heights Drive
Camino, CA 95709
916-626-4833

Folsom Resource Area
U.S. Bureau of Land Management
63 Natoma Street
Folsom, CA 95630
916-958-4474
209-966-3192 (Mariposa)

Forest of Nisene Marks State Park
101 North Big Trees Park Road
Felton, CA 95018
408-335-4598

Henry W. Coe State Park
P.O. Box 846
Morgan Hill, CA 95038
408-779-2728

Henry Cowell Redwoods State Park
101 North Big Trees Park Road
Felton, CA 95018
408-335-4598 (office)
408-438-2396 (campground)
408-335-9145 (district headquarters)

Humboldt Redwoods State Park
P.O. Box 100
Weott, CA 95571
707-946-2409

Inyo National Forest
Forest Supervisor
873 North Main
Bishop, CA 93514
619-873-2400

J.D. Grant County Park
18455 Mt. Hamilton Road
San Jose, CA 95140
408-274-6121

Lake Tahoe Basin Management Unit
P.O. Box 8465
South Lake Tahoe, CA 95731
916-544-6420

Lassen National Forest
Eagle Lake District Office
55 South Sacramento Street
Susanville, CA 96130
916-257-2151

Lee Vining Ranger Station
P.O. Box 429
Highway 120
Lee Vining, CA 93541
619-647-3000

Mammoth Ranger Station
P.O. Box 148
Highway 203
Mammoth Lakes, CA 93546
619-924-5500

Mariposa Ranger District
U.S. Forest Service
Highway 140 at 49 North
P.O. Box 747
Mariposa, CA 95328
209-966-3638

Mono Basin Scenic Area Visitors
Center, Mono Lake Ranger District
P.O. Box 429
Highway 395
Lee Vining, CA 93541
619-647-3044

Mono Lake Committee
  Visitors Center
P.O. Box 29
Highway 395
Lee Vining, CA 93541
619-647-6595

Mount Shasta Ranger District
Shasta-Trinity National Forest
204 W. Alma, Mt. Shasta, CA 96067
916-926-4511

Placerville Ranger Station
3491 Carson Court
Placerville, CA 95669
916-644-2324

Plumas County Visitors Bureau
P.O. Box 4120
Quincy, CA 95971
800-326-2247

Plumas National Forest
  Headquarters
P.O. Box 11500
Quincy, CA 95971-6025

Redwood National Park
1111 Second Street
Crescent City, CA 95531
707-464-6101
(camping reservations:
MISTIX 1-800- 444-7275)

Sacramento County Bicycle
  Coordinator
916-440-5966
(Sacto. bicycle commuter map)

Shasta Lake Ranger District
Shasta-Trinity National Forest
6543 Holiday Dr,
Redding, CA 96003
916-275-1587

Sugarloaf Ridge State Park
2605 Adobe Canyon Road
Kenwood, CA 95452
707-833-5712

Toiyabe National Forest
Bridgeport Ranger Station
P.O. Box 595
Bridgeport, CA 93517
619-932-7070

USGS Map Sales
Box 25286
Denver, CO 80225

Whiskeytown-Shasta-Trinity
  National Recreation Area
Whiskeytown Unit
P.O. Box 188
Whiskeytown, CA 96095
916-241-6584

White Mountain Ranger Station
798 North Main
Bishop, CA 93514
619-873-2500

Yosemite National Park
209-372-0200
(some camping reservations are
through MISTIX, 800-444-7275)

ABOUT THE AUTHORS

Delaine Fragnoli, co-editor of *Mountain Biking Southern California's Best 100 Trails,* works as Associate Editor for *Mountain Biking Magazine.* She is past editor of *Southwest Cycling* and frequently rides with the Pasadena Mountain Bike Club and the Los Angeles F.O.R.C.E. (Female Off-Road Cycling Enthusiasts).

Robin Stuart, co-author of *Mountain Biking For Women,* is a free-lance writer whose work has appeared in numerous bicycling magazines. She lives and rides in the San Francisco area.

R.W. Miskimins, a clinical psychologist with a consulting practice for adolescents and adults, owns and operates Great Basin Bicycles in Reno, Nevada, with his family. He is the author of *Mountain Biking The Reno-Carson Area* and the co-author of *Mountain Biking the High Sierra, Guide 3A, Lake Tahoe South.*

Carol Bonser is the co-author of *Mountain Biking the High Sierra, Guide 3B, Lake Tahoe North* and *Mountain Biking the High Sierra, Guide 3A, Lake Tahoe South.*

Don Douglass, one of the founders and first president of the International Mountain Bicycling Association (IMBA), has written extensively on the need for environmentally sound and responsible riding habits. He has been inducted into the Mountain Biking Hall of Fame.

Réanne Hemingway-Douglass, editor and free-lance writer, published her first book, *Cape Horn: One Man's Dream, One Woman's Nightmare,* in 1994. She led the first women's cycling team across Tierra del Fuego. With her husband Don, she has pioneered many cycling routes in the Eastern Sierra.

RECOMMENDED READING

CYCLING

Cuthbertson, Tom, *Cuthbertson's Little Mountain Bike Book*, Ten Speed Press.

Elliot, Chuck, *Cycling the California Outback with Bodfish*, Bodfish Books.

Gould, Tim and Simon Burney, *Mountain Bike Racing*, Bicycle Books.

Hefferon, Lauren, *Cycle Food: A Guide to Satisfying Your Inner Tube*, Ten Speed Press.

Nealy, William, *Mountain Bike! A Manual of Beginning to Advanced Technique*, Menasha Ridge Press.

————, *The Mountain Bike Way of Knowledge*, Menasha Ridge Press.

Stuart, Robin and Cathy Jensen, *Mountain Biking for Women*, Acorn Publishing.

Van der Plas, Rob, *The Mountain Bike Book*, Bicycle Books.

————, *Mountain Bike Maintenance*, Bicycle Books.

BACKCOUNTRY TRAVEL AND FIRST AID

Graydon, Don, ed., *Mountaineering, The Freedom of the Hills*, 5th edition, The Mountaineers.

Lentz, M.S. Macdonald, and J. Carline, *Mountaineering First Aid*, The Mountaineers.

Rand McNally, *Rand McNally RV Park and Campground Directory: U.S., Canada, and Mexico*, Rand McNally.

Randall, Glenn, *The Outward Bound Map & Compass Handbook*, Lyons & Burford.

Stratton, George, *The Recreation Guide to California National Forests*, Falcon Press.

NATURAL HISTORY

Alt, David and Donald Hyndman, *Roadside Geology of Northern California*, Mountain Press.

Audubon Society Field Guide of American Wildflowers—Western, Knopf.

Carranco, Lynwood, *Redwood Country*, Star Publishing.

Hill, Russell B. *California Mountain Ranges*, Falcon Press.

Little, Elbert L., *Audubon Society Field Guide of North American Trees*, Knopf.

McConnaughey, Bayard H. and Evelyn, *Audubon Society Nature Guide of the Pacific Coast*, Knopf.

Peterson, Roger Tory, *A Field Guide to Western Birds*, Houghton Mifflin.

Whitney, Stephen, *Audubon Nature Guide of Western Forests*, Knopf.

HISTORY

Carranco, Lynwood and John Labbe, *Logging the Redwoods*, Caxton.

Indians of California, Time-Life.

Morgan, Dale L., *Jedediah Smith and the Opening of the West*, University of Nebraska.

ROUTE INDEX

Angel Island Double Loop, 65
Angora Lakes, 203
Annadel State Park/Long Loop
    to Ledson Marsh, 87
Annadel State Park/Short Loop
    to Lake Ilsanjo, 84

Bidwell Park, Upper 148
Bizz Johnson Trail, 161
Bodie to Bridgeport via Geiger
    Grade/Aurora Canyon, 279
Bodie via Cottonwood Canyon, 274
Boggs Mountain Loop, 92
Bolinas Ridge, 74
Borden Hatch to
    Grabtown Gulch, 41
Boulder Creek, 141
Briones Crest Loop, 57
Briones Regional Park/
    Short Loop, 55
Burnside Lake, 209

Calaveras Big Trees State Park/
    South Grove Loop, 248
Canyon Creek/
    Buker Ridge Loop, 125
Carson River Loop, 228
Carter Meadows Loop,130
China Camp State Park/
    Bay View Loop, 79
Clikapudi Trail, 140
Cow Mountain Recreation Area, 94
Crystal Peak, 155
Crystal Springs Reservoir/
    Sawyer Camp Trail, 43

Dixie Mountain Loop, 156
Downieville Downhill, 166

El Dorado Canyon Loop, 179
Ellicotts Crossing/
    Hunters Trail, 197

Feather Falls, 150
Forest of Nisene Marks/
    Sand Point Overlook, 25
Forks of the Salmon/Sawyers
    Bar Loop, 127

Grant Ranch Loop, 29
Grant Ranch/Antler Point, 30
Great Flume Ride, 189
Great Wall of Owens
    River Gorge, 266
Gunsight Peak Loop, 123

Harkins Fire Trail to
    Whittemore Gulch, 38
Headlands Loop, 64
Henry Coe State Park/
    Middle Ridge Loop, 31
Henry Cowell Redwoods
    State Park, 24
Herd Peak Lookout Loop, 135
Hoo Koo E Koo to Phoenix Lake, 68
Horse Canyon/Carson-
    Mormon Emigrant Trail, 207
Humboldt Redwoods State Park/
    Grasshopper Peak, 104
Humboldt Redwoods State Park/
    Peavine Ridge Road, 106

Inyo Craters Loop, 270

Jedediah Smith Redwoods State
    Park/Howland Hill Road, 112
Jumbo Grade Climb, 226

Keystone Canyon Loop, 215
King Range/Kings Peak, 101
Kings Canyon Climb, 230
Klamath River, Upper 121

Lagomarsino Petroglyphs, 221
Lake Chabot Loop, 49
Lake Clementine Loop, 238
Long Valley Loop, 223
Loon Lake Loop, 201
Lower Rock Creek Trail, 262

Martin Dairy/
  Ball Mountain Loop, 133
Merced River Trail, 255
Miller Lake Loop, 184
Mills Peak Lookout, 151
Minaret Summit to
  Deadmans Pass, 267
Mount Diablo/Mitchell Canyon
  to Devils Elbow, 61
Mount Diablo/
  Wall Point Loop, 59
Mount Shasta Loop, 137
Mr. Toad's Wild Ride, 205

Old Emigrant Trail to
  Donner Peak, 173
Old San Pedro Mountain
  Road/North Peak, 36
Olmstead Loop , 236

Pine Mountain Loop, 73
Pine Mountain to Repack, 71
Pioneer Trail, 242
Pony Express Historical Trail, 199
Prairie Creek Redwoods
  State Park/Gold Bluffs Loop,109

Redwood National Park/
  Holter Ridge Loop, 108
Redwood Regional Park/West
  Ridge to East Ridge Loop, 50
Relief Hill Loop, 169
Ridge Fire Trail Loop, 80
Robert Louis Stevenson
  Memorial State Park/
  The Peaks, 90
Rock Creek Lake/Sand Canyon, 265
Rock Creek Trail, Lower 262

Sagehen Loop, 273
Salmon Falls Trail, 234
Samuel P. Taylor State Park/
  Barnabe Peak Loop, 77
Saratoga Gap, 44
Sardine Peak Lookout Loop, 175
Shotgun Lake, 170
Smith River/
  Camp Six Lookout, 116
Smith River/
  Old Gasquet Toll Road, 113
Spanish Springs Canyon, 217
Spencer Meadow Trail, 160
Spicer Meadow Reservoir
  to Sand Flat, 247
Squaw Leap National
  Recreation Trail, 257
Stevens Trail, 241
Sugarloaf Ridge State Park/
  Bald Mountain Loop, 88

Tahoe to Truckee, 187
Three Lakes, 157
Tilden Park/Wildcat Loop, 53

Upper Bidwell Park, 148
Upper Klamath River, 121

Virginia Mountains to
  the Valley, 219

Ward Creek Loop, 182
Wilder Ranch, 21

Yosemite Nationl Park/
  Valley Floor and Mirror Lake, 251

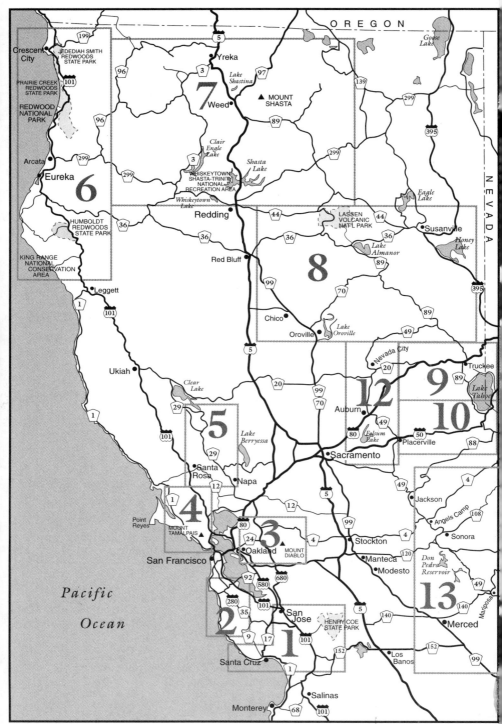